Carnegie Commission on Higher Education

Sponsored Research Studies

WHERE COLLEGES ARE AND WHO ATTENDS: EFFECTS OF ACCESSIBILITY ON COLLEGE ATTENDANCE
C. Arnold Anderson, Mary Jean Bowman, and Vincent Tinto

THE EMERGING TECHNOLOGY: INSTRUCTIONAL USE OF THE COMPUTER IN HIGHER EDUCATION
Robert E. Levien

A STATISTICAL PORTRAIT OF HIGHER EDUCATION:
Seymour E. Harris

THE HOME OF SCIENCE: THE ROLE OF THE UNIVERSITY
Dael Wolfle

EDUCATION AND EVANGELISM: A PROFILE OF PROTESTANT COLLEGES
C. Robert Pace

PROFESSIONAL EDUCATION: SOME NEW DIRECTIONS
Edgar H. Schein

THE NONPROFIT RESEARCH INSTITUTE: ITS ORIGIN, OPERATION, PROBLEMS, AND PROSPECTS
Harold Orlans

THE INVISIBLE COLLEGES: A PROFILE OF SMALL, PRIVATE COLLEGES WITH LIMITED RESOURCES
Alexander W. Astin and Calvin B. T. Lee

A DEGREE AND WHAT ELSE?: CORRELATES AND CONSEQUENCES OF A COLLEGE EDUCATION
Stephen B. Withey, Jo Anne Coble, Gerald Gurin, John P. Robinson, Burkhard Strumpel, Elizabeth Keogh Taylor, and Arthur C. Wolfe

THE MULTICAMPUS UNIVERSITY: A STUDY OF ACADEMIC GOVERNANCE
Eugene C. Lee and Frank M. Bowen

INSTITUTIONS IN TRANSITION: A PROFILE OF CHANGE IN HIGHER EDUCATION (INCORPORATING THE 1970 STATISTICAL REPORT)
Harold L. Hodgkinson

EFFICIENCY IN LIBERAL EDUCATION: A STUDY OF COMPARATIVE INSTRUCTIONAL COSTS FOR DIFFERENT WAYS OF ORGANIZING TEACHING-LEARNING IN A LIBERAL ARTS COLLEGE
Howard R. Bowen and Gordon K. Douglass

CREDIT FOR COLLEGE: PUBLIC POLICY FOR STUDENT LOANS
Robert W. Hartman

MODELS AND MAVERICKS: A PROFILE OF PRIVATE LIBERAL ARTS COLLEGES
Morris T. Keeton

BETWEEN TWO WORLDS: A PROFILE OF NEGRO HIGHER EDUCATION
Frank Bowles and Frank A. DeCosta

BREAKING THE ACCESS BARRIERS: A PROFILE OF TWO-YEAR COLLEGES
Leland L. Medsker and Dale Tillery

ANY PERSON, ANY STUDY: AN ESSAY ON HIGHER EDUCATION IN THE UNITED STATES
Eric Ashby

THE NEW DEPRESSION IN HIGHER EDUCATION: A STUDY OF FINANCIAL CONDITIONS AT 41 COLLEGES AND UNIVERSITIES
Earl F. Cheit

FINANCING MEDICAL EDUCATION:
AN ANALYSIS OF ALTERNATIVE POLICIES AND MECHANISMS
Rashi Fein and Gerald I. Weber

HIGHER EDUCATION IN NINE COUNTRIES:
A COMPARATIVE STUDY OF COLLEGES AND UNIVERSITIES ABROAD
Barbara B. Burn, Philip G. Altbach, Clark Kerr, and James A. Perkins

BRIDGES TO UNDERSTANDING:
INTERNATIONAL PROGRAMS OF AMERICAN COLLEGES AND UNIVERSITIES
Irwin T. Sanders and Jennifer C. Ward

GRADUATE AND PROFESSIONAL EDUCATION, 1980:
A SURVEY OF INSTITUTIONAL PLANS
Lewis B. Mayhew

THE AMERICAN COLLEGE AND AMERICAN CULTURE:
SOCIALIZATION AS A FUNCTION OF HIGHER EDUCATION
Oscar Handlin and Mary F. Handlin

RECENT ALUMNI AND HIGHER EDUCATION:
A SURVEY OF COLLEGE GRADUATES
Joe L. Spaeth and Andrew M. Greeley

CHANGE IN EDUCATIONAL POLICY:
SELF-STUDIES IN SELECTED COLLEGES AND UNIVERSITIES
Dwight R. Ladd

STATE OFFICIALS AND HIGHER EDUCATION:
A SURVEY OF THE OPINIONS AND EXPECTATIONS OF POLICY MAKERS IN NINE STATES
Heinz Eulau and Harold Quinley

ACADEMIC DEGREE STRUCTURES:
INNOVATIVE APPROACHES
PRINCIPLES OF REFORM IN DEGREE STRUCTURES IN THE UNITED STATES
Stephen H. Spurr

COLLEGES OF THE FORGOTTEN AMERICANS:
A PROFILE OF STATE COLLEGES AND REGIONAL UNIVERSITIES
E. Alden Dunham

FROM BACKWATER TO MAINSTREAM:
A PROFILE OF CATHOLIC HIGHER EDUCATION
Andrew M. Greeley

THE ECONOMICS OF THE MAJOR PRIVATE UNIVERSITIES
William G. Bowen
(Out of print, but available from University Microfilms.)

THE FINANCE OF HIGHER EDUCATION
Howard R. Bowen
(Out of print, but available from University Microfilms.)

ALTERNATIVE METHODS OF FEDERAL FUNDING FOR HIGHER EDUCATION
Ron Wolk
(Out of print, but available from University Microfilms.)

INVENTORY OF CURRENT RESEARCH ON HIGHER EDUCATION 1968
Dale M. Heckman and Warren Bryan Martin
(Out of print, but available from University Microfilms.)

The following technical reports are available from the Carnegie Commission on Higher Education, 1947 Center Street, Berkeley, California 94704.

RESOURCE USE IN HIGHER EDUCATION:
TRENDS IN OUTPUT AND INPUTS, 1930–1967
June O'Neill

TRENDS AND PROJECTIONS OF PHYSICIANS IN THE UNITED STATES 1967–2002
Mark S. Blumberg

MAY 1970:
THE CAMPUS AFTERMATH OF CAMBODIA AND KENT STATE
Richard E. Peterson and John A. Bilorusky

MENTAL ABILITY AND HIGHER EDUCATIONAL ATTAINMENT IN THE 20TH CENTURY
Paul Taubman and Terence Wales

AMERICAN COLLEGE AND UNIVERSITY ENROLLMENT TRENDS IN 1971
Richard E. Peterson

PAPERS ON EFFICIENCY IN THE MANAGEMENT OF HIGHER EDUCATION
Alexander M. Mood, Colin Bell, Lawrence Bogard, Helen Brownlee, and Joseph McCloskey

The following reprints are available from the Carnegie Commission on Higher Education, 1947 Center Street, Berkeley, California 94704.

ACCELERATED PROGRAMS OF MEDICAL EDUCATION, *by Mark S. Blumberg, reprinted from* JOURNAL OF MEDICAL EDUCATION, *vol. 46, no. 8, August 1971.**

SCIENTIFIC MANPOWER FOR 1970–1985, *by Allan M. Cartter, reprinted from* SCIENCE, *vol. 172, no. 3979, pp. 132–140, April 9, 1971.*

A NEW METHOD OF MEASURING STATES' HIGHER EDUCATION BURDEN, *by Neil Timm, reprinted from* THE JOURNAL OF HIGHER EDUCATION, *vol. 42, no. 1, pp. 27–33, January 1971.**

REGENT WATCHING, *by Earl F. Cheit, reprinted from* AGB REPORTS, *vol. 13, no. 6, pp. 4–13, March 1971.*

COLLEGE GENERATIONS—FROM THE 1930s TO THE 1960s, *by Seymour M. Lipset and Everett C. Ladd, Jr., reprinted from* THE PUBLIC INTEREST, *no. 25, Summer 1971.*

AMERICAN SOCIAL SCIENTISTS AND THE GROWTH OF CAMPUS POLITICAL ACTIVISM IN THE 1960s, *by Everett C. Ladd, Jr., and Seymour M. Lipset, reprinted from* SOCIAL SCIENCES INFORMATION, *vol. 10, no. 2, April 1971.*

THE POLITICS OF AMERICAN POLITICAL SCIENTISTS, *by Everett C. Ladd, Jr., and Seymour M. Lipset, reprinted from* PS, *vol. 4, no. 2, Spring 1971.**

THE DIVIDED PROFESSORIATE, *by Seymour M. Lipset and Everett C. Ladd, Jr., reprinted from* CHANGE, *vol. 3, no. 3, pp. 54–60, May 1971.**

JEWISH ACADEMICS IN THE UNITED STATES: THEIR ACHIEVEMENTS, CULTURE AND POLITICS, *by Seymour M. Lipset and Everett C. Ladd, Jr., reprinted from* AMERICAN JEWISH YEAR BOOK, *1971.*

THE UNHOLY ALLIANCE AGAINST THE CAMPUS, *by Kenneth Keniston and Michael Lerner, reprinted from* NEW YORK TIMES MAGAZINE, *November 8, 1970.*

PRECARIOUS PROFESSORS: NEW PATTERNS OF REPRESENTATION, *by Joseph W. Garbarino, reprinted from* INDUSTRIAL RELATIONS, *vol. 10, no. 1, February 1971.**

. . . AND WHAT PROFESSORS THINK: ABOUT STUDENT PROTEST AND MANNERS, MORALS, POLITICS, AND CHAOS ON THE CAMPUS, *by Seymour Martin Lipset and Everett C. Ladd, Jr., reprinted from* PSYCHOLOGY TODAY, *November 1970.**

DEMAND AND SUPPLY IN U.S. HIGHER EDUCATION: A PROGRESS REPORT, *by Roy Radner and Leonard S. Miller, reprinted from* AMERICAN ECONOMIC REVIEW, *May 1970.**

RESOURCES FOR HIGHER EDUCATION: AN ECONOMIST'S VIEW, *by Theodore W. Schultz, reprinted from* JOURNAL OF POLITICAL ECONOMY, *vol. 76, no. 3, University of Chicago, May/June 1968.**

INDUSTRIAL RELATIONS AND UNIVERSITY RELATIONS, *by Clark Kerr, reprinted from* PROCEEDINGS OF THE 21ST ANNUAL WINTER MEETING OF THE INDUSTRIAL RELATIONS RESEARCH ASSOCIATION, *pp. 15–25.**

NEW CHALLENGES TO THE COLLEGE AND UNIVERSITY, *by Clark Kerr, reprinted from Kermit Gordon (ed.),* AGENDA FOR THE NATION, *The Brookings Institution, Washington, D.C., 1968.**

PRESIDENTIAL DISCONTENT, *by Clark Kerr, reprinted from David C. Nichols (ed.),* PERSPECTIVES ON CAMPUS TENSIONS: PAPERS PREPARED FOR THE SPECIAL COMMITTEE ON CAMPUS TENSIONS, *American Council on Education, Washington, D.C., September 1970.**

STUDENT PROTEST—AN INSTITUTIONAL AND NATIONAL PROFILE, *by Harold Hodgkinson, reprinted from* THE RECORD, *vol. 71, no. 4, May 1970.**

WHAT'S BUGGING THE STUDENTS?, *by Kenneth Keniston, reprinted from* EDUCATIONAL RECORD, *American Council on Education, Washington, D.C., Spring 1970.**

THE POLITICS OF ACADEMIA, *by Seymour Martin Lipset, reprinted from David C. Nichols (ed.),* PERSPECTIVES ON CAMPUS TENSIONS: PAPERS PREPARED FOR THE SPECIAL COMMITTEE ON CAMPUS TENSIONS, *American Council on Education, Washington, D.C., September 1970.**

INTERNATIONAL PROGRAMS OF U.S. COLLEGES AND UNIVERSITIES: PRIORITIES FOR THE SEVENTIES, *by James A. Perkins, reprinted by permission of the International Council for Educational Development, Occasional Paper no. 1, July 1971.*

FACULTY UNIONISM: FROM THEORY TO PRACTICE, *by Joseph W. Garbarino, reprinted from* INDUSTRIAL RELATIONS, *vol. 11, no. 1, pp. 1–17, February 1972.*

MORE FOR LESS: HIGHER EDUCATION'S NEW PRIORITY, *by Virginia B. Smith, reprinted from* UNIVERSAL HIGHER EDUCATION: COSTS AND BENEFITS, *American Council on Education, Washington, D.C., 1971.*

ACADEMIA AND POLITICS IN AMERICA, *by Seymour M. Lipset, reprinted from Thomas J. Nossiter (ed.),* IMAGINATION AND PRECISION IN THE SOCIAL SCIENCES, *pp. 211–289, Faber and Faber, London, 1972.*

POLITICS OF ACADEMIC NATURAL SCIENTISTS AND ENGINEERS, *by Everett C. Ladd, Jr., and Seymour M. Lipset, reprinted from* SCIENCE, *vol. 176, no. 4039, pp. 1091–1100, June 9, 1972.*

THE INTELLECTUAL AS CRITIC AND REBEL: WITH SPECIAL REFERENCE TO THE UNITED STATES AND THE SOVIET UNION, *by Seymour M. Lipset and Richard B. Dobson, reprinted from* DAEDALUS, *vol. 101, no. 3, pp. 137–198, Summer 1972.*

**The Commission's stock of this reprint has been exhausted.*

Where Colleges Are and Who Attends

Where Colleges Are and Who Attends

EFFECTS OF ACCESSIBILITY ON COLLEGE ATTENDANCE

by C. Arnold Anderson
Director, Comparative Education Center
University of Chicago

Mary Jean Bowman
Professor of Economics and of Education
University of Chicago

Vincent Tinto
Assistant Professor of Education
Teachers College, Columbia University

A Report Prepared for
The Carnegie Commission on Higher Education

MCGRAW-HILL BOOK COMPANY
New York St. Louis San Francisco Düsseldorf
London Sydney Toronto Mexico Panama
Johannesburg Kuala Lumpur Montreal
New Delhi Rio de Janeiro Singapore

The Carnegie Commission on Higher Education, 1947 Center Street, Berkeley, California 94704, has sponsored preparation of this report as a part of a continuing effort to obtain and present significant information for public discussion. The views expressed are those of the authors.

WHERE COLLEGES ARE AND WHO ATTENDS
Effects of Accessibility on College Attendance

Library of Congress Cataloging in Publication Data

Anderson, Charles Arnold, date
Where colleges are and who attends.

"A report prepared for the Carnegie Commission on Higher Education."
Includes bibliographical references.
1. College attendance—United States. 2. School sites—United States. 3. Junior colleges—United States. I. Bowman, Mary Jean, joint author. II. Tinto, Vincent, joint author. III. Carnegie Commission on Higher Education. IV. Title.

LC148.A5 378.1'96'10973 72-2009
ISBN 0-07-010046-2

123456789MAMM798765432

Contents

List of Figures

List of Tables

Foreword

In expanding our system of higher education to provide American youth with more ready access to colleges and universities, if and when they wish to attend, education policymakers have often based their decisions on two widely held assumptions:

1 The geographic proximity of a college to the student's home is an important dimension of his opportunity for a college education (whether or not that opportunity is taken up).

2 Schooling at least to the fourteenth grade is desirable for large numbers of youth who heretofore have not had an opportunity to attend college, and an increase in junior college schooling is one way to assure more equality of opportunity.

The authors demonstrate that the available evidence does not support the first assumption except in very special situations. Attendance is determined mostly by ability and by family status, not by the proximity of a college. Geographic proximity for students from families of low socioeconomic status and for students who have had poor primary and secondary school experiences is not enough. For these students, costs must be low, admission requirements must be minimal, and remedial programs must be available; if these conditions are met, then proximity is of minor importance. Two important qualifications, which the authors note, are: (1) This conclusion does not necessarily apply to metropolitan centers for which there are no adequate data, and (2) attendance by adults may be substantially affected by proximity alone even if that of college-age youth is not.

On the second assumption, the authors raise essential questions about additional investment in the thirteenth and fourteenth years of education as against heavier investment in the earlier years when the real deprivation of opportunity takes place. They also inquire about the most advantageous content of those thirteenth and fourteenth years, if provided, and particularly whether attention should not be concentrated on technical training for the students involved.

The authors conclude that the spread of a thick network of colleges, particularly junior and community colleges, across the nation should be justified on other grounds than the standard argument that proximity contributes to equality for college-age youth. One such ground could be an enlarged opportunity for adults or for employed students of any age. Others would be the dispersal of educational facilities, as against their concentration in a comparatively few larger institutions, or a striving to protect the more academically elite institutions from being diluted in their efforts. And, finally, the creation of local centers for cultural and other community activities could be an important aim.

Professors Anderson and Bowman have long been justly famous for their detailed knowledge of educational practices, their keen analysis of data and arguments, and their independent judgments about accepted generalizations and proposed policies. They constantly point out that more policy options should be explored than the narrow range so often offered, that plans and consequences often diverge, and that what we think is often wrong. They remind us that we cannot have everything we might like to have and that hard choices must be made. Once again, this time with the collaboration of Professor Tinto, Professors Anderson and Bowman have put us in their debt for an excellent analysis of a heretofore clouded topic. This study can greatly clarify the thought that should be behind the policy.

Clark Kerr
Chairman
Carnegie Commission
on Higher Education

July 1972

Preface and Acknowledgments

This report on an involved quantitative investigation designed to test the soundness of new educational policies has been an exciting enterprise for the authors, both methodologically and substantively. We felt privileged that we were asked to undertake the inquiry and were most appreciative for the subvention that made it possible. Though we began with a question that at first glance was deceptively simple, to reach our conclusions we have had to work our way through mountains of computer output. Since the answer proved to be elusive, we had to estimate parameters delicately. At the same time we have tried to be guided—or have been provoked to dissent—by the sage comments and informative studies carried out on similar topics by our predecessors.

Our assignment was to find out whether, generally speaking, the construction of colleges in certain places would bring about a rise in the college attendance rate. In the popular mode of the moment this becomes, "Should we have a junior college in each county?" But there are other alternatives in educational policy, and although we have taken our data from the institutional circumstances of the United States and treat that "system" as our benchmark, we have nevertheless observed a considerable variety of situations. To restate the problem: Among the many facts that influence attendance at college, how important is vicinal accessibility to one or more colleges?

This is not a report on a fresh nationwide inquiry into higher education, nor is it an interpretive essay or a gloss on the subtler controversies about educational policy. It is, rather, a summary of an elaborate statistical analysis of several sets of data, data collected originally by other investigators for the exploration of quite different topics. A new inquiry was impracticable, and guided by hindsight we would say that almost any such inquiry would have been misdesigned. The data we did use actually proved to be astonishingly adaptable to dealing with the question before us.

Obviously it was going to be necessary to use some statistical variant of the technique of "holding other things equal" if our results were to come up to the level of reports done nearly a century ago. We assumed from the outset that we would have to use large bodies of quantitative data to examine a multidimensional complex of interrelationships. We also knew that such a complex procedure would require us to be lucid in expounding our findings. No national sample suitable for our purpose existed, but two large inquiries were offered to us for our use. Combined with a limited review of previous investigations on the same or related topics, our new analyses, we believe, have led us to sound and applicable conclusions. No one of us finds the conclusions wholly agreeable to his personal preferences, and many readers will find our ascetic and cautious generalizations distasteful to their own notions of desirable policies. We hope, however, that we have presented cogent and weighty evidence.

Two sets of data were made available to us for the explicit purpose of preparing this report for the Carnegie Commission on Higher Education about the part that accessibility plays in determining who will use our system of higher education: one set refers to Wisconsin a decade ago and the other to four other states five years ago. Wisconsin high school graduates of 1957 were originally surveyed by Professor J. Kenneth Little and then followed up by Professor William H. Sewell in 1964. Thus we had one set of data for a whole state, a sociolegal entity that provides the money, the students, and the jobs for most of the college-going youth of the area. Dr. Joseph L. Lins of the Wisconsin Coordinating Council for Higher Education supplied additional data on longitudinal enrollment trends. Dr. Vimal Shah, formerly of the University of Wisconsin but now returned to academic work in India, helped us transform the Wisconsin data tapes into working tapes suitable for our purposes.

Dr. Dale Tillery of the Center for Research and Development in Higher Education at the University of California in Berkeley made available to us the data tapes from the SCOPE study (School to College: Opportunities for Post-Secondary Education) and Mr. Denis Donovan of the center staff worked with us in adapting the data for our processing procedures. Dr. Leland L. Medsker, director of the center, not only discussed our problem at length but also aided us generously in reinterpreting results he and his colleagues had obtained.

Of the SCOPE data, which referred to four states, we used data for high school seniors only and for factors related to their continuation into college. The general character of the Wisconsin sample was similar, except that it dealt with all high schools in the state. For Wisconsin we were able also to make some estimates of the flow of youth into postsecondary but noncollegiate schools.

To the data on the tapes loaned to us, Vincent Tinto added computations of distance for each student from his community to the school he attended, with parallel information on the locations of colleges that the student might have chosen to attend. Mr. Tinto also carried out most of the statistical calculations, and in his dissertation has dealt with some topics not included here. The present report is largely written by the two senior authors.

The individuals or agencies lending data to us are responsible in no way for the type of analyses applied to their data or for the interpretations we have placed on our findings. This report has been referred to them in order that we might be assured that no serious misinterpretations have been made. We are extraordinarily grateful for the loan of data in order that we might explore one small but perhaps vital point that has been the subject of much controversy, a point that lies at the base of major commitments in higher education.

Mr. Ronald Skirmont has been of invaluable aid in programming data for the computer. Mrs. Myrtle Tuzar and Mrs. Lillian Rochon carried out most of the incredibly meticulous typing of tables.

We have appreciated many initial suggestions given to us by Dr. Clark Kerr, and by the time this report is published we surely will have received many suggestions for improvements from critics within and outside the Carnegie Commission on Higher Education and its technical staff. We cannot expect that our conclusions or judgments will be accepted by all of them, let alone by the many social scientists who are producing the contemporary revolution in research on education.

We believe our data do support one side of the central question the research has posed. But we of course are aware that one may favor particular structural arrangements among colleges on grounds having little to do with "effects of accessibility upon college attendance." There are also numerous implicit issues that are inevitably raised in pursuing an investigation of this kind. Since we believe our findings have a definite bearing on some of these issues, we have discussed them cursorily in the concluding chapter.

C. Arnold Anderson
Mary Jean Bowman
Vincent Tinto

August 1971

Where Colleges Are and Who Attends

1. *The Analytical Framework and the Plan of Presentation*

Among both laymen and professionals, a salient viewpoint toward education is "more." Successive surges of enrollment occurred first in elementary and more recently in secondary schools. The engorgement of undergraduate and graduate or professional programs is an event of our own lifetimes. Many readers of educational portents would agree at least that the contemporary expansionary tendencies of junior and of community colleges will continue for several decades. But though it seems that these tendencies have a momentum beyond the reach of counterargument, neither the magnitude of this expansion, nor the mixture of types of colleges and of programs—nor the location of new institutions over the national map—is fully agreed upon or predetermined.

To be sure, a major countercurrent is working against preoccupation with merely quantitative questions about education in the United States. Concern about quality (or productivity) of schools and of systems of schools has been growing—in part as a reaction to the unimpressive average records in lower and secondary schools when set against performance in some other countries, and in part as a reaction to discrepant performance between children in central cities and in suburbs. The growing proportion of educational resources—or years—that must be devoted to remedial courses as the typical educational career of youth lengthens also is stimulating a fresh look at many educational operations. Pushing back into the earlier years of socialization, we are becoming aware of the enormous need for effective and costly head-start programs and related forms of earlier compensatory schooling. Even a very rough plotting of the volume of "nonlearning," grade by grade, against the rising median years of schooling dramatizes these dilemmas.

With the rising drain upon public resources for postsecondary schooling and for the projected remedial programs, it becomes every year more essential that we reexamine aims and means in relation to policy options. Within the sphere of higher education, the scope for choice among alternative arrangements may be wider today than it will be even a decade hence. Movements with the momentum (or the inertia) of our system of higher education are not historically reversible; what happens today conditions future options. Plans for higher education can be assessed or interpreted adequately only as they are seen in relation to other major features of postsecondary schooling and learning, including both the momentum of ongoing events and the implications of alternative policies.

The investigation reported in this monograph has been focused narrowly in order to explore from many sides the evidence relating to just one set of questions: does immediate geographic accessibility of a college increase the proportion of high school graduates who will enter upon some form of postsecondary schooling? This limited phrasing of the scope of our inquiry is deceptively simple. What is the response to an accessible college among subpopulations set off by sex, ability, or parental background? What combinations of qualities elicit major variations in attendance at a college? Can we proceed beyond explaining "after the fact" and establish analytical hypotheses about the factors determining college attendance that can be tested with empirical data? The implications of different policies for the seeding of colleges over the face of the nation are not limited to the sector of undergraduate education, nor are they limited even to postsecondary situations. But, aside from wider-ranging questions and contentions in the conclusions, the discussion in the following report will concentrate on analyzing the behavior of new entrants to colleges or universities.

1. THE ANALYTICAL FRAMEWORK

Two logical distinctions call for immediate attention: (1) the distinction between private and political demands for education, and (2) the distinction between the student's perspective on geographic accessibility and the institution's view of recruitment areas. In the following paragraphs we discuss both these distinctions, which will come into play again in Chapters 2 and 3, and we then go on to lay out some college-going decision models that will help interpret the more complex empirical relationships that we probe in Chapters 4 and 5.

Private and Political Demands for Education

A long century ago, in 1862, Congress passed the Morrill Act, thus adding a system of public land-grant colleges to the already emerging system of "state" universities. The shapers of that legislation and of many corollary policies were no more certain, perhaps, of where they were going than we are today. Disputes about goals were acrimonious then, as today; yet some things seem to have been clear to our predecessors. Protagonists of public colleges wanted colleges for the people, and those colleges were expected to serve practical ends; study of agriculture and of the mechanic arts should be honored equally with study of the classics, or even take precedence over these traditionally elitist studies. It was taken for granted also that new colleges for the people would have to be sited where the people were—significantly, a national university has never received more than token public support. To be sure, given the scanty combined resources of all public agencies, networks of transport, and other contributors to nation building, "accessibility" was seen on a more spacious scale then than it is in parallel discussions today. No doubt partly because they confidently relied upon private and local colleges to carry part of the load, men a century ago thought more often in terms of one major public college for each state—though the more humble normal schools were planted more thickly. Despite the enormous growth in scale of every sector of education over the past century, some analogies as well as contrasts with contemporary events are illuminating.

The demands for establishment of the land-grant colleges were *political* demands in that they were voiced by public leaders on behalf of their constituents—whether the latter were electorates or informally adopted populations of reference. The demands were political also in that they voiced both populist and elitist positions, expressions of a national viewpoint as well as shrill clamoring for local self-determination.[1] We can speak about the *private* demands for places in colleges with less confidence. One of the main problems of the new land-grant colleges (as had long been true of private colleges) was to find students, and often that could be done only by first building up a more adequate system of secondary schools in the state. Only slowly, as secondary education came to be more patronized, did private demand for places in the colleges balance the opportunities offered.

[1] Questions about the viewpoints of the Jacksonian era are raised by Cobun (1967, pp. 515–520).

In comparing situations either across the generations or among states or nations, it is fundamental to make the distinction between political and private demands. Analytical care in the matter will contribute to a more adequate appreciation of the nature of historical and current developments and of the interplay of public policies and individual behavior in the educational development process. It was many decades after the Morrill Act before even a tenth of an age cohort completed secondary school; today four-fifths of a cohort formally are qualified to enroll in some college and over two-fifths enter. Private demand for a place in college or university is great, and the rapid rise in enrollments has been a barometer of that demand.

We are not referring merely to the fact that more youth can now meet the easy requirement of having received a high school diploma. Nearly every son's mother and most mother's sons and daughters have come to believe that satisfactory career prospects (i.e., better prospects than the average individual may anticipate) presuppose some training in college. We are observing that the pejorative label of "dropout" is moving up the educational scale until today it is easier to say "he is *merely* a high school graduate." Given these circumstances, a very substantial pressure from self-interested persons is unquestionably behind the political demands of articulate groups for expansion of college opportunities—and without any diminution of the heavy public subsidies to enrollees.

As already intimated, much of the controversy regarding higher education today turns on arguments—occasionally backed up by cogent analysis, though rarely by solid data—asserting the special potentialities of the junior college. It often proves difficult, however, to link up active or latent private demand for places in these schools with the political demands for implanting new two-year (that quickly begin striving to become four-year) colleges thickly over the landscape. Innumerable assumptions underlie each proposal, such as analogies with the "community high school," but this is not the place to scrutinize these many controversies. Equalitarian viewpoints are prominent in these discussions, as they were a century ago in the land-grant movement. But often there are yawning gaps between opportunities to attend a college and individuals' inclinations to make use of those opportunities. Fortunately, the assignment for this report allows us to dodge quibbles about what equality of opportunity means, while at the same time setting out clearly some contrasting empirical evidence about the effects of variation in inequalities. The extent and nature of latent demands for places in college give rise also to many differing judgments and to much contention as to which strategies in higher education might more suitably respond to those demands. While almost every writer about higher education hastens to concede that intelligence tests largely reflect the home environment, not so many confront the implications of the fact that more opportunities for college have little meaning to many youth who find it barely worthwhile to stay in school until the law lets them escape into other spheres of activity.

In studying the effect of college accessibility upon the rate of attendance at college, attention turns first to the latent private demands for college places. Will greater accessibility of a college appreciably raise the rates of enrollment (or of completion of two or four years of college) for high school graduates taken as an aggregate? Will the effects be as marked in low as in high categories of ability or of social status? Will disadvantaged ethnic or cultural groups benefit especially from an improvement in accessibility? Are there distinct state or regional traditions underlying the effects of making college more accessible? Are the reactions of potential college students to variations in accessibility related to the particular type of college?

If we consider the individual's decisions about college, we might expect that effects of accessibility on college attendance would operate in one or more of three main ways: through relationships between immediate geographic access and cost of attending, through effects on preference attitudes, and through diffusion of information or intensity of communications. While it was not possible to deal with each of these relationships directly, the empirical observations are interpreted in this analytical decision framework. Unfortunately, it was entirely unfeasible to conduct a fresh inquiry with a large sample of high school graduates (or entrants); we have had to make use of the few surveys that do exist. Moreover, it has been impossible to identify the time lag in the emergence of latent demand after new colleges were established in particular localities.

Accessibility versus the Market-Area Approach

Just as it is essential to distinguish the political from the private demands for higher education, so is it important when discussing locational policies with respect to colleges to separate the market-area, or "recruitment," perspective from that of accessibility. The former asks, for example, from what catchment area will new enrollees in a given college come. The latter viewpoint looks out to the range of college options available at various distances from the community of residence for a given set of high school graduates. In either studying or planning the spatial structure of higher education, both perspectives are important, and any scheme for enlarging existing colleges or implanting new ones should compare the implications of these two ways of looking at the situation. In this report, the accessibility perspective is the one mainly used, focusing as it does upon what happens to various populations of high school graduates. But when we look at how *types* of college affect the individual's choice of college, the two perspectives come together. Findings from earlier investigations using each approach are summarized in Chapters 2 and 3.

Behavioral Theory and Private Demand

To go beyond the most detailed descriptive picture, we need an appropriate analytical framework that hypothesizes particular determinants of the responses to varying degrees of college accessibility, even though, for the moment, we are unable to mobilize empirical data that are complex enough to match our hypotheses. In weaving back and forth between conceptual scheme and available data that have been processed in new ways, our specification of accessibility should become clearer and at the same time suggest some better-grounded generalizations.

Model 1 It is convenient to begin with a simplified economic model that serves also as a basis for the two ensuing models.[2] The likelihood that individual i will enter college j can be stated as the function P_{ij}.

$$P_{ij}^{1} = P_{ij}^{1}\ (C_{ik},\ W_{ik},\ R_{ik},\ Y_i) \tag{1.1}$$

(The superscript 1 indicates that this equation refers to Model 1.) The set C_{ik} refers to the costs that would be borne by individual i in attending each college of the set k (which includes college j).

[2] The past decade has seen a vast outpouring of theoretical and empirical work on education as an investment in human beings and on the individual's educational investment decision in particular. This is not the place to summarize or evaluate that literature, however. Rather, we will specify here only a broad analytical framework against which to assess evidence from previous researches relating to college location and the results of our analysis of data from the SCOPE and Wisconsin projects.

Other things equal, the lower the costs across the set C_{ik} the greater is the likelihood that an individual will go on into postsecondary education. Likewise, the lower C_{ij} compared to other elements in C_{ik}, the more likely it is that he will attend college j in particular.

The elements of the set W_{ik} (inclusive of W_{ij}) represent the advantages in career prospects for individual i of attending each college as compared with his prospects if he had no postsecondary schooling. In the narrowest interpretation W_{ik} becomes the present value (at some criterion discount rate) of the expected incremental stream of earnings from attending a particular school. W_{ik} could be interpreted even more broadly in terms of a complex utility function of a multidimensional career-opportunity matrix.

R_{ik} specifies nonmonetary constraints on admissions to each college crossed against the individual's characteristics on these same dimensions. Thus, if an institution is highly selective for ability and an individual has low ability, that college does not constitute an option for him. Similarly, a college for women only is not an option for men, and so on.

Y_i is the individual's access to funds for paying the cost of his college education independent of help that may come from the college itself. In the main, Y_i will depend upon family income and wealth.

The likelihood that an individual will attend some college somewhere is the sum of his likelihoods for each separate college: $\sum_j P_{ij}$. Necessarily this sum lies between zero and unity.

By Model 1 the relevance of the location of a college occurs through the effects of the location upon costs of attendance, although the C_{ik} set includes also cost differences among colleges that are quite unrelated to their specific locations. In this model, colleges may differ also in nonmonetary restrictions on entry and in their contributions to career prospects (both monetary and nonmonetary). But Model 1 ignores individual differences in tastes or attitudes while assuming essentially complete information about available college options and their implications along the specified dimensions.

Other things equal, the local presence of a college should increase attendance most directly by lowering its costs. For example, expenditures for room, board, and travel are reduced; though the family still pays the student's subsistence, these costs will normally be less at the relevant margins than for a student living away from home (unless the latter's subsistence is heavily subsidized).

Moreover, the specific cost-reducing effects of geographic nearness are qualified strongly by the level of tuition and fees at the given local college as well as by the lower cost of living at home.

Indeed, by the terms of Model 1, the sheer geographic aspect of accessibility affects costs of attending college not in general but for particular categories of schools that differ along dimensions W_{ik} and R_{ik}. Thus, even using a narrowly economic model, it is essential to identify the basic features of colleges as part of specifying their accessibility. By R_{ik} we are asking, economic considerations aside, accessible to whom? And by W_{ik} we focus upon accessibility to particular prospective career advantages. One could expect that almost any sort of college in a community would facilitate attendance for someone, but a conclusion so general is barely worth stating. The effect of geographic accessibility upon attendance at a college normally is modified by nonlocational components of costs and by what is made prospectively available to a particular sort of person.[3]

The items in equation (1.1) can be specified only broadly and represented by empirical data only approximately. Moreover, data will be confounded by factors relevant to an educational decision but not included in the conceptualization of Model 1. In the later analysis, each individual and school has a specified location, and the use of information on ability, for example, provides a basic element in the R_{ik} matrices. Y_i conventionally is indicated by parental income. Unfortunately, reliable income data are seldom available for families—though we do have them for the Wisconsin sample. But even accurate family incomes for a given year are undependable since they contain a large random or transitory component, which limits their usefulness as an indicator of normal income or of ability to pay. We have no information about family liquidity or about access to loan funds at particular rates of inter-

[3] For his doctoral dissertation at New York University, John Bishop has been doing a cost-accessibility analysis of college attendance in which he takes into account much of what we have designated as the C_k and R_k sets, but at an aggregative level by states. Also, Stephen A. Hoenack included cost estimates of distance in his pricing of the options within the California university and state college system that were open to 1965 graduates of Los Angeles high schools. Two of his results are of particular relevance here: (1) responses to "price" differences among the college options were greater for low-income than for high-income youth (1971, pp. 302–311), but (2) decisions to attend state colleges that were nearby rather than similar institutions at a distance were unaffected by income (1967). The latter was brought to our attention by a remark in Miller (1971).

est.[4] For these and related reasons, economists often rely upon indirect indicators of income or upon instrumental variables in a study of consumption. When the unit of observation is a subpopulation treated as one aggregate, information about schooling or occupation may predict the distribution of home rental, say, just as well as do more direct measures of income. In this report we have to make use of very crude indexes of ability to pay for a college education. At the individual level there are wide and persisting (in addition to transitory) disparities of wealth or income within any category of schooling or occupation. Even for aggregates of families, data on parental education or occupation are extremely crude proxies for income or for ability to pay for a child's college education. Those crude proxies are not merely inadequate indexes for the Y_i; they relate also to information and tastes that are not specified in Model 1.

Specifications for such college characteristics as selectivity, costs, etc., are indicated only crudely and indirectly.[5] We can distinguish private from public colleges and two- from four-year colleges within each of those categories and thus obtain reasonably good assessments of how Model 1 distinguishes responses to accessibility along the major dimensions of the decision nexus. In improving estimates of the extent of latent private demands for higher education that might be activated by an improvement in accessibility, we will need to move on to a broader decision model.

Model 2 By a simple extension of Model 1 we can envisage the location of colleges (for a set of graduates of a given high school) as one of many differentiations of the product, postsecondary schooling. Other dimensions (restrictive academic rules for entry aside) may include size, religious sponsorship, social eliteness, and so on. But as we elaborate this specification, increasingly we

[4] In fact, much more complex and exacting criteria have of course been used to assess "needs" for purposes of determining financial aid to students. The Cartter Panel (1971) suggested yet more sophisticated procedures. Availability of such data, however, awaits implementation of the panel's proposals.

[5] We were unable to distinguish by race, but most of our data, in any event, refer almost exclusively to white high school populations. The important exceptions are for some metropolitan locations, which are distinguished from all other college-accessibility categories. The need for special research on black youth and on youth within urban areas became increasingly evident as we encountered one blockage after another in attempting to work from data collected by others for other purposes.

are introducing elements of attitude or taste relating not only to college going in general but also to aspects internal to colleges beyond those included in Model 1. Such differences among colleges are important because people believe them to be so, and the differences persist only as they are affirmed by differences in student tastes or preferences. In brief, Model 1 is being supplemented by a matrix that specifies the degree of compatibility between the individual's tastes or preferences about the climate of a college and the college's attributes. The Model 2 likelihood (P_{ij}^2) that individual i will enter college j may be expressed as:

$$P_{ij}^2 = P_{ij}^2 \ (C_{ik}, W_{ik}, R_{ik}, Y_i, A_{ik}) \qquad (1.2)$$

where A_{ik} is a supermatrix each component of which is a matrix taking the vector of i's tastes against a vector of characteristics of a particular college (including j).

Inclusion of the A_{ik} matrix has two main implications for our analysis. First, it underlines the inescapable fact that variables used as indexes of parental ability (or willingness) to finance education may contain an element of taste or attitude as well. Second and more important, the A_{ik} matrix emphasizes that there is a sociological as well as an economic aspect to the question of how far the establishment of a local college increases college attendance, how far it mainly substitutes attendance at a local college for that at a more distant one. Whatever the net effect of a nearby college upon aggregate enrollment rates among the high school graduates residing in the community, the local college may draw few (or many) local youth who otherwise would have gone away to school. In other words, the substitution effect and the net effect upon aggregate rates of attendance at college are partially independent. In general, however, we would expect these two phenomena to be positively associated: a college that attracts many local youth who otherwise would have gone to a nonlocal college will also draw in some youth who were marginal in deciding whether to go to college at all.

The "substitution effect" of establishing colleges in widely scattered, nonmetropolitan communities can be of vital importance. (1) They can relieve the pressures of excessive numbers concentrated in a few giant schools. (2) However, there may be effects also on communication links between the local and the wider society and the linkages between individuals who attend college and noncollegiate fellows. (3) If the scattered local colleges offer only two years of higher education, substitution of local attendance for attendance away from home may reduce the proportions who continue through four years of college.

Model 3 Models 1 and 2 each had two important limitations. (1) No allowance was made for limitations in knowledge among high school graduates about educational options. And (2) any possible effects of college location upon subsequent attitudes and tastes for continuing into higher education were disregarded. (Attitudes were exogenous.) Models 1 and 2 were nondynamic, ignoring the possibility that the presence of a college in a community might in due course raise the propensity of youth to attend college somewhere over and above their attendance at the new locally accessible college. The ultimate indirect effect on college-going propensities might even be so strong as to induce an increased enrollment at colleges elsewhere, despite the operation of the local substitution effect. It is extremely difficult in practice to isolate such lagged effects—operating through changes in information and in attitudes or tastes—from the activation of existing but latent demands. Both kinds of response to accessibility of a college are embodied in the available empirical data.

In order to formalize this model conceptually one must stipulate some endogenous intermediate variables. We take the following to be endogenous:

- The vector A_i (of attitudes and tastes of individual i, treated as exogenous in Model 2)
- The vector V_{ij}, specifying individual i's knowledge of the existence and nature of college j
- A term V_i^*, specifying the individual's awareness of educational opportunities and implications of higher education generally, aside from any knowledge about particular institutions

The main location (and other) factors influencing these variables may be hypothesized in the following functional relationships:

$$A_i = A_i\ (L_{kt}, E_i) \qquad (1.3a)$$

$$V_i^* = V_i^*(L_{ikt}, E_i) \qquad (1.3b)$$

$$V_{ij} = V_{ij}\ (V_i^*, A_{ij}, R_{ij}, C_{ij}, L_{jt}, M_j) \qquad (1.3c)$$

The set L_{kt} refers to locations of colleges possessing various attributes already indicated (the subscript t indicating how long the college has been operating). E_i refers to family and environmental background. We have hypothesized (in 1.3*b*) that a youth's knowledge about higher education generally will reflect exposure to and interest in that sector of education aside from information about any particular college. But it is assumed also that such interest or knowledge will be enlarged when local or nearby colleges are of a sort that is pertinent to the given individuals in terms of their general programs and their terms of admission; hence, we add the individual interactive subscript i on L_{ikt}.

Awareness of and knowledge about the particular institution j is presumed to reflect interest in and knowledge about higher education generally, compatibility of these traits of j (including admission policies) with the vectors A_i and R_i, the costs to $i(C_{ij})$, location of the college and its age (L_{jt}), and its enrollment (M_j). In Models 1 and 2 (in equations specifying likelihood of attendance at a particular college) entire sets of A_{ik}, R_{ik}, and so forth were put on the right side of the equation, indicating that the decision was dependent upon the entire range of options. In equation (1.3*c*), however, we concentrate on determinants of knowledge about option j. Taking A_i and V_{ij} as endogenous variables, we may now introduce them into an equation for the Model 3 function (P_{ij}^{3}) as follows:

$$P_{ij}^{3} = P_{ij}^{3}\ (C_{ik},\ W_{ik},\ R_{ik},\ Y_i,\ \widehat{A_{ik}},\ \widehat{V_{ik}}) \qquad (1.3d)$$

where the hats on A_{ik} and V_{ik} specify that these are predicted values from equations (1.3*a*) and (1.3*c*) for the set of colleges. Empirically, it is the determinants of A_i and of V_{ik} that we can observe more or less directly in this study, not the intervening sets $\widehat{A_{ik}}$ and $\widehat{V_{ik}}$ themselves. Indeed, given the nature of the data with which we must work, we are, in fact, inherently picking up all of the sorts of effects included in Model 3. Any effects that the local presence of a college or colleges may have on college attendance rates are included, regardless of whether responses are related directly to the widening of locally available options (Models 1 and 2) or, in addition, reflect cumulative diffusion of attitudes and of information in general related to college going.

Although as yet no unambiguous evidence exists wherewith to separate out the dynamic locational influences postulated in

Model 3, one does expect that college accessibility will enhance attendance through the effects of college visibility upon awareness of and attitudes toward postsecondary education. Presumably as a result, youth become more knowledgeable about the procedures and requirements for admission to college and aware of benefits that college-educated persons believe they will gain. Even if at several removes, this greater visibility should alter attitudes about going to school elsewhere as well as going nearby, and this process may be cumulative. Increased and more accurate information about colleges should foster earlier decisions and more advanced planning by prospective students and their families. Tillery observed that those who made earlier plans to attend college did attend more often (Tillery, 1969, pp. 59–61). One would not expect these facilitating effects to arise from the local presence of just any college or other postsecondary education; the local options must be relevant to particular youth. An advanced charm school for daughters of the newly rich will attract few farmers' sons as matriculants. Mere geographic adjacency will not generate the vivid communication between town and gown in an integrated "information field" through which attitudes and information are diffused.[6]

Our emphasis upon the communication aspects of college location, with resulting impacts upon attitudes or knowledge, is not casual, for it is just by the cumulation of such processes over time that new subpopulations come to participate in the ongoing stream of American life, including its schools.[7] It is through such processes that the gap is reduced between potentially available and actually utilized opportunities for higher education—and even in prior aspirations to reach the culmination of high school graduation. The questions to which Model 3 can be directed are more complex than those covered more traditionally by Model 2 or by the more narrowly economic scheme of Model 1. If economic considerations narrowly defined were our only concern (and we could assume youth were adequately informed), considerations about location of new facilities could be stated solely in terms of

[6] Torsten Hägerstrand's insights and research on diffusion are highly relevant here, as in so many other facets of human behavior and of socioeconomic development. See Hägerstrand (1965, Ch. 12) for brief statements and Hägerstrand (1967) for a fuller discussion.

[7] The process by which new subpopulations are drawn into the schools is traced in C. Arnold Anderson (1959, pp. 27–32).

trade-offs in costs and in compensating payments to youth in more isolated communities. But an adequate analysis must cope with more complex issues.[8]

2. THE DATA AND STRUCTURE OF THIS REPORT

Initially, in getting work started on our problem, we ranged over a mass of scattered and usually quite unrepresentative empirical inquiries relating the location of a college to the rate of attendance. Meanwhile, we explored the potentialities of several available sets of raw data that had not been used for our particular purposes. In Chapters 2 and 3 we will summarize some of the findings from prior studies, though few broad conclusions can be based on those inquiries. The present report, however, rests mainly upon data from two studies. We used some data from *School to College: Opportunities for Postsecondary Education* (SCOPE), which followed up 1966 high school seniors in four states, and we reanalyzed data from the Little and Sewell statewide surveys of Wisconsin high school seniors of 1957, followed up in 1964. The data covered parental social status, measures of each youth's ability, and, for those who went on to college, the name of the college attended.[9] We added to the computer tapes some other data on the characteristics of the colleges and on the characteristics of the high schools and their surrounding communities, with codes for geographic accessibility by types of college. (We cartographically compared locations of colleges and of high schools.) Within each distance category, the colleges were classified by types and mixtures of types. Each of the two main sources of data is described briefly; an interested reader can go to the reports on those original studies.

The Wisconsin Sample

A survey of all Wisconsin high school seniors had been made by J. K. Little in 1957; in 1964 William Sewell followed up a third of

[8] This does not mean that economists must drop the problem at this point. On the contrary, they may be called upon to extend themselves in partnership with sociologists by creatively analyzing "Pareto-optimal redistributions" and by incorporating externalities in the economics of public and private goods.

[9] Before settling on the SCOPE and Wisconsin tapes, we looked into the possibility of using data from Project Talent, but decided against doing so. John Bishop has been making good use of those materials in a concurrent study. However, his work is not directed to locational analysis, which was included only as a part of the process of estimating costs. Other studies using Project Talent data are not, to our knowledge, treating college accessibility as a factor in attendance or completion of college.

the cases, obtaining responses on nearly nine-tenths of his target population.[10] Aside from the care with which the work was done, in the Wisconsin sample we have information about members of a real sociolegal entity; the customs, laws, and the tax-income pool for support of the students and colleges refer to a definite entity of our educational system. Every combination of college accessibility at that time was taken into account. The wholeness of the Wisconsin sample surely outweighs the facts that rates of college attendance have risen some since 1957 and that there have been some (as yet small) changes in the spectrum of collegiate institutions in Wisconsin in the past few years. Wisconsin supplies an important and distinctive type case.

The SCOPE Sample

Project SCOPE is sponsored by the Center for Research and Development in Higher Education of the University of California at Berkeley and by the College Entrance Examination Board. It is following the educational and occupational careers of nearly 90,000 ninth and twelfth graders of 1966 in four states: California, Illinois, North Carolina, and Massachusetts. A multistage, stratified, and proportional random sampling of high schools was designed to obtain about 4,000 pupils for each sex, grade, and state, allowing for probable rates of nonresponse. In each state the counties were clustered by median family income, percentage of white-collar workers, racial composition, mobility of the population, level of school attendance, size of school, and previous proportions of graduates who went to college. From each cluster of counties, school districts and schools were chosen randomly. In three states some metropolitan districts refused to cooperate; the substituted schools in two states did not wholly restore the sample. In the sample from Chicago the distortion was extreme: one university-linked school, one public vocational-technical school, and several parochial schools. Given the concentration of lower socioeconomic status (SES) families in the central city, these biases block us from relating metropolitanism (with its complex of colleges) and rates of attendance. It is possible, however, that averages for a whole metropolitan area would have had little meaning in any case.

[10] Little (1959) and the follow-up study by Sewell. Findings from the latter have been published in a number of articles, e.g., Sewell and Shah (1967, pp. 1–23).

Though we could control for some parental traits, the Chicago sample of low SES families is highly biased;[11] we cannot ascertain whether a corresponding bias exists for Boston. In any event, the Chicago data cannot be used to explore ecological factors within the greater metropolitan area.[12]

The data for Wisconsin became available earlier and the tabulations and regressions developed for those data were used later for Illinois and North Carolina. Despite the poor Chicago sample, the data for Illinois as well as for North Carolina were useful representations of a range of communities and high schools marked off by degree of college accessibility. In California, there was only slight variation in college accessibility; the sample schools were tightly clustered in and around Los Angeles and San Francisco. Although that distribution roughly parallels the population pattern and may be satisfactory for most uses of the data, we could not test relationships between accessibility and rates of entry into college.[13]

The SCOPE sample for Massachusetts presented some of the same limitations as that for California, though in less extreme form. The pattern is unique, however, in that types of institutions are distinctive and the renowned private colleges of the Boston area have for years drawn substantial proportions of students from all parts of the nation. In this respect Massachusetts is at the opposite extreme from the predominantly public systems in Wisconsin and California. One could anticipate making some interesting analyses of the interactions between accessibility and type of school as a joint determinant of rates of attendance were it not that the sample of high schools for Massachusetts has severe

[11] Evidently, lower SES families whose children are going to schools with low proportions of disadvantaged youth are a biased sample of lower SES youth in the city at large.

[12] However, there may be interesting possibilities in this respect for further exploration of the California SCOPE sample.

[13] We have therefore omitted the SCOPE data on California in most of the analyses that follow, despite the prominence of that state as a leader in the junior college movement. Preparing the tapes for the accessibility analysis was the most time-consuming and expensive part of the data processing. Otherwise we would have included some basic cross-tabulations for California, despite the lack of variation in accessibility and the distortions in measuring differences of accessibility within the Los Angeles area.

limitations for such use. So we compromised and used only cross-tabulations without regressions for that state.

The Plan of Presentation

The report that follows is structured in part on the basis of the limitations inherent in the data, in part on what we saw as basic themes and issues of policy, and in part on convenience in laying out the exposition.

Chapter 2 brings evidence from many studies to bear on the question of the implications of "college accessibility," in relation both to distance of the nearest college from the community of the high school and to types of colleges available (and their mix). For the most part only crude relationships between accessibility and rates of college going are reported. Chapter 3 examines local attendance versus migration to college, on the one hand, and college recruitment areas, on the other hand. In these two chapters, the data represent overall rates of attendance in the aggregate; parental background or level of student ability is ignored. (Most of the literature that relates accessibility to attendance rates is limited to gross measures, without controls for parental background or student ability.) Chapters 2 and 3 make more use of findings from prior studies than do the later chapters; correspondingly, these two chapters contain only occasional bits of information from the Wisconsin and SCOPE samples.

Chapters 4 and 5 mine the Wisconsin and SCOPE data. Discussion in Chapter 4 on Wisconsin falls into four main parts: (1) characteristics of the Wisconsin system and growth of its components over time, (2) associations between college accessibility and rates of college attendance by ability and parental status, (3) associations between college accessibility and characteristics (by distance and type) of college destinations, and (4) the place of noncollegiate postsecondary vocational education, with comparisons of student mix in these and in the major categories of colleges and universities. Chapter 5 introduces the four SCOPE states with a few interstate comparisons from other sources as well, comparing these four states and placing them in a national context. The chapter then presents a more intensive analysis of the relationships between college accessibility and rates of attendance by ability and parental backgrounds in Illinois and North Carolina. Each of these states, together with Massachusetts, is compared also with the findings by Medsker and Trent concerning college-going rates by ability/status/college-access categories. The last section of Chapter 5 shifts the focus from college attendance rates generally to relationships between college-accessibility profiles and college destinations among college-bound youth in Illinois, North Carolina, and Massachusetts. Chapter 6 concludes the study.

2. *College Accessibility and the Rate of College Attendance*

One persisting theme in the traditional populist philosophy of higher education in the United States has been that the society needs a plentiful supply of colleges. Tacitly, this outlook exalts the virtues of the local college. At the same time, public opinion strongly supports state colleges or universities. It is then but an obvious question to ask: Do communities that possess a college send larger proportions of their young people to college (or to some other postsecondary institution) than communities that have no local college? Does it matter whether the college is literally within the community or within commuting distance, and are there regular relationships between distance to the nearest college and the proportion of the high school graduating class who will attend? Do different kinds of colleges, different tuition policies, or the presence of various dissimilar colleges in the same place substantially affect the proportions of youth—or, a different matter, of high school graduates—who enter a postsecondary program?

Before displaying findings of the present study or of previous ones, we will review the presumptive biases in data and analyses. Some studies take communities or counties as the units of observation, and such data must be distinguished clearly from evidence about the behavior of individuals. So we open this chapter by speaking of rates of college going in a community (or among the graduates of a given secondary school) rather than speaking of likelihoods that individuals will go to college. These two questions come close to converging when, but only when, we disregard characteristics of the members of a population in order to focus on such community features as its size or the presence of a college. Subsequent chapters will report mainly about individuals possessing specified characteristics (ability, family background, etc.) *and* who live in certain kinds of communities. Since most of the simpler studies summarized in this chapter have used communities or counties as units of observation, we must keep the foregoing distinction in mind, especially as we shift from inquiries that ignore population characteristics to those that include them. It is one thing (1) to predict the likelihood that individuals will attend college on the basis of their personal ability, parental status, or nearness to a college. It is something else (2) to predict community rates of college attendance on the basis of the proportion of high-ability secondary graduates, the proportion of high-status parents, or college accessibility.

To infer a relationship of type (1) from data classified by mode (2) can lead to potentially serious "ecological fallacies" that are all too often ignored. We are tempted to ignore them by the easily overlooked fact that colleges commonly are supported by an "ecological unit" (such as a county), but individuals make the decisions to attend college. Many or most of these individuals actually have characteristics quite unlike the modal features of the community. Also, coefficients of determination typically are larger (and hence more satisfying) when we use geographic or aggregate units of observation than when we use observations on individuals. Averages or percentages or rates used to describe aggregated units of population can eliminate a lot of "noise" from the statistical analysis; variance in the dependent variable will be reduced, but usually there will not be a corresponding (or any) reduction in the absolute amount of variance that can be explained statistically by the independent variable.[1] But this does not necessarily entail bias in the regression coefficients or in the observed differences in percentages attending college among students from communities with and without a local college.[2]

Can we in fact specify, a priori, the directions of bias in an interpretation of observed community differences in proportions attending college as an effect of statistically associated contrasts in college accessibility? The answer cannot be general; it will differ according to whether we are distinguishing among colleges or

[1] There are, of course, special statistical problems in regressions using dichotomous (yes/no) observations as dependent variables. We discuss this in the fourth section of part 1, chap. 4.

[2] Where the independent variables are a single set of mutually exclusive categories that together constitute 100 percent of the sample, simple tabulations of values for the dependent variable will provide the same information as regression coefficients on those (dummy) variables taken in conjunction with the value of the intercept.

treating "a college" as a homogeneous institution, and it could also differ very substantially according to whether the rate of attendance is taken against a total age cohort on the one hand, or high school graduates on the other. One thing seems clear. Short of a past history of consistent and deliberate decisions to locate colleges in comparatively remote or otherwise disadvantaged areas or communities, we should generally anticipate that observed crude relationships between mere presence of a college and college-going rates among members of the relevant age cohort would be biased upward, exaggerating the mean differences in rates of attendance properly attributable to the presence of a college per se. Other characteristics of the populations of communities having a college, not specified in the analysis, could account for a large part, or even for all, of the differences observed. Where the measure of college going is expressed as a rate per high school graduate this positive bias should be less.[3]

1. ACCESSIBILITY AND THE DISTANCE FACTOR

Crude though the estimates may be, it is useful nevertheless to look first at findings relating community and county rates of college attendance to college accessibility, identifying the latter solely in terms of distance to the nearest college—regardless of other characteristics of the schools involved. There are numerous scattered sources of information on this subject, including a number of state reports dating back to the early 1920s, which give college attendance by county of residence and for separate types of college. Here we will draw mainly from studies made during the last generation.

Following in the path initiated in Minnesota by Leonard Koos early in the 1920s, Anderson and Berning (1941) related distance to the nearest college to proportions of 1938 Minnesota high school graduates going on to college. They concluded that a distance of about 10 miles was a breaking point; within that zone rates of attendance were higher than beyond it, but distance otherwise

[3] Under very special conditions the bias could even be reversed. Thus, in a community in which very few youth complete high school, those few are already highly selected and might be participants in quite other cultures and "information fields" than their neighbors; such youth could be exceptionally college-prone. However, careful investigations of this possibility, in the light of supplementary information, has convinced us that for the simple college or noncollege distinction all findings cited in this chapter are biased upward. For particular types of institutions, this is not uniformly the case, as will be pointed out in subsequent discussions.

had no effect. Writing just after World War II, Keller, Kehl, and Berning (1950) identified a somewhat greater critical distance in the same state. They found that the proportions of high school graduates going on to college were 27 percent when the nearest college was within 10 miles, and still 24 percent when it was between 10 and 25 miles, but the rate dropped to 16 percent beyond 25 miles. They suggested that this contrast with Anderson's findings reflected changes in commuting time for any given distance. However, other studies challenge the generalizability of this finding, both for earlier years and for today.

About the same time that these studies were going on in Minnesota, similar investigations were under way in Illinois and especially in New York. The distance factor was viewed in two perspectives already noted. One perspective was to look out from the institution and ask simply how far students attending it commuted. The other was to ask how distance to the nearest college affected the college attendance rate among persons of a particular community of origin. If we compare the results of these two perspectives, how well do they fit together?

In his study of commuting to New York colleges, John Paige (Paige & Russell, 1945) found that 93 percent of the full-time students attending colleges in New York City in the fall of 1941 were living at home; of full-time students in upstate colleges only a third lived at home. Among the upstate students who did live at home, 94 percent lived within 14 miles of their college, and extending that distance another 10 miles brought in another 5 percent; thus virtually no one commuted more than 25 miles. The decided dropping off beyond 10 miles comes closer to the pattern observed by Anderson (for 1938) than to the later findings in Minnesota. In his careful study for the New York State Education Department, Cowen (1946) suggested a distance more like 10 miles as the relevant breaking point for college attendance rates among New York youth.

Cowen's analysis was based on data from all colleges and universities in New York. He identified the places of origin of all enrollees in those institutions in the fall of 1941, using the same data as Paige. Enrollments provided the numerators of his ratios for the various communities in the state, while the denominator was half the population aged 15 to 24. The resulting percentages are lower than for most other studies for two main reasons: they refer to an entire age group and not just to those completing high school, and they refer to total enrollees in college in relation to a generously defined relevant age group instead of taking just college entrants as a proportion of a cohort. (Also, students attending college outside of New York State were not included in the count of college students from a locality.) Whatever the caveats concerning possible upward biases in the first two rows of Table 1 relative to the rest, it is abundantly clear that distance had little effect on college attendance rates once the nearest college was more than 10 miles away.

TABLE 1 ***Percentages of youth attending college in New York State, fall 1941, by distance from hometown to nearest college***

*Distance from town to nearest college**	*Percentage of youth attending college*		
	Total	*Full time*	*Part time*
College in the town	11.1	7.2	3.9
Within 10 miles	8.0	5.9	2.5
11–20 miles	6.6	5.2	1.8
21–30 miles	6.6	5.1	1.7
31–40 miles	5.7	4.6	1.7
Over 40 miles	6.6	5.6	1.3

* Excluding towns having no college students, those having fewer than six students per 100 square miles, and New York City.

SOURCE: Cowen, 1946, p. 19.

In their study of the 1957 Kansas high school graduates, Daughtry and Hawk (1957) found that in communities with two or more colleges, 53 percent of the graduates enrolled in college, and in communities with one college, 51 percent. When there were no colleges in the community, distances to the nearest college made no difference; thus the proportions enrolling were almost a third whether the nearest college was within 10 miles, 11 to 25 miles, 26 to 50 miles, or 51 to 100 miles distant. This sharp split between rates of attendance where there is a college within the community and all other situations (even at short distances) may very well characterize other Plains states with similar settlement patterns; it may be in part a contrast between rural and urban populations, having no direct connection with local accessibility of a college. It would be hazardous, however, to generalize this finding.[4]

The Wisconsin and the SCOPE data refer to quite different sociogeographic entities than do the data for Kansas. A summary of results for four states, using a simple three-step scale of college

[4] A number of studies dealing with college intentions are also concerned with these questions.

accessibility, is presented in Table 2. For the noncollege communities, having a college within 20 miles brought no appreciable increment in attendance over having to go beyond 20 miles—except for males in North Carolina. Indeed, for females the less accessible situations were marked by slightly higher enrollments. For Massachusetts and North Carolina the differences in rates of attendance between the two kinds of community were negligible, but the contrasts were substantial for Wisconsin and Illinois. As the data for Kansas showed, whatever part the generalized college-accessibility factor may play in raising attendance rates, a short commuting distance to just any college cannot be given the credit. From Table 2 one can contrast the situation where no college lies within 20 miles of the high school community and that in which the community has a college (column 2 minus column 4). For females the effect is positive but slight and for males the difference is around 10 percent. Apart from any positive inferences that might be drawn from these

TABLE 2 ***Percentages of high school graduates entering college, by sex and distance to nearest college; Wisconsin and SCOPE samples***

			No college within community	
	All locations	*College within community*	*College within 20 miles*	*No college within 20 miles*
*Wisconsin, 1957**				
Males	38.3	43.7	33.2	30.2
Females	25.9	29.0	20.4	23.8
Illinois, 1966†				
Males	55.3	57.3	48.6	48.3
Females	47.2	48.8	40.4	43.4
Massachusetts, 1966†				
Males	59.3	60.5	58.4	‡
Females	53.5	52.9	54.1	§
North Carolina, 1966†				
Males	43.1	46.0	42.1	34.0
Females	41.2	45.2	37.3	41.5

* From the accessibility analysis (as of 1957–58) prepared by Vincent Tinto, and the Little-Sewell Wisconsin tapes described in Chapter 1.

† From the SCOPE tapes and 1966–67 accessibility analysis prepared by Vincent Tinto.

‡ No cases.

§ The sample included only one community having a girl's school. The college-entry rate in that case was 48.7 percent.

crude comparisons, they do indicate the possibility that it is not so much the presence of a college as it is the associated community characteristics that underlie the rises in attendance.

Despite these perhaps unneeded cautions against premature causal inferences, it may prove helpful to display a collection of recent estimated rates of college going for communities that do or do not possess a college (Table 3). The results differ considerably, ranging from a "college effect" of almost 20 percent among communities in Kansas to no effect in Massachusetts. In Wisconsin and North Carolina a span of half a dozen years brought striking contrasts. In Wisconsin shrinkage in the differential was due mainly to growing enrollments for noncollege communities; since these data rest on statewide samples, the conclusion would seem to be fairly firm. For North Carolina the sources for the two years are disparate, yet that bias does not, in our opinion, explain the tendency toward more rapid growth in college going among youth

TABLE 3 ***Percentages of high school graduates entering college from localities with and without institutions of higher education; selected sources for 1957 to 1968***

		College(s) in locality	
Source		*One or more*	*None*
California communities	1959[a]	45	42
Illinois communities	1966[b]	53	45
Kansas communities	1957[c]	52	33
Kansas counties	1963[d]	54	47
Kentucky counties	1957[e]	37	26
Massachusetts communities	1966[b]	56	56
New York counties	1968[f]	65	63
North Carolina counties	1961[g]	40	31
North Carolina communities	1966[b]	45	39
Wisconsin communities	1957[h]	36	27
Wisconsin counties	1963[i]	34	33

[a] Beezer and Hjelm, 1961.

[b] SCOPE, 1966.

[c] Daughtry and Hawk, 1957.

[d] The Advisory Committee on Junior Colleges, 1964.

[e] Kentucky Council on Public Higher Education, 1958.

[f] Drawn from data presented in *College Going Rate of New York State High School Graduates: 1968–1969,* 1969.

[g] Hamilton, 1962.

[h] Data taken from present study, based upon work of William Sewell and J. Kenneth Little. See Little, 1959.

[i] Tuckman, 1969.

from the noncollege communities. The tendency in some instances for lagging areas to catch up in college going, even without benefit of a local college, constitutes a clear warning against premature conclusions that reducing distance to college by opening more colleges is a prerequisite for wider utilization of postsecondary schools. Since installation costs of any college are gigantic, and since other sectors have at least equally urgent claims upon resources, a more sensitive analysis of the accessibility factor should prove to be a good investment of research time and money.

2. INSTITUTIONS AND SYSTEMS OF HIGHER EDUCATION

It is not unusual to hear someone say that it is not the presence of a private college but only that of a public college that matters.[5] Although these remarks may or may not stand up to a test, institutional and system characteristics must be considered. Ideally, one would wish to align institutional features with the analytical scheme set forth in Chapter 1 and then proceed to identify each component factor. In practice, however, colleges are seldom categorized in terms of the criteria that we should like to identify.[6] There are mixed advantages and disadvantages in this noncongruence between analytical categories and the forms in which information about higher education are reported. On the one side, we are unable to specify tidily the econometric or other models on a national scale. Without extremely elaborate specification, however, this would not be possible in any case, and many of the difficulties in making comparisons over time and across states would remain. Colleges are unlike in many ways and we are unable to draw any neat national picture of what we casually call the system of higher education. It is indeed beneficial in some ways that so many studies have been or are being carried out within particular states, for within these limited universes it is easier to identify the characteristics of separate types of institutions.

Despite all the pressure toward attainment of a national educational policy, especially in higher education, one cannot avoid being impressed by the strength of our *federal* heritage. Broad contrasts in regional history and in events peculiar to certain states produce

[5] In fact, several studies explicitly confine their interest to public colleges and universities only. The pioneering work by Medsker and Trent (1965) is focused in this way and disregards the presence of private institutions.

[6] This situation is changing as researchers push toward more precise and fuller econometric and sociometric models of demands for places in institutions of higher education. These new models, however, have not as yet been joined in an analysis of accessibility effects per se (even when geographic data are used).

a richly varied national mosaic of colleges and universities. Interaction of these historically evolving systems of education with the local socioeconomic features of the society generates the variation we observe and sets limits upon the policies open to us in the years ahead. Nowhere is this more evident than at the transition from secondary to further (presumably higher) education, in particular with respect to the functions, scale, and location of two-year colleges or alternative postsecondary types of schooling. With pertinent events in the history of the land-grant system in mind, it may be useful to bring out some of these variations.

The belated interest of southern New England in land-grant colleges was not accidental; the area had long been studded with many sorts and qualities of private colleges providing a wide range of educational options. In earlier generations many of these private schools had been "peoples' institutions" in that economic constraints were not a major barrier to individuals who qualified for entry.[7] But in the more populist sense (often misleadingly called Jacksonian) or in the sense used by advocates of junior and community colleges today, they were not colleges for the populace. Meanwhile, changes have been going on in the economics of access to higher education and in the financial operations of private colleges. In this region the impact of opening new colleges designed to enhance popular enrollment cannot remain unaffected by the widespread, even national, patronage of the dominant private sector, with its worldwide prestige. Problems of realigning the structure of this more European sort of higher education present policy issues that are quite different from those in states that have long been dominated by public colleges of equal prestige.

Land-grant history in New York was different; even Cornell (often called the most successful exemplar in this movement) began as a fusion of public funds with private philanthropy. It preserved some of the flavor of Ivy League colleges at a time when these colleges were being exhorted to serve "the people" better and to offer what was even then called a more relevant higher education.[8] In Rensselaer, New York boasted the first high-quality technical institute (aside from West Point), established a good many decades

[7] Harvard was still running a preparatory section to provide a supply of students in the years immediately after the Civil War. But if this was a "compensatory program" in that it sought to upgrade attainments at entry to the freshman year, it was certainly not "compensatory" in the sense of providing special programs for disadvantaged minority youth.

[8] For a summary, see Bowman (1962).

before the Morrill Act. Even today, in the conventional sense there is no "University of New York," despite many State University of New York (SUNY) campuses. The state moved easily into founding local community colleges and multicounty or regional junior colleges. Though always kept separate from high school districts, these schools were affected by the statewide high school accreditation scheme and the regents examinations at termination of secondary school.

Meanwhile, New York City has acquired many and large public and private universities (along with innumerable sorts of other postsecondary schools). The traditional controls by examination are being set aside in favor of "open entry" and compensatory programs, so that the effect of junior colleges is blurred. It remains to be seen whether these innovations will raise the rate of completion of the bachelor's degree, will affect the "quality" of college graduates, or will enlarge the output of college graduates beyond what would have occurred through transfer from two-year to four-year schools. Unfortunately, we can obtain no data with which to explore the locational aspect of colleges within large metropolitan areas, so upstate New York becomes more central for our discussion. New York has combined systematic development of a common-school system that includes separate local and regional junior colleges and more recently the four-year SUNY campuses, without a preeminent state university at the top of the structure.

Turning to the South, the steeply hierarchical status structures among whites, together with racial segregation, found expression in the systems of higher education. Effects included a retarded participation in land-grant development, a high relative frequency of private junior colleges, and the low rates of persistence through four years of college (until recently even among Southern elites). Furthermore, in some parts of the South, and in some of the Appalachian states in particular, there are often wide cultural distances between remote, backward areas and the richer agricultural and urban centers. The private junior colleges grew up mainly as socially elite institutions. Where the generally more recent public community colleges have been located mainly in poorer or more isolated rural sections, responses to the presence of those institutions must be very different from the more common situation in which colleges are located in relatively advantaged communities. So must the roles of the educational institutions themselves. Further complications arise in the South, as elsewhere, because of the varying patterns of local or state teachers colleges and their recent transformations, usually to four-year state colleges.

The Midwest was the most receptive environment for colleges spawned by the Morrill Act. Whether joined with existing state universities or established separately, the land-grant schools often had to face competition from old and even new denominational liberal arts colleges. Turnover among these small colleges has been high for two centuries, but some of them have sustained a high quality and remain among the world's best examples of higher education. Today the liberal arts colleges of the Midwest vary widely in quality and in the geographic range over which they attract students, whether or not they have retained their ties to the sponsoring denomination. With the more rapid expansion of public colleges, the private ones are perhaps becoming less visible, but their presence widens the options (compared, say, to the Mountain and Pacific states)—and certainly complicates the analysis in any study of this kind.

We may recall William Rainey Harper's comments on the private liberal arts colleges of his day. Scanning the varied intellectual landscape, with its large proportion of intellectually and financially weak private schools, Harper argued that many second-rate four-year colleges might better become first-rate junior colleges. We can hardly test Harper's prescience, for today, as then, colleges are diverse in atmosphere, in cost, and in quality and reputation. No statistical analysis of the college-going behavior of youth who live near to or far from stronger and weaker colleges will permit us to reiterate his advice or to call his prescription self-serving. A policy to guide the reorientation of assorted colleges must rest on more penetrating and creative thought than statistics alone could generate.

In the Far West generally, and in California in particular, a state system of public institutions dominates the total range of higher education available to the youth of the area. New policies and remedial reactions to emerging defects of the present system are constrained by this slant. But it does not follow that domination by public institutions predetermines the structure of a system.[9]

[9] The proportions of entering freshmen in public institutions is, of course, increasing across the nation. This reflects both the policy of restrained growth that many private institutions have adopted to maintain their character (in contrast to the monolithic public universities), and the financial constraints on these institutions, which have been aggravated by the competition from public institutions with heavily subsidized tuitions. But this is now changing.

In fact one of the most important distinctions for this study is epitomized in a comparison of the public systems in California and Wisconsin.

The junior college system of California grew up locally in response to demands for postgraduate work in the already excellent secondary schools. It has been policy in California to encourage the formation of separate districts for junior colleges in order to bring into them a stronger flavor of higher education. At the same time, perhaps paradoxically, an open-door, free-tuition policy has been pursued in a manner that makes junior colleges part of the state's "common school" system. Where a junior college is linked closely to a high school (or to a set of high schools in a district coterminous to that for the junior college), the continuation rate into junior college would be maximized, other things being equal. A clear majority of California college entrants are enrolled in junior colleges; indeed one-third of all junior college students of the entire nation are enrolled in the California system. (Adding Illinois and New York accounts for almost half the national total.) But here we have to choose which road our reasoning will follow: are we interested in providing community colleges for a diversity of roles and clientele, or in the volume of direct transition from high school to so-called postsecondary enrollment, or in the output of baccalaureate degrees? The last of these aims cannot be very accurately gauged from the degree of popularity of the junior college segment of the system. Neither do such data help us draw up policies for nonacademic postsecondary education, especially in technical subjects or in adult or continuing programs.

Using California criteria, one could argue that Wisconsin does not have a system of junior colleges, despite having some public municipal schools. The independent, local, two-year colleges that have been spread widely through rural Wisconsin have been small county teachers colleges, and these are now being phased out. But Wisconsin does have a lower-division, postsecondary system, and one that maintains criteria of ability for entry. These Extension Centers provide easy transfer to the University of Wisconsin, but there are entrance qualifications. Though widely scattered geographically, the centers are not tied to localized districts—nor are they part of the "extension service." Broadly, they are more like the regional junior colleges of New York than the junior colleges of California. Because these Wisconsin Extension Centers are both more selective by ability and less localized than the junior colleges of California, it would not be surprising that for any given impact on college attendance the Wisconsin Centers would exert a somewhat lesser immediately local effect, at least for students who are of less than top ability. On the other hand, Wisconsin has a significant and growing array of noncollegiate municipal community and vocational institutions; some of these are being pushed today toward the junior college model by rising public demands for the symbols of academic certification.

3. ACCESSIBILITY PROFILES AND COLLEGE ENTRY RATES

It is appropriate to open a summary of empirical investigations of the effect of college accessibility profiles upon attendance rates by quoting from the work of Leonard Koos. Fifty years ago he collected information for North-central and Northwestern states showing that 10.9 per 1,000 high school graduates went to college

TABLE 4 ***Summary of Koos' findings on percentages of Oregon high school graduates entering college in 1948 and 1949****

College opportunities	*Total counties*	*Median*
Counties:		
1948		
Without opportunities	25	30.1
High tuition only	4	28.8
Low tuition	6	43.6
	35	
1949		
Without opportunities	22	27.7
High tuition only	3	30.0
Low tuition	9	30.8
	34	
School districts:		
With 500 or more students in grades 9–12		
1948		
Without opportunities	19	31.8
High tuition only	3	33.6
Low tuition	3	56.7
	25	
1949		
Without opportunities	18	25.8
High tuition only	3	34.7
Low tuition	2	48.5
	23	

* Koos, 1950.

if they lived in a community possessing a junior college and 5.6 per 1,000 did so in other communities (1924). In 1948–49 he made a detailed study for Oregon (1950), classifying counties and independent school districts according to the character of available postsecondary opportunities (Table 4). The findings are somewhat erratic and Koos' explanations do not always seem to be lucid. He reported that among counties the presence of a high-tuition college (if there were no other colleges) did not improve the rate of college going by youth from that county; in the independent school districts there did seem to be some positive effect of the high-tuition colleges. The presence of a low-tuition college seemed clearly to exert a marked attraction—except for the inexplicable case of counties in 1949.[10] One suspects that much of the effect of the low-tuition schools actually reflects associated traits of the communities in which they are located. In part we are observing the cost-reducing effects (as of low tuition or lower subsistence cost) when these all occur together; but the response no doubt is picking up other, noneconomic factors. Some of the related factors (such as the comparatively open entry more often found in public colleges) have little relationship to proximity. But nearness to home (costs aside) is part of the picture; proximity may serve the preferences of some individuals and also diffuse knowledge and shift attitudes about colleges among new sets of potential enrollees (as Model 3 specified). Some of the intricacies in the relationship of college accessibility to enrollment emerge from examining the collation of findings presented in Tables 5 and 6.

The first of these tables refers to total enrollments (at colleges within the state) as proportions of the college-age population rather than as ratios to high school graduates. The figures are therefore cumulative counts of retention through high school, into college, and in college. Even for locations without a college, the enrollment rates differ strikingly among these few states. In Michigan and Virginia, particularly, the metropolitan communities and those possessing multiple colleges display more retention into college than do the more rural areas of the state. In these same two states it is counties with public four-year colleges that display the highest enrollments. But in Florida, places with no college do as well as or better than those with colleges, whatever be the type or combination of types. Clearly we cannot draw any firm conclu-

[10] With one exception, all the low-tuition schools were public and all the high-tuition schools were private.

TABLE 5 ***Differentials in percentages of college-age population attending college by college-accessibility and type of home area***

	Michigan counties, 1956	*Virginia counties & independent urban areas, 1964*	*Florida counties, total 1953*	*Florida counties, white schools only, 1953*
Percentages enrolled in college from noncollege locations	17	10	6.5	9.2
Excess rates over those in noncollege locations:				
Community college or public two-year college	+ 7	+ 2	+3.0	+1.9
Private two-year college		0		
State college only	+31	+22	+0.9	−1.0
Private college only	+11	+ 7	+0.4	+0.7
Multiple institutions	+ 6	+15	+4.4	+9.1
Metropolitan	+21			

SOURCES: Column 1: Russell, 1957, pp. 10–12. Column 2: Russell, 1965, pp. 34, 44. Columns 3 and 4: Brumbaugh, 1956.

sions about the impact of a local college unless we know something about the characteristics of the various communities. Nevertheless, even on the surface, these data do not suggest that community or junior colleges (whether public or private) have a marked effect upon the inclination of high school graduates to continue for more schooling (nor do they tell us anything about persistence after entry to college). It is possible that junior colleges encourage more youth to enter college, yet they probably also hold back some youth who otherwise would have continued all the way to a bachelor's degree.

That the rate of continuation into college is related in complex ways to various characteristics of home communities (aside from mere nearness to a college) is revealed by the data of Table 6, which identify the mixture of types of college locally available, i.e., "college-accessibility profiles." Generally there is indeed a positive association between college attendance rates and residence in the college communities, as one would expect from the data of Table 3. But some of the differences are quite modest, and even negative. Let us be more specific.

The California experience with junior colleges—and with their presumed enhancement of college attendance—has received

TABLE 6 ***Differential rates of entry to college among high school graduates by college-accessibility categories in selected studies***

	Rate of college going from noncollege locations (1)	*Public two-year college only* (2)
California communities, 1959[a]		
Percentage to college	32	+17
Percentage to college and/or other postsecondary institution	42	+12
Illinois counties, 1940–41[b]	20	+ 7
Illinois communities, SCOPE, 1966[c]		
Percentage to college, male	48	0
Percentage to college, female	41	+ 8
Kansas counties, 1963[d]	47	+11
Kentucky counties, 1957[e]	26	
New York counties, 1968[f]	63	+ 1
North Carolina counties, 1961[g]	31	
North Carolina communities, SCOPE, 1966[c]		
Percentage to college, male	40	+ 8
Percentage to college, female	38	− 6
Massachusetts communities, SCOPE, 1966[c]		
Percentage to college, male	58	+ 5
Percentage to college, female	54	− 1
Wisconsin counties, 1957[h]	25	
Wisconsin counties, 1963–64[i]	33	− 1
Wisconsin communities, 1957[j]		
Percentage to college, male	32	
Percentage to college, female	23	
Medsker and Trent (16 communities), 1959[k]		
Percentage to college, male	35	+25
Percentage to college, female	32	+14
Percentage to college and/or other postsecondary institutions:		
Male	38	+24
Female	49	+ 4

SOURCES: [a] Beezer and Hjelm, 1961. [b] Griffith and Blackstone, 1945. [c] SCOPE, 1966. [d] The Advisory Committee on Junior Colleges, 1964. [e] Kentucky Council on Public Higher Education, 1958. [f] Drawn from data presented in *College-Going Rate of New York State High School Graduates: 1968–1969,* 1969. [g] Hamilton, 1962. [h] Little, 1959. [i] Tuckman, 1969. [j] Data taken from present study, which draws from studies by Little and Sewell in Wisconsin. [k] Medsker and Trent, 1965.

Excess rates of college going over rates from noncollege locations by home area college-accessibility type							
Private two-year college only	*Teachers college only*	*Extension center only*	*State four-year college only*	*Private four-year college only*	*Multiple colleges*	*Other specifications*	
(3)	*(4)*	*(5)*	*(6)*	*(7)*	*(8)*	*(9)*	*(10)*
		+1	+13		+10		
		−1	+8		+3		
	+15		+17	+5	+16	+3	
+3		−4	+5	+26			
		+3	+15				
+6			+6	+3	+6		
+13			+8	+6	+10		
−3				+1	+3		
			+10	+8	+14	+3	
+12			−17	0	+2	+10	+8
+10			−3	+1	+17	+10	+8
					+23	+5	−8
						+16	−4
				+8	+7	+3	
		−2	+5	−1	+2		
	+2	+9	+9	+13	+9	+18	+23
	+2	+2	+8	+3	+7	+7	+11
		+10	+14		+14		
		−7	+13		+8		
		+10	+14		+14		
		−10	+4		−4		

extensive discussion and publicity, and the effects of accessible two-year colleges in that state a decade ago seem impressive (Table 6, column 2). Perhaps equally striking effects would have appeared for Texas if we had comparable data. But for other states the evidence is at best ambiguous. The SCOPE data for communities outside the Chicago area (the only ones that could be included in column 2) show no advantage in male rates of entry over counties with no colleges at all. Yet the percentages for females are positive relative to female college going from noncollege communities, bringing the rate for women to a par with that for men. Taking both sexes together, the earlier 1940–41 figures for Illinois showed a clear positive differential in the junior college communities, though still a difference much smaller than that for California junior college communities in 1959 or for the Illinois communities with state teachers colleges in 1940–41.

The negligible figure (— 1 percent) for Tuckman's data on Wisconsin community colleges for 1963–64 can be set aside; these are not directly comparable to junior colleges elsewhere. Nor should we be surprised at the slight differences for Massachusetts high school graduates of 1966; it would have been surprising to find positive effects for junior colleges matching those for California. With North Carolina, the puzzle is less the lack of a differential between communities with public junior colleges and with no college (for the sexes combined) as it is the opposite effects for the two sexes. Since identical communities are involved and the net sex difference is 14 percent, there appears to be a definitely selective impact. Perhaps the newer public junior colleges may be eliciting a quick pragmatic economic response among males while a lag persists among females. Insofar as these colleges happen to be in the less advanced sections of the state, the evidence in Table 6 may understate the full impact of these colleges among local males. The strong positive response in both sexes suggested by the North Carolina data for communities with private junior colleges is consistent with the history of these schools and their location (discussed further in Chapter 5); the causation may well run mainly from attitudes toward college to establishment of a private junior college. The evidence for extension centers suggests negligible effects except in Wisconsin, where, for males, the 1957 figures suggest a strong response. These positive results for Wisconsin and the virtual lack of effect of California extension centers are reasonable enough, given the differences between the two systems of higher education and the contrasts in the nature of an extension center remarked on a few pages earlier.

That public institutions will have more effect upon local college attendance often is asserted, and such, indeed, was the implication that Koos wished to draw from his data for Oregon. But by combining with communities possessing public colleges those having both private and public colleges, he weighted his results for what he called "public college communities" toward the educationally intensive and larger communities. Little divided his 1957 data for Wisconsin counties into three sets: communities with some kind of private but no public college, those having either a two- or a four-year public college but without any private school, and communities with various mixtures of private and public colleges. Attendance rates were lower for communities with only public colleges than for those with only private colleges, even though public colleges charged lower tuition. But the seeming contradiction between the Koos and Little findings is spurious. In Wisconsin, public and private colleges are located in different sorts of places. In particular, rural communities with county teachers colleges have other attendance-depressing features so that these schools could exert only a modest influence on the plans of local high school graduates.

If we limit our observations to localities that have only public colleges offering at least a four-year course, there is a positive differential across all the states (except for the strongly negative figure for males in North Carolina). The existence of generally positive differentials raises questions about associated traits of communities that have four-year public colleges but no others. How do such communities compare with others in any of these states? Were public four-year colleges located initially in areas with particularly strong demands for college places[11] or were they sited at random? We need to know more about state conventions or laws that shift responsibility for proposing or initiating a college to state central officials or to local people. And we need much more information about the balance between the community and the academic flavor of different sorts of colleges in the various states. In addition, a college community attracts certain types of in-migrant families, including many who move there to bring college more within reach of their children. Should one expect that the

[11] The processes determining locations of four-year state colleges suggest that this sort of response to demands may be very important in recent California history, as in public systems elsewhere.

present rash of upgrading two-year colleges to four-year colleges and of transforming normal schools to state colleges will change the picture given by Table 6 within a few years? The SCOPE data for North Carolina show that a community may have a four-year public college without having been or becoming especially college prone. Surely the presence of the college does not reduce the frequency of college going. Clearly we have to find some way to identify and isolate the effects of community population features that confound interpretation of statistical associations between college accessibility and rates of attendance.

One piece of evidence from the state data of Table 6 is particularly worthy of note before we examine the evidence presented by Medsker and Trent. This is the longitudinal evidence for Wisconsin, which can be taken essentially at face value since sample biases are negligible. Between 1957 and 1964 there was an 8 percent increase in rates of college going from localities lacking a college, and at the same time differences among such communities became more uniform. It appears that, Milwaukee aside, the state now is quite homogeneous in this respect, almost regardless of variations in accessibility of a local college—and even before adjusting the data for socioeconomic features of the populations or individuals involved.

The study by Medsker and Trent is almost certainly the most cited attempt to trace the effects of college accessibility upon college going. Indeed, it is the only prior study that has attempted directly to identify that association among sets of students individually identified simultaneously by ability and by the social status of their families. We will have occasion to return to their findings as we push behind the analysis presented in this chapter to look at individuals' characteristics. It is important, therefore, that the nature of the Medsker and Trent sample of high schools be made clear—not only for interpreting the data in Table 6 but for subsequent references as well. This is done best by listing the 16 communities they used, their categorizations of those communities, and our checks on the colleges available in their sample communities (Table 7), along with data for community population and median adult schooling. Although their conscientiously chosen sample may be quite satisfactory for many purposes, it has severe limitations when (as in Table 6) each community is treated as one unit of observation. They had only two noncollege communities and both were low in level of adult schooling. So were the com-

TABLE 7 ***Communities in the Medsker and Trent study; population size, median education, and college profiles***

*Medsker and Trent classifications and communities**	*Number of participating high schools*	*Population (thousands)*	*Median grade completed*	*College availability comparison†*
Noncollege communities				
Freeport, Illinois	1	22	9.4	Same
Lorain, Ohio	1	51	9.5	Same
Junior college				
Bakersfield, California	3	35	11.5	Same
Danville, Illinois	1	38	9.2	Same
Hutchinson, Kansas	1	34	11.0	Also technical institute
Joplin, Missouri	1	39	9.9	Also technical institute
Port Huron, Michigan	1	36	10.1	Also technical institute
Extension centers				
Altoona, Pennsylvania	2	77	9.5	Also technical institute
Racine, Wisconsin	4	71	9.5	Also private four-year college
South Bend, Indiana	5	116	10.1	Also technical institute and adjacent private four-year university
Zanesville, Ohio	2	41	9.2	Technical institute only
State college				
Eau Claire, Wisconsin	2	36	10.8	Same
Kalamazoo, Michigan	4	58	10.7	Also one private college and one technical institute
Muncie, Indiana	3	58	10.0	An upgraded teachers college
Springfield, Massachusetts	3	67	10.6	Also private four-year college and a technical institute
Multiple				
San Francisco, California	3	775	11.7	Same

* Medsker and Trent, 1965, p. 107.

† According to *Patterson Education 1957–58,* 1957, "Same" indicates colleges as specified at the left and no others.

munities with extension centers, and for these the rate of college going did not differ from that for noncollege towns. The communities labeled junior college and state college, by contrast, had higher medians for adult schooling as well as higher rates of college going. It should be noticed that three of the five junior college communities also had a postsecondary technical school. According to our information, one of the towns with an extension center also had a private four-year college, three had a technical institute, and one of these had Notre Dame University on its doorstep. Of the four state college communities (with 12 high schools), one had, in addition, both a private college and a technical institute and one of the state colleges had been a teachers college. In conducting the sampling, amidst all the foot-dragging from selected schools, there must have been strong unstated assumptions about the local irrelevance of either private colleges of any kind or technical colleges (public or private) in towns that have general public junior colleges or both a junior college and a state college. Generalization from the Medsker and Trent sample to the national level is the more questionable in view of the fact that Bakersfield (California) accounts for three of the seven high schools in the junior college set; that town has drawn special acclaim and it is moving speedily to acquire a four-year state college.

These data, accordingly, must be read as containing a bias toward the large effects of public institutions. Later we will go behind the gross figures. But any conclusions about the stimulating effect of a local junior college remain exaggerated by the sample of towns used. Nor can a study of this type sort out the ways in which a given kind of college affects college going among youth when the college is moved to very dissimilar settings. Therein lies the paradox, that state by state analysis is at once both more and less useful than a national sample.

3. *Student Migration, College Recruitment Areas, and Locational Substitution Effects*

The central question discussed in Chapter 2 was whether the presence of a college (or certain sets of colleges) near a high school enhanced the rate of college attendance among the high school graduates. In this chapter we focus upon a related but distinct pair of questions. On the one hand, we try to delineate the spatial features of student "supply sheds" or catchment areas; on the other hand, we try to find out whether college locations divert the streams of student migration. We are asking from what localities a college will draw students and we are asking how likely it is that a youth will attend college at various distances from home, depending upon the nature of his options at those distances and upon the geographically intervening opportunities. Both questions must lead to considering, among other things, the extent to which immediate availability of a local college may merely substitute attendance at the local institution for attendance at an institution farther from a given community.

In section 1 we review relevant models of migratory behavior that can be applied to the study of student flows. This discussion will serve as background for later sections, though each is laid out around its own theme. The discussion cannot be kept tidy, since empirical evidence cuts across methods, models, and substantive problems. However, section 2 mainly explores reports on interstate student migration that are of special interest even in a less aggregative context. Section 3 puts the college at the center of the picture, analyzing the spatial patterns from which its students come. Finally, in section 4 we return to the community of origin and raise questions about how much and what kind of locational substitution may occur in the choice of a college.

1. DISTANCE, OPPORTUNITY, AND MIGRATION MODELS

Model 3 (set forth in Chapter 1) allows grouping of elements in order to focus upon a more aggregative aspect of the patterns of college destination among high school graduates. Moreover, instead of aggregating P_{ij} over j to assess the likelihood that an individual will attend college, we could aggregate P_{ij} over i or over subcategories of i to identify the nature of student "supplies" to a particular college or set of colleges. Either way, it is ultimately the probabilities P_{ij} that lie back of more aggregative empirically observed relationships. In Model 3 the distances of the various colleges from the individual's home community enter into each of the P_{ij} values in three ways:

- Through relationships between distance and costs (in the C_{ik} matrix)
- Through dynamic effects on and interactions with preference attitudes (in the A_{ik} matrix)
- Through increased information and intensity of communications (in the V_{ik} matrix)

Many studies of migration skim over these elaborations when they do not just ignore them. Much of the research on migration is the work of rather empiricist-minded demographers and is mainly oriented to aggregative analysis. It often has not seemed important to them to look into the "black boxes" or to try to bring these intervening variables out into view. But the demographic models are relevant for the study of student migration, because along with their emphasis on sheer aggregative scale factors they can be interpreted in the contexts of communication and of decision theory.

Three basic aggregative models have been used in efforts to identify the effect of distance or of spatial structures upon human migrations; each model, with suitable modifications, can be applied to analysis of migratory students. The models are best known in the sparse terms of population density and distance, but other forces of attraction or restraint have sometimes been incorporated into empirical applications of the models. We may call the three models by the following shorthand terms: (1) the gravity model, (2) the population-potential model, and (3) the intervening-opportunity model.

The gravity model This model is derived by analogy with Newtonian physics, using ideas of mass and attractive force. Later applications to migration (and most recently to the planning of transportation systems) were anticipated by Ravenstein's 1885 paper on migration. Zipf (1946) made a rather simplistic application: migration between two cities is proportional to the product of their populations and inversely proportional to the distance between them. An ingenious application of the gravity model to 1963 student migration will be summarized below.

The population-potential model This is an asymmetrically elaborated variation on the gravity model. It can be applied to decisions about the location of a college or business enterprise that will serve a set of consumers or it can deal with the spatial aspects of supplies of labor or materials. The analogy between a college and a business may be taken either way; students are consumer clients and they are also raw material that will be processed. In this model, the drawing potential of a locality z is a function not only of its own population but also of the populations of other localities weighted inversely to their distances from z.[1] Consideration need not be confined to population only, but may embrace any pertinent characteristics; thus estimates of "market potential" may be weighted by income or purchasing power, or by qualifications of potential workers or of students—and usually some types of personnel are recruited from wider areas than are others. In considering possible decisions about college location, one would wish to consider the type of college visualized, to what sort of individuals it will appeal, whether applicants are likely to be youth who prefer to remain near home or to be more footloose, whether they can pay high fees or not, possess high academic capability or not, and so on. Service areas of colleges differ substantially with the type, size, and academic quality of a college. Consideration of market or population potentials is tacit in most systematic efforts to make optimal decisions about location of colleges, especially where the intent is to serve a localized population of students.

The intervening-opportunity model In this model there is explicit acknowledgment that individuals balance the merits of different options. Like the other two models, this one was devised by demographers; Stouffer developed it in 1940 and revised it in 1960 for

[1] The initial concept of population potential was developed by Stewart (1947).

studying intercity migration (Stouffer, 1940, 1960). But as far as we know, the full form of this model has never been applied to an analysis of college choices. Because of its potentials for the study of decisions in education, it will be useful to lay out its elements in detail.

The dependent variable *(Y)* is the flow from one given locality to another; for example, the number of high school graduates from community *w* who enroll in a college in community *z.* Using the notation of Model 3, we then predict:

$$Y_{wz} = \left[\sum_{j=1}^{m} \sum_{i=1}^{n} (P_{ij}) \right]_{wz}$$

As before, P_{ij} is the likelihood that individual i will attend college j. The vector $i = |1 \cdots n|$ refers to high school graduates in w and the vector $j = |1 \cdots m|$ refers to colleges in community z. But as yet we have no operational hypothesis about distance or about the geographic factors affecting the values of P_{ij} and hence of Y. Stouffer emphasized the spatial distribution of opportunities rather than the constraining effects of distance, as one would do if using either the gravity or the population-potential model.

Stouffer defined *opportunity* empirically as the total migration into a city from all other cities. So for students we might think of opportunities in a given college as the total of enrollees (or more narrowly, those from other than the home community in which the college is located). To simplify we will speak of all entrants. One can add further constraints such as the race, religion, or ability of applicants. *Intervening opportunities* appeared in two variants. In the earlier formulation, with respect to movement from w to z, say, they were all opportunities for new entrants to colleges at places within or on the perimeter of a circle around w with a radius equal to the distance from w to z (Figure 1). The opportunities bounded by this circle constitute the variable X_A in Stouffer's first model. The predictive equation in that model was:

$$Y = K(X_M) / X_A \tag{3.1}$$

In a slightly modified version this becomes:

$$\text{Log } Y_A = \text{Log } K + b_M \text{ Log } X_M - b_A \text{ Log } X_A \tag{3.2}$$

FIGURE 1
Intervening opportunities and competing migrants

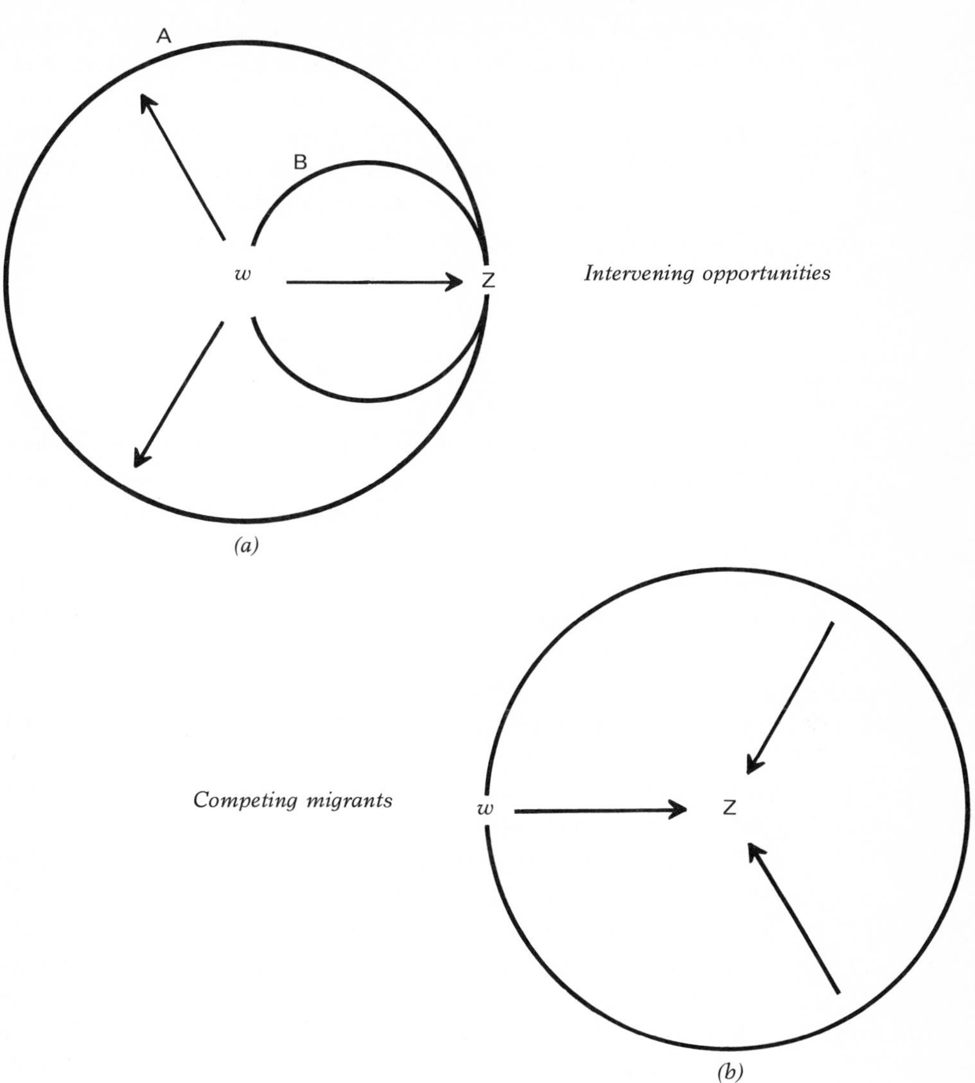

The variable X_M is a scale factor; in Stouffer's analysis it was the total migrants into z multiplied by the total migrants out of w. By analogy we could conceive it as total new enrollees into colleges at z multiplied by total high school graduates from w who went on to college anywhere. The coefficient b_M allows for exponential scale effects on attraction between two places. Stouffer found that this value was always above unity in all variants of his model; there is, in other words, an exponentially disproportionate intensity of migration flows between major centers in comparison with flows among smaller places or between a large and a small place. This phenomenon probably recurs in student migration in the sense that intermetropolitan flows are disproportionate to others.

It will be noticed that Stouffer's model disregarded the geographic directions in which the intervening opportunities lie relative to the line between w and z. Taking X_A as the measure of intervening opportunities, it would make no difference whether they were concentrated between w and z or in another direction from w. This measure of intervening opportunities would weight entrants into colleges lying to the rural side of w from z exactly the same as entrants into colleges lying between w and a more urban z, and vice versa. In application this model gave Stouffer poorer predictions of migration from St. Louis to Denver than from St. Louis to New York. He therefore took as the area delimiting intervening opportunities the circle around the midpoint between w and z (and of radius equal to the distance from that midpoint to either w or z); he called this X_B rather than X_A. Though results were improved, systematic biases persisted. So Stouffer was led to the notion of "competing migrants" (or "competing freshmen"). Stouffer's X_C (interpreted as the number of competing freshmen) would be the total number of college-bound high school graduates in localities as close as or closer to z (including residents of z) as is community w—but excluding the college-bound persons in w. The appropriate picture now is of a circle centered on z, with radius equal to the distance from w to z. We are, so to speak, looking out the windows of a college onto its recruitment area. Though Stouffer did not go beyond ordinary least-squares regressions, the variables X_A and X_C could be viewed as the demand and supply sides of an equation for the determination of the flow of students from w to z, which suggests development of a simultaneous equation model. Although such a model might well be applied to flows of students, its utility would depend upon adequate specification of the determinants of the P_{ij} likelihoods (in the light of factors discussed in Chapter 1). It is unfortunate that resources did not permit this type of analysis in the present inquiry.

2. INTERSTATE STUDENT MIGRATION

Between 1890 and 1920, over a fourth of the individuals attending college had migrated across state borders to do so, excluding students in teachers colleges and, of course, those in the few junior colleges that existed. If we include students in teachers colleges, about a fifth of the students were migrants; this proportion has remained steady since 1930 (Groat, 1964). During this period the overall proportion of youth attending colleges has grown dramatically, with public colleges absorbing a rising proportion of the total. Moreover, the interregional pattern of student migration has altered appreciably. Since the end of the last century the total volume of student in-migration to the several states was more uniform over the country, as was the ratio of students to population from each state. Today, fewer states account for a large proportion of all student out-migration. Even though migrant students are more likely than nonmigrants to attend private colleges, states that rank high in out-migration to private colleges also rank high in out-migration to public colleges, a pattern quite unlike that for student in-migrations. The Northeast has shifted from being a region of strong student in-migration to one of net out-migration, and the West has become a region of net in-migration. These summary figures are supported by studies for recent decades.

Without powers of clairvoyance, one may anticipate a substantial rise in the actual numbers of migrant students in coming decades; in fact, that has occurred since 1958 (Groat's terminal date). If junior colleges become increasingly an adjunct to high schools, the proportions of students who migrate could decline, a result that could occur also due to restrictions imposed for fiscal reasons on out-of-state students at public four-year colleges and universities. Less important than prediction, however, is the need to highlight salient issues. There is especially a need to take account of the spreading pressures not only to expand junior colleges but to institute open-door policies and compensatory schemes—all seen in the light of the growing financial squeeze on higher education.

Gossman and his associates (1968) made an interesting application of the gravity model in a 1965 study of migrant students. They used a highly generalized form in which instead of the populations at origin and destination they specified only R_i as "a parameter representing a factor relating to out-migration at i and A_j to represent in-migration at j." Taking M_{ij} to represent migration volume from i to j and D_{ij} as the distance between the two localities, they obtain

$$M_{ij} = k \frac{R_i A_j}{D_{ij}^{\,b}} \quad \text{where } k \text{ and } b \text{ are constants} \qquad (3.3)$$

Instead of using regression analysis to fit this gravity model to the data on migrant students, the formula was interpreted in terms of the probability of migration from i to j. The origin factor R_i and the destination or "attractiveness" factor A_j were treated as unknown parameters and estimated for each state by use of a maximum likelihood procedure from data on observed volume of migration and distance. The exponent b was taken as 1 and 2 respectively in two versions of the analysis. The maximum likelihood estimators $\widehat{R_i}$ and $\widehat{A_j}$ for R_i and A_j, respectively, are plotted in Figure 2 for migrant undergraduates in public colleges (using the estimates obtained with the exponent 2 on distance, which gave the best fit of the likelihood migration estimates to their observed values for public colleges). In Figure 3 we have plotted $\widehat{A_j}$ for undergraduates in public colleges against the same value for those attending private colleges (in the latter instance taking an exponent of 1 on D, which gave the best fit for private colleges).

As the authors point out, the high rank of California on both $\widehat{R_i}$ and $\widehat{A_j}$ (in Figure 2) reflects not only a large numerical magnitude of migrations both into and out of that state, but also, and primarily, its isolation from the other states that are major sources and destinations of migrating students. In fact, even for migrants to private colleges the value of $\widehat{A_j}$ was largest for California; it exceeded the value for Massachusetts even though only about 11,000 students in this category came into California as against over 38,000 into Massachusetts. "Under the gravity hypothesis, the high value of $\widehat{A_j}$ for California signifies that this state would attract more migrants than Massachusetts were its neighboring states areas of high potential out-migration" (Gossman et al., 1968, p. 161).

The East-West contrast in the drawing power of private compared to public colleges is dramatized in Figure 3. In the lower right corner (with relatively low public but very high private "attraction") we find all of the New England and Middle Eastern states plus Illinois; the extreme cases are New York and Massachusetts. The opposite pattern (high public with low private values) is displayed by Hawaii and Arizona followed by New Mexico and a scattering of northern Plains and Mountain states. For both public and private institutions, there is a generally high drawing power of the Far West, Colorado, and Texas.

The implications with respect to effects of distance were clear; usually an exponent of 1 for distance gave a good fit, especially

FIGURE 2

Pull and push factors in migration of undergraduates to public institutions, 1963

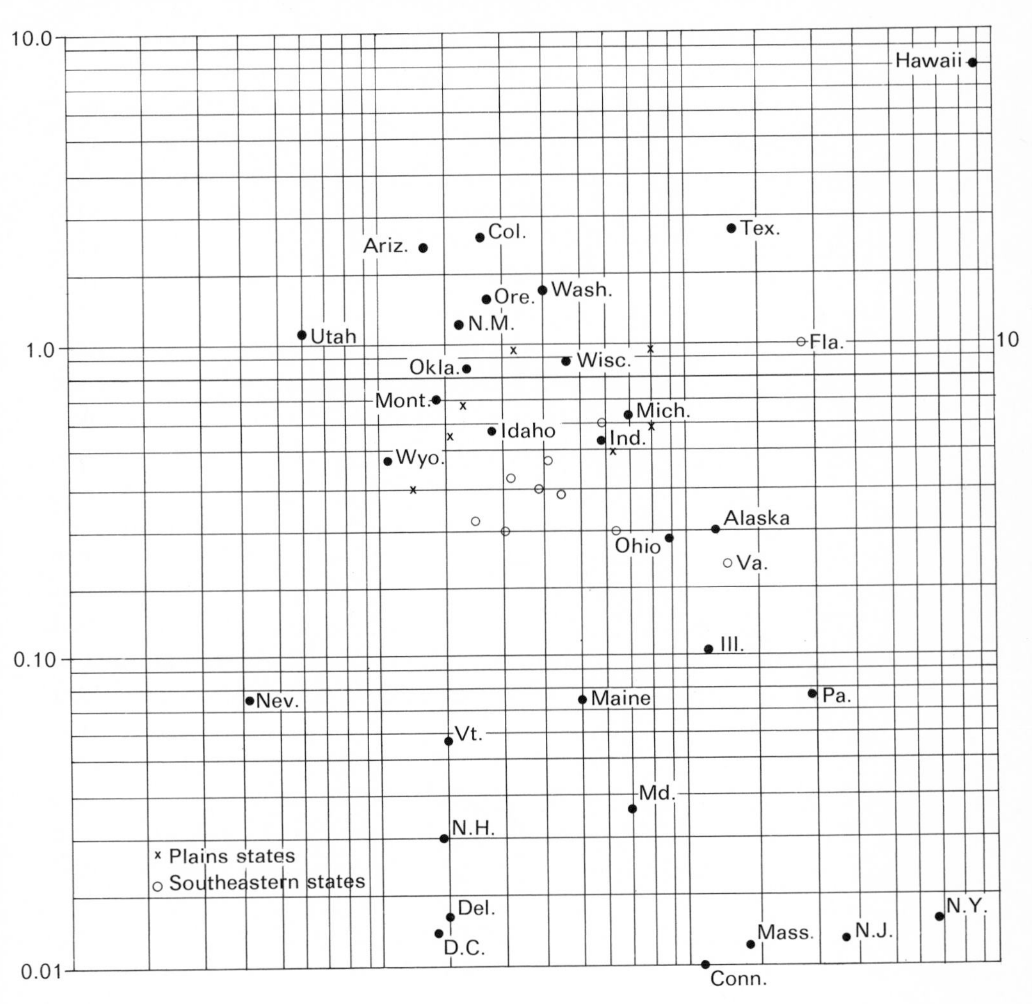

SOURCE: Gossman et al., 1968, pp. 159, 160.

FIGURE 3

Attraction factors in migration to public and private institutions

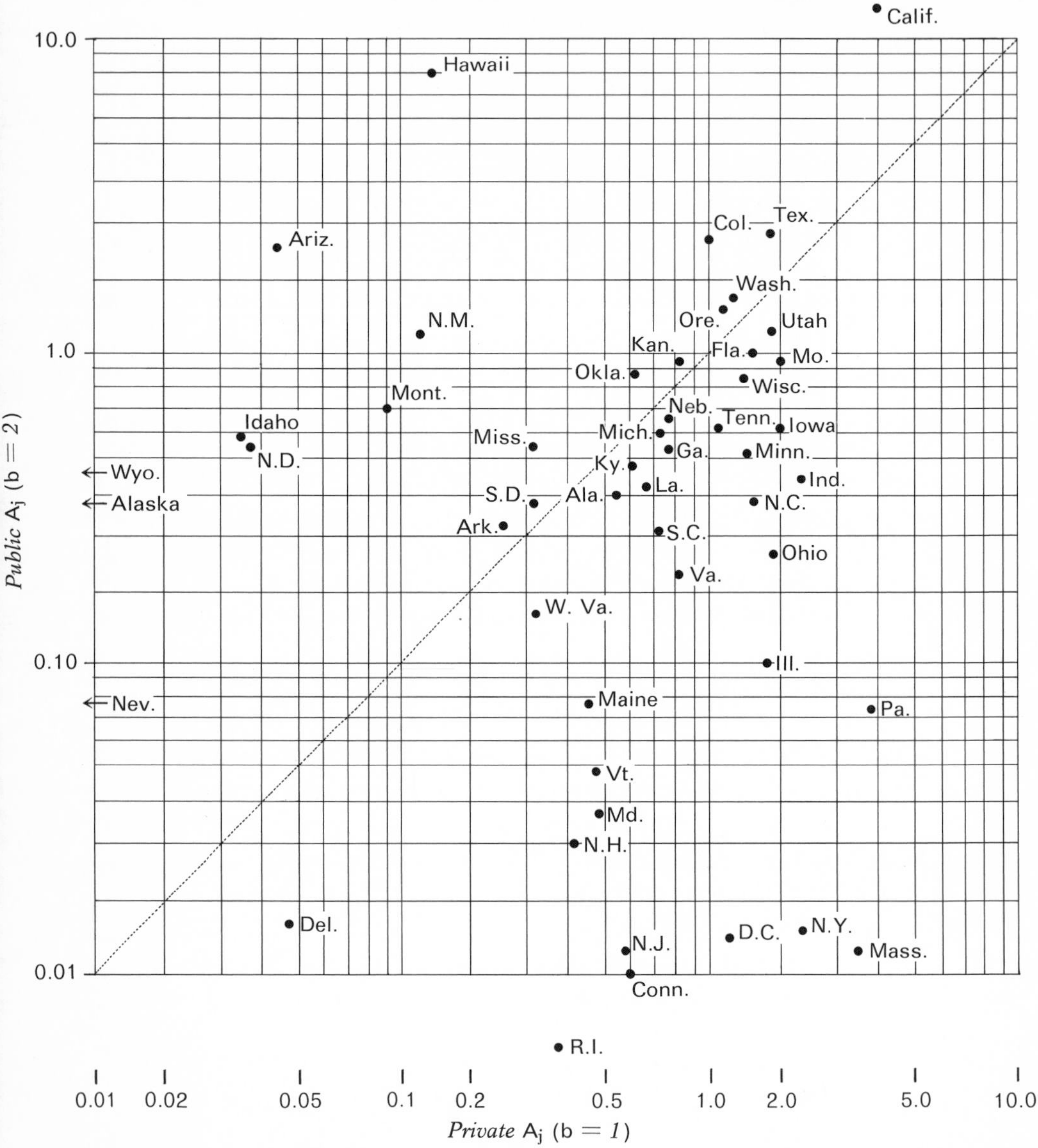

Public A_j (b = 2)

Private A_j (b = *1*)

SOURCE: Gossman et al. 1968, pp. 159, 160.

for graduate students—though for undergraduates in public colleges an exponent of 2 was preferable. Holding constant the influences measured by R_i and A_j, the authors concluded that undergraduates attending public institutions were the least willing to travel long distances to attend college. Nevertheless, they do travel almost as far as undergraduates who attend private colleges; this seeming paradox reflects the well-known regional contrasts in student densities and in concentration of private colleges that were reflected in Figure 3.

As a last step in their analysis, Gossman and his associates examined the correlates of $\widehat{R_i}$ and $\widehat{A_j}$ using stepwise regressions; it was found that in each case a single independent variable accounted for most of the explainable variance. For explanation of variance in $\widehat{A_j}$ (among both graduates and undergraduates in public colleges) the main variable was the income that the state's public colleges received from federal sources. For private colleges the main variable was income to the college from private gifts and grants. The various coefficients of correlation ranged from .76 to .93. Scale effects, quality effects, tuition subsidies, and scholarships are all picked up by such variables.

As an explanation of variance in the origin estimator or scale value $\widehat{R_j}$, 1960 urban population predominated, correlating .90 or higher for all sets of students except undergraduates in public colleges. Though these values are high, they do *not* tell us whether adding another institution in a particular community would increase college attendance among youth in that vicinity.[2] They *do* tell us that young people migrate out of major population centers in large numbers (a trivial scale effect) to attend schools that are well-financed and in which there are available places (a not-so-trivial effect). And they tell us generally that migrant college youth choose the nearer rather than the more distant options, especially in their undergraduate years and if they are attending a public college. We may make surmises about costs in relation to ability to pay or about communication or information fields, but the study just examined provides no direct evidence on these topics.

Finally, by placing the various states on a national spectrum, the investigation of interstate student migration provides a useful background for studies of college locations and student flows on

[2] The negligible effect of distance as a factor in attendance rates at the higher levels of an elitist educational system has been documented in European studies and should hardly cause surprise. Thus, for example, Jef Maton (1966) found that in Belgium area differences in rates of enrollment in higher levels of secondary education and in the universities were significantly related to income per head but bore no relationship to distance from higher institutions (or to local industrial structure).

a smaller scale and in a finer within-state perspective. We will have occasion to refer back to the study by the Washington group when we look intensively at the SCOPE states in Chapter 5.

3. STUDENT RECRUITMENT AND LOCAL SERVICE AREAS

Many studies have been made for the purpose of guiding the choice of location for a new or branch establishment of higher education. Some of these surveys contain little beyond maps of populations with designations of the localities that already possess a college, distinguishing categories of school by level and type. Some of the studies are more sophisticated in their handling of data, and the cumulative yield from these many reports begins to shape up into a coherent pattern.

Two Formal Studies of Spatial Interactance

Models relating to formal gravity structures, population-potential, or intervening opportunities have been used to analyze the spatial pattern and reach of particular colleges in two studies of the origins of particular student bodies. Both studies introduce explicit references to communication or "spatial interactance" for interpreting their data. Harold McConnell studied the county of residence of Ohio undergraduate students at Bowling Green State University (McConnell, 1965). He tried several formulas to define migration potentials ${}_jM_i$ to Bowling Green at the jth location from each other point i, using the following formula:

$$ {}_jM_i = \frac{P_i}{D_{j-i}} \qquad (3.4) $$

in which P_i is the population at i and D_{j-i} is the distance from i to Bowling Green. The migration potential was then used in a zero-order regression to predict enrollments in Bowling Green from each county, expressing all variables in logarithmic form.[3] In his tests of this first formula, McConnell (1965, pp. 31–32) observed by inspection that

> Enrollments for counties located nearer other large public and private universities than they are to Bowling Green and those farthest from Bowling Green are, in general, over-predicted. Those counties located nearer to Bowling Green than to other large universities, those with largest populations and those having highest per capita income are generally areas of underestimation.

[3] Notice that this changes the nature of the hypothesis. On this point, see Gossman et al. (1968, pp. 156–157).

He therefore tried out several versions of the formula. In some an aggregate measure of income was substituted for P_i, simply taking the product of P_i and per capital income to get AI_i; this is a way of picking up income effects on the likelihoods of attending college as well as of migrating to Bowling Green in particular. To allow for possibly exponential effects of travel time, the distance factor in the denominator was tried with exponents of both 2 and 1. And another pair of formulas (with P_i and AI_i, respectively, in the numerator) were tested replacing distance in the denominator by a measure of intervening opportunities (O_i), defined as the number of colleges nearer the population center of the county of origin than is Bowling Green, regardless of direction.[4]

All variants of the model explained the flows very well, as we should expect, given the substantial size factor that was built into them; and for much the same reason there was little difference among the variants. Coefficients of determination ranged from .790 for the migration-potential P_i/O_i to .884 for AI_i/D_j^2–i. Unfortunately, as with other conventional applications of gravity and related models, there is underdetermination of results and failure to discriminate with respect to the critical factors at work. Scale factors swamp other effects so long as the dependent variable is an aggregate flow rather than a measure of rates of movement. It would have been better to carry the analysis further and to control for scale effects of the population at origin in an exploration of how other factors may have affected the migration-distance patterns. To suggest this, however, is to raise a quite different set of questions.

A study of enrollments at Western Washington State College (at Bellingham) by H. G. Kariel (1968) is of conceptual interest because of his attempt to specify information fields by the use of data on telephone toll messages to other parts of the state (for 10 days in June of 1962). His design draws peripherally upon the ideas of the human geographer, Hägerstrand.[5] Unfortunately, scale effects again swamp the analysis. However well such models may predict student market or supply-area potentials from a recruiter's point of view, they are far too crude for a discriminating analysis of the effects of policies for locating colleges.

[4] It is unfortunate that this measure was the number of institutions, without regard to their size or type.

[5] See Hägerstrand (1965, 1967). The subtleties of Hägerstrand's analysis seem to have been unappreciated, however.

Competing Colleges and Recruitment Ranges

There is much to be said for going back to see what can be learned from descriptive-quantitative compilations of a less formalized sort (even without using complex statistical or econometric models). Many data are widely scattered through reports on the higher education systems of many states, especially in studies intended to determine the need for additional colleges. Much of the material is unorganized, and most of the older studies paid little attention to migration distances beyond a mere local-nonlocal distinction. Some reports present data on the putative effects of available college alternatives in the area, or relate type of institution to the proportions of students recruited locally. These reports are a kind of reverse image of the studies on rates of college going discussed in Chapter 2.

How the presence of other colleges, and the combination of types of colleges, affects the number of entrants to a given college has received attention in many reports over the past 40 years and more—and was exemplified in the 1965 McConnell study discussed above. Perhaps the earliest survey of the geography of higher education in relation to presumptive needs was that conducted for Indiana in 1926 by Judd (Judd et al., 1926). He and his associates began with four maps of enrollments from each county in each of four state colleges, expressing these as ratios of youth in the 1925 school census for each county of origin. Informal scanning of these maps revealed no systematic effect of distance for attendance at Indiana University, moderate effect for Purdue (the land-grant school) and for the normal school at Terre Haute, and a decided negative distance factor for attendance at Ball Teachers College. (The latter being a new institution, the authors assumed its recruitment area would expand.) The effect of what we would now call "intervening opportunities" was noticed for the presence of a private or denominational college in a county—what we will call "locational substitution." "As a general rule, a county containing such an institution will show a relatively small percent of its school census enrolled in state institutions, irrespective of its distance from them" (ibid., p. 54).

Few would risk saying how far that observation could be generalized for the 1920s, let alone for today. One would hardly challenge the vague conclusion that, other things being equal, the drawing power of an individual college will be affected by the mixture of opportunities available in the same area.[6] Just how these mixes

[6] This was asserted in the 1932 study by Reeves et al. It has been reasserted over four decades by a number of writers, but with little or no evidence.

of colleges exert their effects, and even in what directions, is another matter; the relationships will surely not be simple. One recent study indeed contends that being located near other colleges sometimes could be a facilitating factor: "Schools located near SUNY campuses at which the major developments have taken place did substantially better than the 48 school average" (Nelson, 1967). It would be interesting to know what may lie back of this observation. Just what was it in the developments on these SUNY campuses from 1961 to 1966 that spilled over onto nearby private colleges? Proximity in general to SUNY campuses evoked no such effects, and private colleges near the CUNY sites (in greater New York City) grew more slowly than did those in other localities.

The study of 35 colleges (all associated with the Methodist church) by Reeves and his associates (1932) had the advantage of dealing with colleges scattered widely over the map. Half the colleges were on the approved list of the Association of American Universities. When the college was located in a city of 100,000 population or more, about 46 to 47 percent of students commuted in the approved and nonapproved colleges alike. However, the commuter proportions dropped sharply among the approved colleges as the college community became smaller (to 13 percent for towns under 40,000), whereas among the nonapproved colleges the decline in proportions commuting was slight. (Even nonapproved colleges in places with under 40,000 population had 38 percent commuters.) Greater visibility or a wider geographic appeal of high- over low-quality colleges is to be expected quite generally, and in other sets of colleges with quite different affiliations.

The comments by the Reeves team concerning the effects of competing colleges have a definitely modern sound, and remain timely for the most basic disputes about policy today. For example, they had this to say concerning competition between liberal arts and junior colleges (p. 34):

> Junior colleges are beginning to be an important factor in higher education in the territories served by several of the institutions included in this study. During the course of the survey visits, the question was frequently raised as to the probable ultimate effect of the junior college movement upon the service of the four-year college of liberal arts. It now seems clear that the strong and well-administered colleges of liberal arts have nothing to fear from the competition of the junior college, although a few of the weaker four-year colleges in this group may ultimately find it desirable to become public or denominational junior colleges. While the development of public junior colleges in neighboring centers of population has at some

of these colleges resulted in temporary decreases in the enrolments of the freshman and sophomore years, when the situation once becomes established this loss is more than made up by the additional enrolments in the junior and senior years. . . . The situation is perhaps best illustrated in California, where the junior college movement has reached its most extensive development. The College of the Pacific, which is located so as to feel the full effect of the junior college competition, finds that it has larger enrolments in the two upper years than in the lower division, and has also a rather large postgraduate student body.

The sweeping expansion in college attendance over the country together with the singular position of California in higher education underlay the last observation. The remark also presaged developments in the public colleges of California during the 1960s, with the further expansion and specialization of junior colleges, four-year state colleges, and universities. The Reeves group saw the competition of strong, neighboring four-year colleges as a much more serious threat to the liberal arts colleges than the potential competition from junior colleges.

Recruitment Areas and Destinations by Type of College

In a 1941 study of higher education in New York State, Philip Cowen analyzed local proportions in recruitment to various colleges (Table 8). Some of his findings were quite to be expected: municipal colleges were of the commuter type and enrolled local residents only. Colleges in New York City drew a large majority of students from that metropolis. Students attending low-tuition colleges were preponderantly local (78 percent). The localism of Catholic colleges doubtless reflects their location mainly within high-density population centers. Conversely, high-cost colleges, those in the smaller communities, and colleges with high-ability entrance requirements drew large proportions of enrollees from nonlocal places. There was also a monotonic order of direct costs to students with size of place. Beyond these limited generalizations, further conclusions from these data should be made with care.[7]

Another study of particular interest was carried out in the 1940s by Strayer and associates in the state of Washington; some of the results are given in Table 9. The teachers colleges (of great importance then and only recently being transformed into state

[7] The low-tuition, local-attendance syndrome should be noted in view of the cost-lowering effect of this combination. Unfortunately, Cowen's report did not go beyond the local-nonlocal dichotomy in recruitment as related to distance.

TABLE 8 Local recruitment of students in New York institutions of higher education in 1941

Characteristics of colleges	*Number of institutions*	*Median percentages of students from local area*
Classification I (table 10, p.30)		
Municipal colleges	4	100
Universities	12	41
Liberal arts colleges	34	36
Separate engineering schools	5	21
State teachers colleges	11	18
TOTAL	66	36
Classification II (table 11, p.37)		
Roman Catholic	19	62
Other church	5	20
Nonchurch	27	21
Sex of student body (table 12, p.37)		
Men only	16	52
Women only	20	37
Coeducational	30	30
Tuition and other direct costs to student; excludes zero tuition institutions (table 13, p.41)		
$467 and over	10	4
401–466	14	36
301–400	14	51
300 and less	11	78
Size of college-age population (table 14, p.41)		
New York City (628,049)	20	76
4,630–62,508	26	36
644–4,588	20	10
Preferred ability cutoff (table 15, p.42)		
Highest 10%	1	1
Highest 25%	9	24
Highest third	14	41
Upper half	20	27
Lower half	12	49
No information	10	

SOURCE: Cowen, 1946.

TABLE 9 ***Geographic selectivity of recruitment and destination among entering freshmen to higher education in the state of Washington, 1945***

	Washington state institutions				
			State colleges of education		
	University	State college	West	Central	East
Recruitment areas					
Percentages from:					
Home county	67	9	62	26	54
Adjacent counties	13	22	15	43	25
All others	20	69	23	31	21
Destinations from designated origins					
Percentages of:					
Home county students	95	92	44	61	15*
Adjacent county students not near other schools	73	55	18	18	15
Adjacent county students also in or adjacent to other schools	35	24		1†	16‡
Other places (nonadjacent) in or adjacent to other schools	32	5	1	6	2
Neither in nor adjacent to other schools	58	35	3	4	1
School's percentage of all students entering state institutions from any in-state location	73	20	3	3	2
Number of students	8,721	2,340	329	355	196
Population of home county	63,760	5,100	6,630	2,720	21,700
Population of adjacent counties	56,650	4,758	6,960	86,270†	8,720‡

* Also adjacent to the state university.

† Includes the home county of the state university.

‡ Includes the home county of the state college.

SOURCE: Computed from data in Strayer, 1946. The population figures are from the U.S. Census of Population, 1950.

colleges) recruited from a narrower radius in Washington than in New York. But the heavy draught of the University of Washington from its home county occurred largely because that county contained the greatest concentration of potential students to begin with, not because the university lacked a statewide appeal. Washington State College (at Pullman), by contrast, was in a rural locale.

Indeed, when we turn the figures around to explore destinations of youth residing in home or adjacent counties for the given colleges, the pattern looks quite different. Over 90 percent of state college enrollees in 1945 who resided in the home counties of the state university and the state college entered the home institution. So also did majorities of those residing in adjacent counties that lacked (and did not lie adjacent to other counties possessing) other public colleges. The effects of competing local opportunities can be seen as we move from row (5) to row (6) and again in the contrast between row (7) and row (8) insofar as concerns the two major state-supported colleges. Indeed, 58 percent of college-going youth from counties lacking local or neighboring colleges entered the university and 35 percent entered the state college. The percentages paralleling those just given were 32 and 5 for youth residing in nonadjacent localities possessing (or lying next to a county that possessed) public colleges. These data for Washington underline the importance of looking at student migration from the perspective of the college as well as from that of the locale of origin of students or prospective students. The data also make clear the importance of comparing the net expansionary effects with the substitution effects of establishing a new college in any given location.

The recruitment areas of state institutions of higher education in Michigan (in 1955) are summarized in Table 10, which barely skims the surface of the rich data in the report. The spatial patterns in recruitment to Michigan colleges reflect the interaction of population distributions in relation to the sites of colleges with the visibility of different colleges and with the range of geographic orientation observable among various sets of students. One striking finding (that appeared also in the 1941 New York study) is that specialized technical schools draw students from a very wide area.

Wisconsin is one of the states for which we have the fullest information, and a substantial part of the new analysis in later chapters relates to that state. Combining the detailed appendices in the Hawthorne-Lins study of Wisconsin students for 1964 and 1967, it is possible to contrast the recruitment areas by type of college (Table 11). The University of Wisconsin in Milwaukee is a truly municipal-state institution, with nearly all students coming from adjacent counties. The truly statewide college is the university at Madison; and though Madison draws considerable numbers from outside the state, the state colleges also recruit widely. The strong local representation in the University Extension Centers

TABLE 10 ***Geographic origins of students enrolled in public institutions of higher education in Michigan, 1955***

State institutions	*Estimated college-age population of home county 1955*	*Estimated college-age population of adjacent counties 1955*	*Number of counties represented by students*	*Percentage of enrollment from:*	
				Home county	*Home and adjacent counties*
University of Michigan	5,433	158,033	83	22	66
Michigan State University	9,035	20,096	83	20	31
Wayne State University	117,563	46,348	82	83	93
Western Michigan University	6,198	18,609	74	33	56
Central Michigan College	1,876	10,108	77	13	29
Eastern Michigan College	5,433	158,033	60	24	86
Northern Michigan College	2,737	7,648	35	44	77
Michigan College of Mining and Technology	2,240	2,415	82	14	21
Ferris Institute	1,229	7,508	81	8	16

SOURCE: Russell et al., 1955, tables 1 and 5.

TABLE 11 ***Percentages of Wisconsin freshmen from home counties, adjacent counties, and other states, 1964 and 1967***

Type of institution	*1964*			*1967*		
	From home county	*From home and adjacent county*	*From other states*	*From home county*	*From home and adjacent county*	*From other states*
University of Wisconsin, Madison	19	29	34	19	25	28
University of Wisconsin, Milwaukee	80	93	2	80	92	3
University Extension Centers	73	87	2	79*	94*	2*
State colleges	20	41	11	16	34	14

County teachers colleges: there were 34 listed in 1964 of which six had closed by 1968. Students were virtually all from home or adjacent counties and in the aggregate these colleges took in about 600 students annually.

Private colleges enrolled 3,248 freshmen in 1964 and 3,529 in 1968.

* Excludes two centers established in 1968.

SOURCE: Computed from data and maps in Hawthorne and Lins, 1968.

(the two-year branches of the state university) testifies to their distinctive role as arms of the university reaching out into rural localities; this pattern of enrollment in the centers occurs despite the fact that ability criteria for entry match those applied at the university. Not only does "the state is our campus" remain a vivid ideal in Wisconsin, the walls and not only the extramural programs have been extended to draw in students who will finish their baccalaureate work in large numbers at Madison. Obviously this is not the California pattern; the few community colleges and specialized local-municipal colleges could be omitted from Table 11 without major alteration of conclusions.

Junior Colleges and the Concept of Service Areas

One of the most detailed delineations of the spatial dimensions of estimated needs for new colleges is to be found in the study by Hamilton and his associates (1962) for North Carolina. Their work rested upon the principle that distance to college is related directly to the choice to attend it. They developed the notion of "service area" for individual colleges, areas bounded by a travel time of not over 45 minutes. The criteria included present and potential densities of student populations and the growth potentials of the respective areas.

Even more elaborate use of the notion of service areas has been made by the California agencies concerned with planning for higher education. But the California situation has many distinctive features; for example, a large proportion of the service areas and their centers are highly urban or belong to conurbations. Consequently, the most difficult issues about location are intra-urban, and social distance within large cities may be more important for recruitment to college than is geographic distance. In less metropolitan states (and notably in such regions as Appalachia) social distance is more closely linked to time or costs distance as service areas become stretched out from cities into large or inaccessible hinterlands. In addition to distinctive settlement patterns, Appalachia and some other regions have distinctive levels of adult education and of outlooks upon the utility of education.[8]

4. LOCATIONAL SUBSTITUTION EFFECTS

Our discussion several times has edged up to the question: How far does the location of a college (of any given kind) within a community simply substitute enrollment of local residents in that new

[8] Willingham (1970) and Medsker and Tillery (1971) are two very useful studies of the open-door or free-access college.

institution for what would have been attendance elsewhere? To what degree is a college an expression of preexisting educational interests, and how far does it bring about a net increase in college attendance? The data for the state of Washington (in Table 9) were especially relevant, but the question of substitution is attacked more directly in Table 12 (using data that are more exhaustively

TABLE 12 ***Summary analysis of net location and locational substitution effects: Wisconsin, 1957, and SCOPE samples for Illinois and North Carolina, 1966***

	Wisconsin communities (excluding Milwaukee), 1957 (Sewell data)*		*Illinois communities†, 1966 (SCOPE sample)*		*North Carolina communities† (SCOPE sample)*	
	Noncollege	*College*	*Noncollege*	*College*	*Noncollege*	*College*
			Male students			
a *Total number*	2,276	1,784	968	3,305	2,897	2,584
b *Number to college*	731	729	469	1,892	1,171	1,190
Percentages to college:						
c *Total*	32.3	40.8	48.5	57.4	40.4	46.0
d *Maximum net location effect* $= C_w - C_o$	(8.5)		(8.9)		(5.6)	
e *Within community*		14.1		20.4		14.4
f *Beyond 60 miles or out of state*	21.9	22.8	31.6	30.8	27.9	25.2
Percentage distribution of college entrants by distance to destination (row b = 100%)						
g *Within community*		34.6		35.5		31.3
h *Within 20 miles, outside community*	14.2	3.7	14.9	6.4	16.9	.9
i *20–60 miles*	17.5	5.9	20.1	4.3	14.2	13.2
j *Beyond 60 miles, in state*	49.6	36.4	47.1	25.3	61.3	43.5
k *Out of state*	18.6	19.4	17.9	28.4	7.5	11.0
TOTAL	99.9	100.0	100.0	99.9	99.9	99.9
Indexes of locational substitution effect						
l $S_1 = [(g + h)_w - (g + h)_o]$	24.1		27.0		15.3	
m $S_2 = C_o S_1$	7.8		13.1		6.2	
n $S_3 = (e - d)$	5.6		11.5		8.8	

TABLE 12 ***(continued)***

		Wisconsin communities* (excluding Milwaukee), 1957		Illinois communities†, 1966		North Carolina communities†, 1966	
		Noncollege	College	Noncollege	College	Noncollege	College
		Female students					
a	*Total number*	2,244	1,929	928	3,485	3,106	2,790
b	*Number to college*	493	555	381	1,702	1,171	1,260
Percentages to college							
c	*Total*	22.0	28.7	41.1	48.8	37.7	45.1
d	*Maximum net location effect* $= C_w - C_o$	(6.7)		(7.7)		(7.4)	
e	*Within community*		9.2		14.4		11.4
f	*Beyond 60 miles or out of state*	13.7	16.1	30.6	26.4	26.5	26.6
Percentage distribution of college entrants by distance to destination (row b = 100%)							
g	*Within community*	0.0	32.1	0.0	29.5	0.0	25.2
h	*Within 20 miles, outside community*	15.6	5.6	10.5	12.0	14.3	1.1
i	*20–60 miles*	22.3	6.1	15.3	4.4	15.4	14.7
j	*Beyond 60 miles, in-state*	40.7	36.6	56.7	27.2	63.6	45.8
k	*Out of state*	21.3	19.6	17.5	26.8	6.6	13.2
	TOTAL	99.9	100.0	100.0	99.9	99.9	100.0
Indexes of locational substitution effect							
l	$S_1 = [(g + h)_w - (g + h)_o]$	22.1		31.0		12.0	
m	$S_2 = C_o S_1$	4.9		12.7		4.5	
n	$S_3 = (e - d)$	2.5		6.7		4.0	

SOURCE: * Data obtained from a 1963 Wisconsin study by William Sewell. See Sewell, 1963. † SCOPE, 1966.

analyzed in later parts of the present report). The indexes are crude; thus, all sorts of colleges are combined to yield a simple dichotomization between college and noncollege communities. As yet the students are not differentiated for ability or family status and their options are only foreshadowed; nevertheless, the data are suggestive.

The gross differentials in attendance rates between college and noncollege communities are shown in line *(d)*—for males and females in the upper and lower parts of the table, respectively. In rows *(g)* through *(k)* the youth attending college were distributed by distance between home and college. Among youth of Illinois and North Carolina, irrespective of sex, those residing in communities with a college were much more likely to attend a college outside of the state; in Wisconsin the excess was slight. Surely this difference—seemingly in paradoxical opposition to one's expectations—reflects characteristics of communities in which colleges are located more than it does the simple presence of a college. At the other extreme, one cannot attend a college locally where there is none, and for a fair proportion of youth in noncollege communities there was no college within 20 miles. Conversely, except for areas of relatively large population concentrations, existence of a college within one's community reduces the likelihood that there will also be another college outside of the community but within 20 miles. These situations, so clearly portrayed in the table, may help to account for the comparatively large proportions of college-bound youth from noncollege communities of Illinois and Wisconsin who attended schools lying between 20 and 60 miles from home, but there is no parallel distinction between youth from college and from noncollege towns in North Carolina. (Percentages going to out-of-state colleges were remarkably small for North Carolina.)

The effort to identify location-substitution effects by the aid of these data can be pursued along several paths. We can simply compare the college-bound youth from communities with and without colleges in respect to their destinations; row *(g)* provides the simplest measure of this kind.

A slight modification is to compute the index of substitution S_1: the difference in percentages attending college within 20 miles of home for those going to college from communities with and without a local college. This index ranged from only 12 for girls in North Carolina to 31 for girls in Illinois.

The quite different substitution index S_2 is expressed in relation to total high school graduates in noncollege towns; S_2 is multiplied by the overall rate of college attendance (C_o) among youth from noncollege communities. Choice of the noncollege communities for the base multiplier reduces most of the estimates of S_2 compared to what we would get if we took C_w as the multiplier. S_2 turns out, nevertheless, to constitute a major fraction of or even substantially to exceed the differentials between college and noncollege communities in overall rates of college attendance.

Finally, we assigned the entire aggregate differential in rates of college going (row *d*) to destinations within the community; this figure was then subtracted from the percentage of youth from college locations attending at home (row *e*) to get a net local substitution figure, S_3, for the youth from college communities. Any indirect effects of the presence of a college in positively encouraging attendance elsewhere are ignored. In most situations this assumption is justified if only because any indirect effects are too fine-grained to rise above other unmeasured but relevant community traits. It turns out that S_3 constitutes well over half of the home-community rates of attendance of men in college towns of Illinois and North Carolina, but well under half among men in Wisconsin and among women generally. Some of the factors that may explain these and other contrasts will emerge in ensuing chapters as we push into a more intensive examination of the patterning of options and responses among youth in the states we studied in detail.

SUMMARY Our main task in this chapter was to find and lay out evidence about the determinants of recruitment areas for various kinds of colleges and for the geographic subpopulations from which students come. On some points, evidence about this complex of problems is clear, but on others it is ambiguous. It all depends on how we ask the questions and how we specify the key variables. Studies designed to determine where new colleges or branches should be sited typically start by making overly simple assumptions about the critical relationships and the probable responses by youth. They then collect data on distribution of people and of the college places needed in the light of particular assumptions they chance to have chosen. Where studies have probed more deeply the emphasis has usually been upon estimating local versus nonlocal recruitment rather than upon determining recruitment distances. There is good reason for this; many inquiries have shown the existence of a sharp breaking point beyond commuting range, and "local" tends conveniently to be seen in terms of "commuting areas." One can list several tentative generalizations from these various surveys:

1 Some sorts of colleges have high visibility and draw students from wide areas.

2 The size of recruitment areas is related inversely to local population density, especially for public colleges.

3 Recruitment areas are larger for schools that set higher ability criteria for admission.

4 Distance response patterns in choosing a college have differed substantially over time and across states in association with contrasts in characteristics of systems of higher education, in settlement patterns, and in cultural-educational heritages.

5 College-going students from counties that are relatively remote from major educational centers are considerably more likely to attend the big state (and national) institutions when no local colleges are at hand than they would otherwise. However, effects of college mix are otherwise ambiguous with respect to "supplies" of students.

6 Serious underspecification and the dominance of scale variables in statistical applications of migration models to the analysis of spatial patterns in student recruitment limits the value of the models, despite high coefficients of determination.

Few of these generalizations are startling. What is not included is important. Above all, these ommissions relate to characteristics of individuals, of high schools, and of communities of origin as all these affect sensitivity and selectivity of response to college options and to the location of those options. Among other things, even when the questions are posed from the market-recruitment point of view we may have to work our way back into the communities of origin and to individuals residing in those communities.

Student recruitment areas, effects of the local presence of a college upon "supplies" of students, and substitution effects of local colleges upon the distance that youth will go to attend college are interrelated phenomena. Ultimately, we must use simultaneous-equation models, but prior to that we need samples more stringently selected than any as yet available (other than the 1957 sample for Wisconsin). It is absolutely critical, also, to disaggregate colleges by types and related characteristics, on the one hand, and to disaggregate potential students on the other hand. Finally, to ask whether the addition of a college will raise attendance because of its presence is almost useless information unless we at the same time ask what attendance is going to be displaced by enrollment in the newly accessible school.

4. *From High School to College in Wisconsin*

Thus far, in relating college attendance to college accessibility we have used evidence that pertains to populations or aggregates, not to individuals, and no allowance has been made for differences in ability among the potential students or for differences in family background. The unit of observation has been a whole community or a county. These aggregate units were distinguished to some extent by size and density of population as well as by some indicator of college accessibility; we could have made a more intensive analysis of these units but that would have been a less profitable procedure than the one we used and it was impracticable to do both. In the remainder of this report we will try to find out, with considerable definitiveness, how much personal ability or family social status affects the interaction between college accessibility and rates or patterns of college attendance. We begin in this chapter with an examination of the data for Wisconsin; despite being a decade old, these are the most suitable data obtainable for the central questions of this investigation.

1. SOME PRELIMINARY OBSERVATIONS

To go beyond the rough comparisons of the preceding two chapters, we must be specific about the main characteristics of a given system of higher education. Accordingly we will lay out what we believe are the pertinent features of the Wisconsin system, tracing some alterations in its scale and composition over the last decade. Next we will recapitulate a few relationships between accessibility and attendance discussed in Chapter 2, from which we will move directly into critical questions concerning determinants of attendance rates as related to accessibility and to certain other elements in the "college decision." But first it is important to comment on statistical methods and on the confounding effects of association between the size of a community and its degree of college accessibility.

Higher Education in Wisconsin

From its establishment in 1848, the university at Madison has been the core of the Wisconsin system. It became the land-grant college by virtue of the Morrill Act, and the "Wisconsin Plan" for a vast university adult education program for rural areas became a model much copied in other states. Meanwhile, this extension of the extramural university to serve a widely spread noncollege population was paralleled by the opening of the two-year Extension Centers designed mainly to serve as routes to the university at Madison (and later also in Milwaukee). This system now enrolls about 12 percent of all those who finish high school in the state; in 1967 the Extension Centers accounted for a third of that 12 percent. Adding freshmen in the regional four-year colleges and branches of what is now called the "State University System" to the freshmen in the "University of Wisconsin system," a third of the state's 1967 high school graduates became part of that state system, which in all accounted for five-sixths of the total entrants to collegiate institutions in Wisconsin. In addition to these entrants into the state system in 1967, 3,500 high school graduates entered private colleges in their home state; this was 5 percent of the total high school graduating cadre or about one-seventh of all Wisconsin youth who that year began college. Six percent of the 1967 high school graduates entered colleges in other states; half again as many freshmen for Wisconsin colleges came from other states. A trickle of youth entered the state teachers colleges (about 600–700 annually over the past decade).

Up to 1967, the statistics did not include entrants to vocational, technical, and adult education schools (mainly municipal), and they were not included in the above accounts for college freshmen. Recently, their numbers have been substantial, however, and in the year of 1967 the count of entrants to these schools who had had no prior postsecondary schooling was 15,000, amounting to an impressive 36 percent of all new Wisconsin entrants into public or private colleges and noncollegiate institutions taken together.

Changes over nearly a decade in the relative importance of various college institutions (exclusive of vocational-technical or adult-education institutions) as absorbers of new high school graduates are shown in Figure 4. Most conspicuous is a near doubling of the proportions entering regional state colleges. These, along with the Extension Centers, absorbed nearly all the increased intake of youth from Wisconsin high schools. Private colleges

FIGURE 4 ***Percentages of Wisconsin high school graduates entering college by type of institution, 1959–1967***

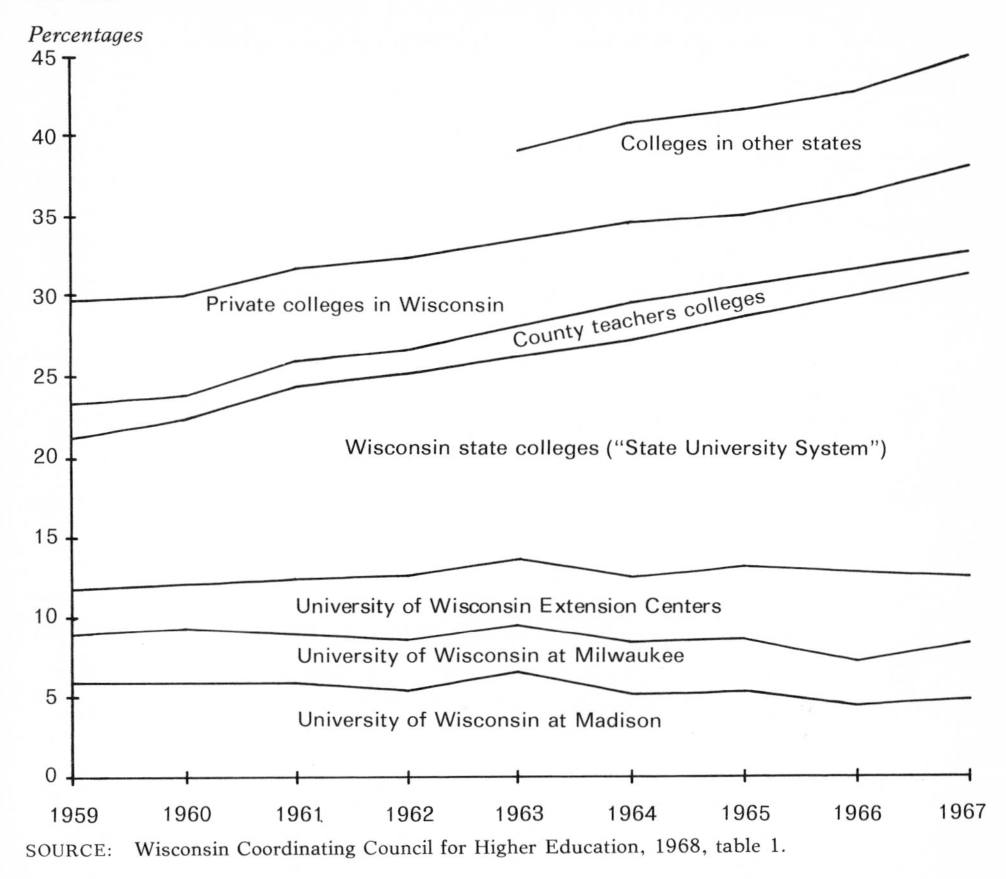

SOURCE: Wisconsin Coordinating Council for Higher Education, 1968, table 1.

experienced a slight loss in the proportion of high school graduates they attracted.

As the term "junior college" is commonly used, there has been no marked development of this kind of school in Wisconsin. The two-year county teachers colleges play a negligible role, and, as anachronisms, are about to lose their state subsidies. The two-year Extension Centers are distinctive in being part of the university, with full transfer of credits to the university when desired. Some of the vocational-technical or adult schools are comprehensive, conferring a two-year associate degree and offering a variety of other adult programs; other schools offer programs quite closely tailored to local requests. Wisconsin has the elements of a junior or community college system, but colleges that explicitly warrant that title are scarce and are located where other colleges also are operating.

The College-Accessibility Profiles

To identify the effects of college accessibility upon the rates and selectivity of college attendance, we had to specify the local college "profiles" in accordance with the locations of colleges in 1957, when the youth in the sample were graduating from high school. Two designations were used: the community, meaning the town or city in which the youth finished high school; and a zone that included the community but extended outward for 20 miles. The categories used to derive the profiles within-community college accessibility were as follows:

1. None (noncollege communities)
2. State colleges: four-year parts of the state college system, now called state universities
3. Private four-year colleges
4. County teachers colleges
5. University Extension Centers
6. Madison: this community (capital of the state and home of the university) is sufficiently distinctive to be treated separately
7. Milwaukee
8. Milwaukee Region A (Shorewood, Whitefish Bay, Wauwatusa, all north of the city)
9. Milwaukee Region B (Cudahy, Greendale, South Milwaukee, West Milwaukee, West Allis)
10. "Multiple" (referring to other locations with more than one college). In each of these locations at least one institution offered less than a four-year program; in other words, each included a University Extension Center, a vocational-technical college, or some kind of teachers college, in addition to one or more four-year collegiate or university (public or private) institutions.

When the local area was defined by the 20-mile radius, the classifications were essentially the same, except that the Milwaukee areas were combined and the "multiple" classification (which now becomes considerably larger) was subdivided to distinguish types of mixtures in the local college profiles. The city of Milwaukee itself was excluded from most of the regressions, but it is included

FIGURE 5 ***Distribution of the population of Wisconsin, 1960***

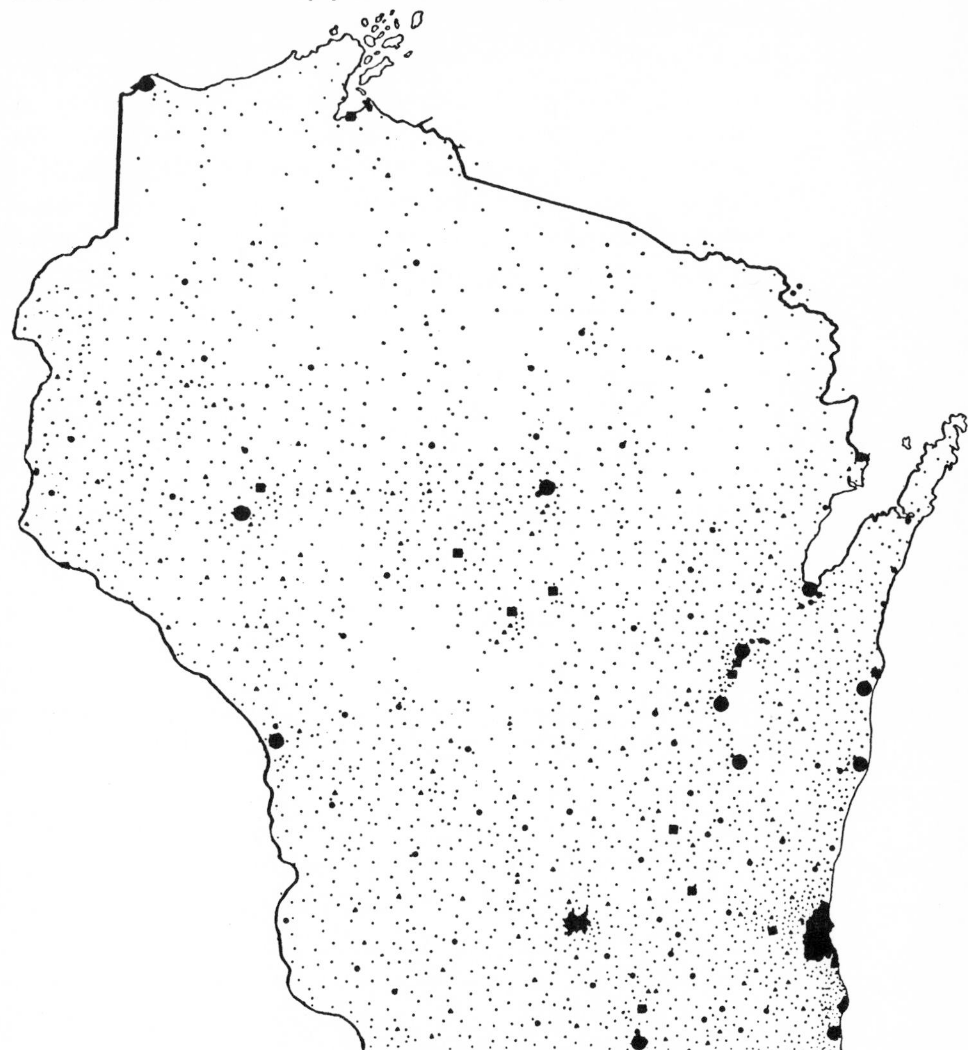

in the cross-tabulations.[1] Figures 5, 6, and 7 map the distribution of total population of Wisconsin in 1960, of the high schools in the 1957 sample, and of the colleges that existed at that time.[2]

[1] Special regressions were run to analyze the operation of ability and various family characteristics with respect to college attendance within a large city. By eliminating Milwaukee from the other regressions, we avoided confounding ability and status factors in other parts of the state with conditions that were peculiarly metropolitan. Milwaukee has a wide diversity of colleges, from the state's only private university and the University of Wisconsin in Milwaukee to community colleges and vocational and technical institutes.

[2] Notice that Figure 7 includes noncollegiate technical and vocational institutions.

FIGURE 6 ***High schools in Wisconsin, 1957***

College Accessibility and Attendance Rates

In Table 2 we compared college attendance rates for communities with one or more colleges with rates for communities that had no college even within 20 miles. The respective rates of college going for 1957 Wisconsin high school graduates were 44 and 30 percent for males and 29 and 24 percent for females. A definite association of attendance with accessibility of a college is indicated, especially for males; clearly the sex differences are not negligible. It is no less important to recall that over the ensuing six or seven years these community differences have largely disappeared (Table 3).

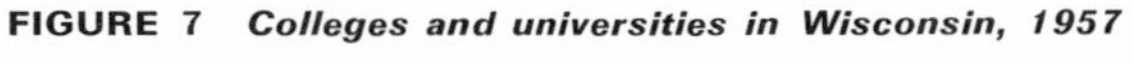

FIGURE 7 ***Colleges and universities in Wisconsin, 1957***

Considering the types or mixes of colleges and not merely whether one was present locally, the highest college attendance rates for males were in Madison and Milwaukee, and the lowest rates were in communities without colleges or with only a teachers college (Table 6). Proportions of males entering college appeared to be associated closely with degrees of urbanism, which makes it difficult to separate these influences from the ones determining the distribution of various kinds of college. Urbanism seems to have been less important among girls: Madison stood out, but

Milwaukee was little different from any place having a four-year college. This and much other evidence for many states supports the proposition (which is sufficiently plausible) that the education of males commonly is seen as a direct investment in formation of human capital whereas education of girls is more often seen as a consumer luxury.

Several questions arise from a perusal of these findings. For example, just how close are the associations between college-accessibility profile and size of the community? How far might observed differentials among communities in college attendance rates reflect biased mixes in abilities, however measured? To what degree do communities with different college-accessibility patterns have populations of different socioeconomic composition? Given a particular profile of college accessibility, are the rates of college going linked with a youth's ability or with the status of his family? And what are the interactive effects, taking all of these dimensions into account? Before turning to these substantive questions, some comments on statistical procedures are called for.

Methodological Explanations and Caveats

The most often-used technique in this monograph is simple cross-tabulation, with rates of college attendance (or the rate for a particular sort of college destination) entered in each cell. By nesting tables we could go a long way toward identifying relationships without running into unspecified problems of interactions among the independent variables; in this way we could observe key interactions directly. The main summary tables explicitly show differences in percentages.

Multivariate regression was used as a way of incorporating a wider range of independent variables into the analysis without losing too many degrees of freedom (or finding too many under-populated or empty cells). The regressions were run for total samples by sex and then by taking ability quarters and father's education in turn as *design variables* for analysis of accessibility and of other determinants of college attendance within each ability and paternal education category.

Prior to running the regressions, each independent variable was converted into (1,0) dummy-variable sets. For example, the set of within-community types of college accessibility was transformed so that each category (e.g., no college, Extension Center, etc.) became a dummy variable, which was either 1 or 0 (yes or no). All independent variables were so converted to produce sets of dummy variables which were then used in the multiple regression equations. The latter were run using one dummy variable out of each set as the omitted dummy, which was the base (or referent) with which all other dummy variables of that set were compared.

In all regressions the dependent variable was simply college attendance. Such a dichotomy for individuals, when treated as a dependent variable, becomes a cardinal quasi-probability or likelihood variable. In this study, when running a multiple regression of such a dichotomous dependent variable against several independent variables one may interpret the calculated values of the dependent variable as an approximation to the conditional probability of going on to college for given values of the independent variable. When applied to sets of individuals (for example, quarters of the ability scale), the dependent variable may be interpreted as the predicted proportion of the group that will go on to college.

Use of a dichotomous dependent variable in a multivariate regression has several limitations (Tobin, 1958; Coster & Wager, 1965). Most important, there is a distortion involved in treating a bounded variable with asymptotic upper and lower real limits as though it could (and did) take a linear form throughout.[3] Several methodological alternatives have been used. Ideally, so long as we stayed with observations on individuals only, maximum likelihood iterations could have been used. However, that procedure would have been extremely expensive, probably not adding commensurately to the substantive findings. Quite a different alternative, which was pursued where the data permitted, was to group observations for each sex by ability quarter, socioeconomic status of the family, and college-accessibility types, taking proportions in each cell who went to college as the observations. These values were transformed into logits, on which we did analysis of variance.[4]

Coming back to the regressions with college attendance as a dichotomous dependent variable, three points are worth mentioning. (1) There is no distortion so long as only one set of mutually

[3] A minor problem is the inefficiency in the estimation of the coefficient of determination because the error terms do not fulfill the independence condition. However, biases on that account are small over the range (or ranges) in which there is a good approximation to linearity.

[4] See Theil (1970). An alternative to the logit is an arcsine transformation, which, though intuitively less appealing, has some mathematical advantages and gives essentially the same statistical results. On this, see Bock and Jones (1968).

exclusive dummy variables is used. (2) Even when multiple sets are introduced, the linear model can provide a good approximation over likelihood ranges from the 20th to the 80th percentile on the dependent variable. (3) When the population is subdivided into ability quarters (or categories of paternal schooling), there is a shift along the percentile distribution that can (and does) also shift the slope coefficients in the regression equations. In effect, by separating the sample into ability quarters we are testing whether and how the slopes of relationships shift over the full percentile range of underlying likelihoods covered by the total sample. Distortions still remain at the extremes, especially for the lowest-ability quarter, but they are decidedly damped by our use of ability quarters or of father's schooling as design variables. (The later analysis using logits provides a further methodological check on the regression results.)

Multiple regressions have been run on the total male and total female samples starting with the set of dummy variables for college-accessibility types or profiles, then adding other sets of independent variables. We then reverse this procedure to enter ability and family background first, adding college accessibility last. Metric beta coefficients are used throughout; they can be read as simple differences in predicted proportions or likelihoods of youth attending college as compared with the proportions in the "omitted-dummy" category who do so.[5]

Community Size, College Profiles, and Attendance Rates

A few pages back we recapitulated the crude evidence about rates of college attendance in Wisconsin that had been presented in Chapter 2. The first question concerned the confounding effects of associations between college-accessibility profiles of communities and their degree of urbanism in other respects. For Wisconsin there is a close association between college profiles and the population of a community (Table 13). Indeed, an equation using five categories of community size to explain college attendance rates gave the same coefficient of determination as an equation that contained nine dummy variables for college accessibility (Table 14). This table may be used also to illustrate how to read the more complex regressions that follow. Interpretation of Table 14 is simplified because each equation contains only one set of categori-

[5] Standardized beta coefficients, in which each variable is expressed in units of its own standard deviation, are difficult to interpret with a dichotomous dependent variable.

TABLE 13 ***Distribution of 1957 sample of Wisconsin high school communities among various college-accessibility and community-size categories***

College type	Community size: Under 2,500	2,500–5,000	5,000–10,000	10,000–20,000	20,000–50,000	50,000–100,000	Above 100,000	Milwaukee
00	254	25	25	10	3			
11							*	*
12								†
13		1	4	1	7			
14	1	2	1	1	4			
15	5	8	5	1				
18				1	3	7		
19								
29				2	4	1		
49							5	
39								22
59				6		3		

Where 00 = None
11 = State university
12 = Private university
13 = State college
14 = Private college
15 = Teachers college
18 = State Extension Center
19 = Technical, vocational, religious
29 = Multiple
49 = Madison
39 = Milwaukee
59 = Milwaukee suburbs

* The University of Wisconsin in Madison and in Milwaukee.

† The only private university is in Milwaukee.

cal or dummy variables, which makes it directly comparable with a simple cross-tabulation.

Thus, equation (1) tells us that 32.1 percent of the male graduates from high schools in communities with no college (the omitted dummy) went on to attend a college somewhere; that value is shown as the intercept, or constant term of the equation. The metric beta coefficient on each of the college-accessibility categories (independent dummy variables) specifies the *difference* in proportion of boys in the designated category and boys from noncollege towns who entered a college. For state college communities the difference is 9.5 percent; for communities with Extension Centers

TABLE 14 Regressions of college attendance on college-accessibility profiles and community size, Wisconsin males, 1957

Equation number	*(1)*	*(4)*
R^2	0.018	0.017
F	9.34	19.08
Constant	0.324	0.306
Access within community		
None	. . .	
State college	0.095	
Private college	0.125	
County teachers college	0.008	
Extension Center	0.089	
Multiple	0.097	
Madison	0.225	
Milwaukee region A	0.203	
Milwaukee region B	0.043	
Community population		
Under 2,500		. . .
2,500–9,999		0.039
10,000–24,999		0.085
25,000–99,999		0.126
100,000 and over		0.276

8.9 percent; for Madison 22.5 percent; and so on. Thus 32.1 + 22.5 or 54.5 percent of Madison boys entered college. In equation (4) we observe a consistent monotonic (but nonlinear) rise in proportions attending college with growing population of the high school community.[6]

Though some distinctions in college accessibility could no doubt be found within broad categories by city size, overall estima-

[6] For the state of Washington for the years 1939–1941, Landis (1945) reports the following:

Size of place (population)	*Percentage of high school graduates entering college within six months*
100,000 and over	40
10,000–31,000	33
2,500–10,000	25
250–2,500	21
Under 250	20

tion of the effects of college accessibility upon rates of attendance will tend to be biased upward by the operation of factors associated with size of place. These ambiguities are less likely to occur if one controls for parental traits. Indeed, these traits may be part of the complex associated with size of place and pattern of college accessibility that encourages or discourages continuation into higher education.

2. EFFECTS OF ABILITY AND PARENTAL BACKGROUND

Personal ability and family status can be handled in two main ways when we are seeking to ascertain the effects of college accessibility upon college attendance. One can treat ability or family status as control variables: we ask what will be the effects of college accessibility on attendance from a community as a whole *once we control* for ability and social-status traits of the local population.[7] The other procedure is to divide the sample by pupils' ability (or family backgrounds, or both simultaneously) and then relate college attendance to accessibility for each of these categories. This second procedure reveals interesting interaction effects (see Section 3 below). First, however, we will explore the determinants of college attendance for the whole population of secondary graduates.

College Accessibility and Community Size

In Table 15 an X shows that the indicated set of mutually exclusive dummy variables has been included in an equation. Adding sets of independent variables for ability and for father's education, as was done in equations (2) and (5), substantially raises the coefficients of determination and their F values; these unambiguously indicate highly significant relationships, since with our crude treatment of the dependent variable they are, in fact, minimum

[7] The measure of ability used in the Wisconsin survey was the V. A. C. Henmon and M. J. Nelson test (Henmon & Nelson 1942). The test was administered to all Wisconsin high school juniors (the scores quartered by Sewell). The measure of SES is a weighted index that included (1) father's occupation, (2) father's education, (3) mother's education, (4) estimated funds the family could provide if the student were to attend college, (5) the degree of sacrifice this would entail for the family, and (6) the approximate wealth and income status of the student's family. These variables are specified without regard to effects of college proximity and were analyzed using the principal-components method with varimax rotation, which produced a three-factor structure. Sewell and Shah (1968, p. 562) explain that "the composite SES status index was developed by squaring the loadings of the principal items on each factor as weights, then multiplying the student's scores on the items by the respective weights, and finally, summing the weighted scores of the principal items on each factor."

TABLE 15 ***Regression analysis of college attendance rates of male 1957 Wisconsin high school graduates; details for college-accessibility and community-population variables only***

Equation number	*(1)*	*(2)*	*(3)*	*(4)*	*(5)*	*(6)*
R^2	0.017	0.212	0.226	0.018	0.212	0.225
F	9.34	75.54	68.39	19.08	102.99	87.39
Constant	0.324	0.053	0.016	0.306	0.049	0.020
Independent variable set						
Ability		X	X		X	X
Father's education		X	X		X	X
Father's NORC score			X			X
Access within community						
None	. . .	. . .	. . .			
State college	0.095*	0.070*	0.065*			
Private college	0.125*	0.051†	0.057*			
Teachers college	0.008	0.009	0.010			
Extension Center	0.089*	0.017	0.019			
Multiple	0.097*	0.036†	0.035			
Madison	0.225*	0.081*	0.062*			
Milwaukee region A‡*	0.203*	0.051†	0.010			
Milwaukee region B§	0.043	—0.028	—0.049†			
Community population						
0–2,499				. . .	. . .	. . .
2,500–9,999				0.039*	0.014	0.007
10,000–24,999				0.085*	0.005	—0.012
25,000–100,000				0.126*	0.052*	0.030†
Over 100,000				0.276*	0.108*	0.083*

* Significant $F_{.01}$ and $t_{.05}$ (one-tailed).

† Significant $F_{.01}$ but not $t_{.05}$ (one-tailed).

‡ Contains the towns of Shorewood, Whitefish Bay, and Wauwatusa.

§ Contains the towns of Cudahy, Greendale, West Allis, South Milwaukee, and West Milwaukee.

estimates. The *further* addition of parental occupational status, in equations (3) and (6), has only a small effect.[8]

Contrasting equation (3) with (1), we observe that the larger initial regression coefficients on the college-accessibility variables

[8] The sum of mean values for all variables in a given set, including the omitted dummy, must add to unity; a youth's father must be in some education category, even if the category is "no response." There were very few incomplete responses in the Wisconsin data, and the nonresponse cases closely matched distributions for all respondents on other items. Nonresponse cases were deleted from the regressions for Wisconsin but retained in those using the SCOPE tapes.

are reduced substantially. Thus, in equation (3), communities in "Milwaukee Region A" no longer stand out in college attendance from noncollege towns or from towns having only a county teachers college. And in this equation the coefficient on the dummy variable for communities with four-year state colleges now matches that for Madison; the latter was distinctly higher when neither youth's ability nor parental schooling was included. The effect of community size likewise is reduced [compare equations (5) and (6) with (4)], and it becomes clearer that urbanism alone has "significant" effects only when we reach a population of 25,000 or even 100,000.

What should we mean by "big" or "small" or "significant" effects in reading results such as those shown in Table 15? An author whose name has been lost by us wrote pointedly of the "fully-only" syndrome in interpretations of findings in the social sciences. Applied in the present context, a (statistically significant) increment of 5 percent in rates of continuation into college becomes "fully 5 percent" for the proponent of one policy but "only 5 percent" for his opponent. To the first man, the difference is societally significant, or perhaps significant in relation to its cost; to the second man, a 5 percent difference seems negligible. But the first man might be shaken if told that despite a large sample the 5 percent was "statistically insignificant." On the other hand, the "only 5 percent" man may well continue to say *only* 5 percent despite a high level of statistical significance, because he judges that the implied policy is not worth its cost.

In Table 15 we have extremely small but nevertheless significant coefficients of determination even in equations (1) and (4); indeed, the .018 would appear to be too small to be worth notice, and it must be acknowledged that its being significant is due to the large sample. On the other hand, some of the regression coefficients are substantial in their intuitive societal relevance—or would be if we agreed upon a causal framework. But when we move on to the other equations the "fully" interpretation used to bolster a strategy for encouraging attendance at college must get at least a small check. The coefficients of determination have risen, but the rise reflects factors that have nothing to do with options in college location. Nor are these factors—ability of youth and social status of the youth's family—subject to the student's control. Whether the regression coefficients (for college accessibility or type of place) are *now* of the "fully" rather than the "only" order societally, and whether they are properly interpreted as guides to strategy have become new questions.

Importance of Ability and Family Background

The maximum range in proportions attending college across the categories of college accessibility was 21 percentage points for women and 23 points for men. Although this is not a negligible disparity, it has been shown that controlling for youth's ability and parental status substantially reduced the influence of college accessibility. It is useful, therefore, to look from the other direction and ask just how far the ability and background variables explain college attendance—and how stable those effects are after allowing for college accessibility.

The effects of youth's ability, parental status, and paternal education are given a quick overview in Table 16. As one would expect, on each of these variables (and for each sex) there is considerable selectivity for college attendance. When communities were grouped for college accessibility, the range among them in rates of college attendance was just over 20 percentage points. Here, using traits of individuals, attendance rates vary by about 50 points among males; for paternal schooling the effect is of similar magnitude among girls, but the ranges are about 10 points less for girls on the other two traits.

TABLE 16 ***Mean rates of continuation into college by ability, SES, and father's education; Wisconsin males and females, 1957***

	*Percentages going to college**			
	Male		*Female*	
Ability quarters				
1. Low	12.5		9.0	
2.	28.7	(16.2)	18.4	(9.4)
3.	43.6	(31.1)	29.4	(20.4)
4. High	67.0	(54.5)	47.6	(38.6)
SES quarters				
1. Low	17.9		11.2	
2.	26.5	(8.6)	13.6	(2.4)
3.	41.8	(23.9)	27.3	(16.1)
4. High	65.1	(47.2)	52.6	(41.4)
Father's education				
Elementary	24.8		15.8	
High school 1–3	33.0	(8.2)	21.0	(5.2)
High school 4	47.8	(23.0)	31.7	(15.9)
College 1–3	59.8	(35.0)	47.3	(31.5)
College 4+	73.0	(48.2)	65.0	(49.2)

* Figures in parentheses are the differences in percentages as compared with the first category in each set.

When the ability and parental status traits are entered in the same regression equation, there is of course some dampening of the coefficients on each variable as compared to what was observed when only one set of categories was used. (Compare equation (1)*M* of Table 17 with the increments given in parentheses in Table 16.) Nevertheless, the pattern of association with college going remains strong, even when allowance is made for type of high school course (as in equations (2)*M* and (2)*F*).

Of particular interest are the persisting steep gradients on ability (in Table 17) when controlling for background and the much steeper gradient for ability among males as compared with females. The strong effect of maternal education is impressive. Moreover, despite a correlation between the effects of father's and mother's education, both variables display coefficients consistent with what might have been anticipated for each set taken alone. This situation will be explored further when we treat paternal education as a "design" variable for the purpose of setting up subpopulations.

The advantage for college going of coming from a family in the upper half, and especially in the upper quarter, of the income distribution comes through strongly for both sexes in these Wisconsin data. This finding impresses us the more in that other parental traits that doubtless reduce the coefficients for income are in these equations. The coefficients for income, like those on parental education and on youth's ability, are unaffected by the inclusion or exclusion of college-accessibility profiles.

The presence of significant coefficients for graduates of the college preparatory course (see equations (3)*M* and (3)*F*) is to be expected, and if our college preparatory courses were more like the upper-secondary academic courses in Europe, the coefficients presumably would have been much larger. That these coefficients are here so modest reflects the ambiguous nature of most secondary curricula in the United States. But to use this variable raises some questions about the processes that determine college going. Does the presence of a college (or of a certain sort of college) in a community encourage local youth to attend the college preparatory course of the high school more often than they would otherwise? If so, this curriculum variable is picking up indirect effects of college accessibility upon rates of college attendance. A comparison of equation (3) of Table 17 with equation (3) in Table 15 suggests that this may be the case. However, correlations between having studied in the college preparatory course and various indexes of

TABLE 17 ***Regression analysis of college attendance rates of male and female 1957 Wisconsin high school graduates***

	Males			Females	
Equation numbers	*(1)M*	*(2)M*	*(3)M*	*(2)F*	*(3)F*
R^2	*0.209*	*0.292*	*0.293*	*0.263*	*0.265*
F	*159.15*	*72.12*	*54.31*	*64.12*	*48.54*
Constant	0.064	—0.026	—0.033	—0.009	—0.009
Ability					
1. Low	. . .	. . .	. . .	. . .	. . .
2.	0.145*	0.084*	0.084*	0.017	0.017
3.	0.253*	0.146*	0.147*	0.070*	0.069*
4. High	0.456	0.306*	0.307*	0.151*	0.149*
Father's education					
1. Elementary	. . .	. . .	. . .	. . .	. . .
2. High school 1–3	0.056*	0.015	0.015	0.021†	0.021†
3. High school 4	0.169*	0.085*	0.085*	0.035*	0.036*
4. College 1–3	0.274*	0.122*	0.118*	0.087*	0.085*
5. College 4+	0.334*	0.103*	0.104*	0.161*	0.156*
Mother's education					
1. Elementary		. . .	. . .	. . .	. . .
2. High school 1–3		—0.003	—0.004	—0.014	—0.015
3. High school 4		0.045*	0.044*	0.051*	0.049*
4. College 1–3		0.119*	0.118*	0.180*	0.177*
5. College 4+		0.136*	0.134*	0.197*	0.196*
Father's occupation					
1. Farmers		—0.010	—0.006	0.046*	0.046*
2. Laborers		—0.046*	—0.044*	—0.020	—0.020
3. Private household, service		0.013	0.013	0.029	0.026
4. Operatives		—0.058*	—0.057*	—0.014	—0.014
5. Craftsmen, foremen, etc.		0.016	0.018	—0.015	—0.016
6. Clerical, sales		. . .	. . .	. . .	. . .
7. Proprietors		0.098*	0.101*	0.082*	0.082*
8. Managers, officials		0.100*	0.100*	0.116*	0.118*
9. Professionals		0.070*	0.071*	0.057*	0.056*
10. Other		0.108†	0.108†	—0.025	—0.024
Parental income					
1. Low		. . .	. . .	. . .	. . .
2.		0.017	0.015	—0.017	—0.017

	Males			Females	
Equation numbers	*(1)M*	*(2)M*	*(3)M*	*(2)F*	*(3)F*
R^2	*0.209*	*0.292*	*0.293*	*0.263*	*0.265*
F	*159.15*	*72.12*	*54.31*	*64.12*	*48.54*
Parental income (cont.):					
3.		0.062*	0.060*	0.030*	0.028†
4. *High*		0.123*	0.124*	0.116*	0.115*
High school program					
"Vocational"		...	...	...	...
College preparatory		0.236*	0.235*	0.205*	0.208†
College(s) in community					
00 None			...		...
13 State college			0.036†		0.023
14 Private college			0.018		−0.028
15 Teachers college			0.011		−0.009
18 Extension Center			−0.008		−0.047*
29 Multiple			0.028		0.007
49 Madison			0.036		−0.004
39 Milwaukee region A			−0.019		0.061*
59 Milwaukee region B			−0.042		0.031

* Significant $F_{.01}$ and $t_{.05}$ (one-tailed).
† Significant $F_{.01}$ but not $t_{.05}$ (one-tailed).

college accessibility display very low coefficients in a zero-order matrix.[9]

Finally, Table 17 makes it clear that addition of variables for college accessibility has little effect on any other coefficient or on the coefficients of determination. The contrast with the results shown in Table 15 is dramatic; there we moved in the other direction, starting with college accessibility and then adding other variables. These results cast doubt in a major degree on any hypothesis that location of a college *by itself* has substantial effects upon college attendance. But that conclusion leaves unanswered

[9] For this reason, we decided early against using a recursive model in which the type of high school course would have been predicted in a first stage by college accessibility; we would then have traced college-accessibility effects as these might operate both directly, at the point of graduation from high school, and indirectly, through earlier orientation of secondary programs in the community.

the question as to whether the location of a college significantly enhances the likelihood of college attendance for members of certain social or ability categories, even if not for all categories. It is to such questions that we now turn.

3. THE SELECTIVE IMPACT OF COLLEGE ACCESSIBILITY

Studies to trace out the later careers of high school graduates have been of two kinds. Some policy advocates have stressed talent loss, often with special reference to the able offspring of uneducated or poor parents. Other advocates, and their numbers have of late been increasing, focus on the fate of less-qualified youth, particularly those from disadvantaged backgrounds.[10] However we view these questions, any assessment of the effects to be expected from making college more accessible must give attention to specifying the effects upon particular subcategories among secondary graduates. Indeed, such an analysis almost surely will lead us to concern about the teaching of pupils at an early age. In this section, we first examine separately some effects by ability categories and by parental status; their joint effects will be taken up later. We start by exploring cross-tabulations, then look at regressions in which the samples were divided first by ability and then by father's education. And finally we consider the three factors together—expressing the proportions attending college in logit transforms.

An Overview: Some Cross-tabulations

The effects of the basic three variables were shown separately in Table 16; they are now shown in cross-tabulation separately against college accessibility (Tables 18 and 19).[11] Disregarding type of college to focus only on contrasts between college and noncollege communities, a good summary emerges from Table 18. Few youth who were of low ability attended college in any case, and for high school graduates in the lowest quarter of ability the local presence of a college made very little difference. It does seem to have had some effect among youth of higher ability, especially among boys in the upper half of the ability scale. The local presence of a college appears to have had about the same effect upon attendance among sons of better and of lesser-educated fathers. The noteworthy point here, perhaps, is that father's

[10] Reconsiderations and revisionism piled on revisionism about "hereditability of ability" have vastly complicated all these discussions.

[11] Negative differences are bracketed, whether significant or not.
In Table 19, figures below those in column (1) are bracketed.

TABLE 18 ***Percentages of male and female 1957 Wisconsin high school graduates from college and noncollege locations who attended college, by ability and parental background***

	Males			*Females*		
	No college	*One or more colleges*	*Columns (2) — (1)*	*No college*	*One or more colleges*	*Columns (5) — (4)*
Entire sample						
Percentages	32.1	43.7	+11.6*	21.9	29.0	+ 7.1*
Number at 100%	(2278)	(2586)		(2244)	(2854)	
Ability quarters						
1. Low	11.7	13.6	+ 1.9	8.8	9.2	+ 0.4
2.	25.1	31.8	+ 6.7*	14.8	21.3	+ 6.5*
3.	37.7	48.2	+10.5*	26.6	31.4	+ 4.8*
4. High	60.4	71.7	+11.3*	42.4	50.9	+ 8.5*
SES quarters						
1. Low	16.6	20.7	+ 4.1*	12.0	9.9	— 2.1
2.	24.7	29.0	+ 4.3*	14.9	12.4	— 2.5
3.	38.0	44.6	+ 6.6*	27.1	27.4	+ 0.3
4. High	64.0	65.6	+ 1.6	49.4	53.8	+ 4.4
Father's education						
Elementary	22.1	28.2	+ 6.1*	15.8	15.7	— 0.1
High school 1–3	26.7	37.2	+10.6*	17.2	23.4	+ 6.2*
High school 4	43.3	51.1	+ 7.8*	30.4	32.5	+ 2.1
College 1–3	65.5	57.0	— 8.5*	39.8	51.9	+12.1*
College 4+	65.7	76.6	+10.9*	58.7	67.0	+ 8.3*

**z* test significant at 0.05 level.

schooling picks up so little of the effect of measured ability.[12] Presence of a local college does seem to have stimulated attendance by girls whose fathers were comparatively well educated.

Using the composite measure of family status (SES), a local college is of no more than moderate effect at any level of status. That this composite index of status mutes the apparent effect of having a locally accessible college suggests again that much of the attendance difference in the two types of community (top row of

[12] The exceptionally high rate of college going among the small subset of sons whose fathers had one to three years of college and who are living in a community without a college distorts the pattern of differences for males.

TABLE 19 ***Percentages of male and female 1957 Wisconsin high school graduates who attended college; within community college-accessibility types, by ability and parental background***

	Within community college-accessibility types				
	No higher institutions	*Four-year college only*		*Teachers college (county)*	*Extension Center only (state)*
		Public	*Private*		
	(1)	*(2)*	*(3)*	*(4)*	*(5)*
					Male graduates
Entire sample					
Percentages	32.1	41.6	44.9	33.1	41.2
Number at 100%	(2273)	(365)	(198)	(355)	(306)
Ability quarters					
1. Low	11.7	[10.3]	16.2	13.5	15.4
2.	25.1	42.4	39.2	25.3	[24.7]
3.	37.7	51.6	49.1	38.7	48.3
4. High	60.4	73.3	65.5	61.8	63.6
SES quarters					
1. Low	16.6	17.7	[15.2*]	18.9	25.5
2.	24.7	31.6	[23.3*]	[19.7]	[19.7]
3.	38.0	44.8	41.5	38.4	48.4
4. High	64.0	[60.6]	75.4	66.6	[52.2]
Father's education					
Elementary	22.1	28.1	31.1	[20.3]	31.4
High school 1–3	26.7	37.5	[25.0*]	28.6	39.4
High school 4	43.3	47.1	49.0	50.0	44.7
College 1–3	65.5	[61.0]	78.6*	[55.6*]	[37.5*]
College 4	65.7	71.4*	81.5*	68.0*	71.4*
					Female graduates
Entire sample					
Percentages	21.9	30.3	25.7	24.5	24.5
Number at 100%	(2244)	(297)	(249)	(367)	(281)
Ability quarters					
1. Low	8.8	9.2	[7.8]	14.3	[4.7]
2.	14.8	25.4	23.7	24.7	17.7
3.	26.6	36.2	26.9	[24.7]	[26.1]
4. High	42.4	49.4	45.8	[37.5]	47.8
SES quarters					
1. Low	12.0	[9.2[	[8.0]	[10.1]	[5.7]

	Madison	Milwaukee	
Multiple (Extension + other) *(6)*	*(State university + other)* *(7)*	*City* *(8)*	*Suburbs* *(9)*
41.3	55.0	50.1	36.9
(266)	(149)	(803)	(144)
16.0	23.8*	13.7	[7.1*]
26.2	47.1*	29.9	29.7*
38.2	53.5	54.5	[35.9*]
71.1	74.5	78.9	65.0*
25.5	25.0*	20.8	[11.8*]
29.2	31.7*	30.2	[17.1*]
42.9	[26.7*]	50.2	39.0*
[61.8]	78.7	67.7	[56.9]
31.9	30.8*	31.4	[18.8*]
41.9*	38.9*	43.4	37.0*
49.4	61.0*	56.9	[39.5*]
[60.0*]	[42.9*]	[60.7]	‡
[50.0*]	86.5	80.4	77.8*
29.7	43.3	29.4	31.2
(413)	(159)	(925)	(163)
12.0	11.4*	[7.9]	[3.1*]
17.3	38.5*	18.9	24.4*
30.2	45.2*	33.2	31.7*
52.5	64.3	53.2	55.1*
13.1	6.3*	[10.5]	[12.5*]

TABLE 19
(continued)

	Within community college-accessibility types				
	No higher institutions (1)	Four-year college only: Public (2)	Four-year college only: Private (3)	Teachers college (county) (4)	Extension Center only (state) (5)
					Female graduates
SES quarters (cont.):					
2.	14.9	17.7	[6.8]	[11.8]	[13.5]
3.	27.1	37.8	[24.3]	32.1	[26.3]
4. *High*	49.4	50.0	55.7	50.6	[44.9]
Father's education					
Elementary	15.8	19.0	[13.6]	[13.7]	[15.1]
High school 1–3	17.2	30.9	25.0*	27.0	17.2
High school 4	30.4	32.5	[29.3]	[30.1]	30.8
College 1–3	39.8	50.0	‡	52.9*	45.5†
College 4+	58.7	64.0	61.5*	63.6*	60.0*

* From 15 to 49 cases in denominator.

† From 10 to 14 cases in denominator.

‡ Fewer than 10 cases in denominator.

NOTE: Underlined percentages: significantly above attendance rates on column (1) using z test at 0. 05. Bracketed percentages: below percentages in column (1).

Table 18) may be picking up biases in the mixtures of characteristics of the subpopulation rather than effects of college accessibility —especially among girls.

With the use of Table 19 we can begin to examine how particular combinations of types of colleges can affect the rate of college going. For all communities with a college, all cases are underlined for which proportions going on to college differed significantly (at the .05 level) and positively from attendance rates for comparable kinds of youth in noncollege communities.[13]

Eight particularly interesting features can be observed in Table 19:

1 There is a negligible effect of college accessibility among the least able boys for almost every variety of college profile—as had been noted for

[13] Out of 103 comparisons for males and 104 for females, there were 24 and 26 negative differences respectively; however, twice as many negative instances could have been expected at random, and few of those occurring are significant.

	Madison	*Milwaukee*	
Multiple (Extension + other) (6)	*(State university + other)* (7)	*City* (8)	*Suburbs* (9)
[14.7]	[11.8*]	[13.1]	[4.4*]
27.1	34.2*	[21.9]	27.3
54.9	71.8	51.2	68.1*
17.0	19.1*	16.0	[13.3]
28.9	[16.0*]	20.6	20.6*
31.7	39.5*	33.5	37.5*
55.0*	69.2†	51.6	50.0†
67.6*	88.9*	60.2	84.2*

Table 18. For girls, by contrast, county teachers colleges do attract the less able in small communities. Among boys of low ability, the exception is Madison, with a distinctively high rate of college entrance. Perhaps the local traditions of college attendance in Madison put more pressure on low-ability sons of better-educated parents to go to college *somewhere,* even if not in Wisconsin. (To be sure, the number of low-ability boys coming out of the Madison high school was small.) Overall, among the less able Wisconsin youth we should expect to observe only a modest effect of college accessibility on attendance. Ability is a major element in academic motivation, and most Wisconsin colleges still have ability restraints on entry, as they did in 1957. Wisconsin is not marked out for its concern about low-ability youth or about needs for compensatory programs at the college level even today.

2 Within each sex, among students of middle to higher ability and family status, residing in Madison was associated with substantially higher likelihoods of entering college. Excess attendance by Madison boys (compared with all noncollege localities) was marked at every ability level, as it was for girls—also excepting those of least ability. For SES categories, how-

ever, only at the top did the differentials definitely favor Madison; the effect is striking among both boys and girls whose fathers had finished college. Presumably, a considerable proportion of Madison youth are offspring of university faculty and state administrators.

3 Living in the metropolis (Milwaukee) went along with higher rates of college attendance among the more able youth of both sexes—and quite generally among the boys. When we control for socioeconomic status, however, residence in Milwaukee appears not to have much effect, especially among girls. The complex urban patterns of pro and antischool influences are reflected in the shifting figures. If one were instead trying to trace out relationships within a giant metropolis, the problems of analysis would be even more intractable.

4 Next to Madison, it was communities with public four-year colleges that had the broadest impact on college going, regardless of sex, except for the least able individuals. Sorting the potential students by family SES, the advantages of the state-college communities was greatest in the third quarter of status for both sexes. However, these differentials are much smaller than those between the public four-year and the noncollege communities for each of the ability categories among boys. One might infer that the presence of a four-year public institution had its main effects on able youth in the middle of the SES range; however, more definite inferences must await the three-way cross-tabulations to be discussed later.

5 The presence of private four-year colleges seemingly affected boys more than girls, but only in the upper reaches of the SES scale. As among the ability quarters, presence of a private college had no marked differential effect among girls but appears to have affected the middle ability range among boys.

6 Residence in a community possessing a university Extension Center (but no other postsecondary school) apparently induced few girls to continue into college, but boys from homes with low SES standing or whose fathers were less educated were markedly more likely to attend college if they resided in these communities.

7 Each multiple college community included at least one four-year school and another offering a two-year program. College attendance rates in such communities, as in those with Extension Centers only, were relatively high among boys of modest social origin (with less-schooled fathers) and among the most able boys. Among girls the biggest effects were on the distinctly able and on daughters of college men. Living in a town with more than one college or with a public four-year college made a significant difference also, it would seem, among daughters of men with some high school education.

8 The presence of a county teachers college did not enhance college attendance among boys, as it well might have done in an earlier generation. But the pattern among girls is quite different: attendance was seemingly stimulated among the less able half of the girls, but for the most able ones attendance was less frequent among residents of communities with teachers colleges than in noncollege towns.[14]

Regression Analyses within Ability Categories

The sort of questions that have been explored through cross-classifications can also be examined by the use of multiple regressions; indeed a larger number of presumtively relevant independent variables can be handled (if we accept linearity assumptions).[15] In all the following regression tables for Wisconsin, college accessibility is entered in two ways. First there is the set of categories already used, characterizing the community itself. Second is a set characterizing the community plus an area extending 20 miles around it. Mostly we will look at the first (within community) set only.

We continue to use the dichotomous dependent variable, viewing results as first approximations. This procedure does raise problems in interpreting the regression coefficients, especially as they bring predicted likelihood (or proportions) toward the extremes (at which the coefficients become positively or negatively too large). Again this problem arises mainly as we approach (and even "predict") beyond the lower limit of a zero rate of college attendance. The problem is aggravated by multicollinearities among the sets of independent variables, and (given our selection of omitted dummy variables) it finds virtually full expression in a downward bias of the constant term, especially in regressions for categories

[14] Teaching in primary schools has long been a conventional occupation for rural girls, and the county teachers college epitomized that tradition in what is now almost a vestigial guise. Perhaps it is not an accidental variation in the data that they show responses to proximity of a teachers college to be most positive among daughters of men who had entered a schooling stage (e.g., secondary or higher education) but had not completed that stage. (There is some evidence also that the less-able girls from families rating fairly high in SES were responsive to the proximity of these schools.)

[15] As in regressions already examined, independent variables are categorized and sets of dummy variables are constructed even on measures (including income along with youth's ability and family SES scores) that could have been treated as cardinal. This procedure frees the analysis from linearity (or other specified functional) constraints on relationships within each set of attributes or each "dimension" of the analysis.

of less-able youth. Compared to the earlier regressions, the present ones have the advantage that the subdivision of the sample by ability quarters allows the slopes of the regression coefficients to shift as we move from propositions centering around mean rates of attendance at 12.5 percent for boys and 9.0 percent for girls in the lowest quarter of ability to mean values of 67.0 and 47.6 respectively in the highest quarter of ability (Table 16). Some of these shifts are substantial, as we should anticipate from consideration of the contrasts between ability categories that were pointed out when discussing Tables 18 and 19. Indeed, these multiple regressions will be used mainly to check on the evidence provided by those two tables. We have drawn seven main conclusions from Tables 20 and 21 when they are viewed in relation to the cross-tabulations.

1 It is boys of the two middle-ability quarters and girls in the two top-ability quarters whose likelihood of attending colleges seems to have been affected most by other factors (among those we could examine). This summary emerges from a quick look along the line of R^2 in those two tables. Doubtless the downward bias in R^2 (contrasted to what would have occurred with the more expensive and sophisticated maximum-likelihood techniques) is largest for the bottom quarter of ability because this group comes closest to a limit (in this case the zero limit) and the linear fit is therefore poorest. Visualization of a sigmoid curve should provide intuitive appreciation of this fact. Pulling the asymptotic tails into line either in logits or in probit units, the distance between the 5th and 10th percentiles will be roughly three times greater than that between the 45th and 50th.[16]

2 Within each ability category and for each sex, the regression coefficients on characteristics of family and school are insensitive to inclusion or exclusion of dummy sets on college accessibility. This finding is in line with what we observed earlier for the total sample.

3 Again we find that living in Madison is associated with higher rates of college attendance for both sexes (despite controls for parental background) in equations run for the next-to-lowest ability group. However, for males these effects disappear among the most able and become negligible among the least able (here even negative for females, though not significantly so). Seemingly it is the middle range in ability that is susceptible to the atmosphere and immediate presence of the University of Wisconsin as a stimulant to college attendance.

[16] This is taken into account, of course, in the z tests for differences between percentages.

4 The regression analyses support the earlier evidence that all but males of the lowest ability are more likely to go to college if they reside in communities with a four-year state college. Controlling for family characteristics does not change this relationship. Among girls, however, it was only among the next to least able quarter for whom the association remained positive after applying the controls for parental background. That social status plays a special part in the response of girls to college opportunities has been shown many times, but not often has the solidity of this conclusion been demonstrated so unequivocally.

5 Residing in a community possessing a four-year private college did not raise boys' rates of college going in any ability category, once controls for parental background have been effected. Some positive effect seems to remain for girls in ability group 2, but among the ablest girls the negative effect was equally large. All in all, there seems to be no unchallengable effect for girls either. College attendance by youth from communities with private colleges must be explained by characteristics of the people who live there, not by the presence of that sort of college.

6 Controlling for family status, residents of communities with Extension Centers were no more (and sometimes even less) likely to continue their schooling beyond high school than were youth in communities with no college.[17] By contrast with the within-community set, the coefficient on Extension Centers (and that only) *within 20 miles* is strongly positive for boys in the next-to-top ability quarter and remains positive in the top quarter.[18]

7 The selective impact of a teachers college, suggested by the earlier cross-tabulations, emerges also from the regressions. There is no effect on boys. College attendance seems to be encouraged among girls in the second quarter of ability, but coefficients were decidedly negative among the more able girls. As with the Extension Centers, the data again must be telling us more about unmeasured characteristics of the communities where these schools are located than about the effects of the school's presence.

Regression Analyses within Categories of Father's Education

Reading from Tables 20 and 21 one could notice that the education of boys' mothers or family income appeared to be especially important for the second quarter on ability. Among girls, mother's school-

(Text continued on p. 102)

[17] The only exception (therefore suspect) is for boys of top ability living in communities having both Extension Centers and some other college, but this instance raises questions not so much about the effects of the centers as about the bases on which their siting was determined.

[18] The only other significantly positive coefficients for males in the second college-access set were for state college only in ability 2 and 4, and for Madison in ability 2.

TABLE 20 ***Regression analysis of college attendance rates of male 1957 Wisconsin high school graduates by ability quarters***

	Ability 1 (N = 1117)			*Ability 2 (N = 1010)*	
Equation number	*(1) M.A1*	*(2) M.A1*	*(3) M.A1*	*(1) M.A2*	*(2) M.A2*
R^2	*0.139*	*0.152*	*0.149*	*0.193*	*0.201*
F	*8.40*	*6.71*	*5.77*	*11.24*	*8.48*
Constant	−0.024	−0.027	−0.027	0.037	0.029
Father's education					
1. Elementary	. . .	. . .	. . .	. . .	. . .
2. High school 1–3	0.016	0.022	0.015	0.033	0.037
3. High school 4	0.023	0.031	0.023	0.072*	0.071*
4. College 1–3	0.139*	0.169*	0.143*	0.162*	0.149*
5. College 4+	0.287*	0.277*	0.281*	0.097†	0.109†
Mother's education					
1. Elementary	. . .	. . .	. . .	. . .	. . .
2. High school 1–3	−0.017	−0.024	−0.019	0.052†	0.048†
3. High school 4	0.024	0.020	0.028	0.056*	0.057*
4. College 1–3	0.118*	0.122*	0.128*	0.117†	0.117†
5. College 4+	0.122*	0.122*	0.117*	0.213*	0.202*
Father's occupation					
1. Farmers	0.037	0.034	0.036	−0.040	−0.030
2. Laborers	0.041	0.040	0.041	−0.071†	−0.066
3. Private household, service	0.123*	0.132*	0.134*	−0.058	−0.056
4. Operatives	0.002	0.014	0.009	−0.058	−0.051
5. Craftsmen, foremen	0.080*	0.093*	0.091*	−0.057	−0.056
6. Clerical, sales	. . .	. . .	. . .	. . .	. . .
7. Proprietors	0.090*	0.093*	0.092	0.030	0.035
8. Managers, officials	0.133†	0.130*	0.141*	0.048	0.048
9. Professionals	0.031	0.056	0.041	0.054	0.041
10. Other	0.122†	0.136†	0.128†	0.295*	0.289*
Parental income					
1. Low	. . .	. . .	. . .	. . .	. . .
2.	0.006	0.010	0.009	0.096*	0.093*
3.	0.034†	0.041†	0.038†	0.050†	0.053†
4. High	0.096*	0.109*	0.103*	0.204*	0.209*
High school program					
Vocational	. . .	. . .	. . .	. . .	. . .
College preparatory	0.151*	0.155*	0.148*	0.232*	0.232*

	Ability 3 (N = 1060)			Ability 4 (N = 1039)		
(3) M.A2	*(1) M.A3*	*(2) M.A3*	*(3) M.A3*	*(1) M.A4*	*(2) M.A4*	*(3) M.A4*
0.207	*0.200*	*0.203*	*0.211*	*0.176*	*0.180*	*0.184*
7.73	*12.38*	*9.06*	*8.31*	*10.32*	*7.66*	*7.07*
0.012	0.069	0.062	0.108	0.223	0.216	0.196
. . .	. . .	. . .	. . .	. . .	. . .	. . .
0.025	—0.015	—0.016	—0.010	0.012	0.012	0.010
0.062*	0.141*	0.139*	0.142*	0.075*	0.075*	0.071*
0.137*	0.190*	0.177*	0.198*	—0.007	—0.009	—0.018
0.097†	0.151*	0.143*	0.158*	—0.015	—0.010	—0.019
. . .	. . .	. . .	. . .	. . .	. . .	. . .
0.050†	—0.020	—0.018	—0.019	—0.035	—0.040	—0.037
0.053†	0.028	0.027	0.027	0.096*	0.094*	0.099*
0.135*	0.142*	0.140*	0.148*	0.151*	0.148*	0.155*
0.215*	0.138*	0.140*	0.128*	0.140*	0.139*	0.138*
—0.039	0.013	0.018	0.011	—0.021	—0.008	—0.016
—0.065	—0.077†	—0.077†	—0.078†	—0.055	—0.054	—0.060
—0.060	0.150†	0.153†	0.138†	—0.165†	—0.167†	—0.171
—0.059	—0.038	—0.041	—0.034	—0.107*	—0.108*	—0.110*
—0.059	0.062	0.063	0.067	0.003	—0.001	—0.000
. . .	. . .	. . .	. . .	. . .	. . .	. . .
0.038	0.236*	0.240*	0.229*	0.040	0.043	0.052
0.041	0.131*	0.129*	0.131*	0.105†	0.102†	0.111†
0.046	0.089†	0.087†	0.086	0.096†	0.087†	0.105*
0.310*	—0.001	—0.002	0.011	—0.060	—0.080	—0.092
. . .	. . .	. . .	. . .	. . .	. . .	. . .
0.091*	—0.018	—0.019	—0.018	—0.029	—0.034	—0.021
0.049†	0.124*	0.123*	0.134*	0.038	0.031	0.044
0.205*	0.084*	0.089*	0.104*	0.102*	0.098*	0.118*
. . .	. . .	. . .	. . .	. . .	. . .	. . .
0.231*	0.261*	0.259*	0.261*	0.362*	0.360*	0.362*

TABLE 20 ***(continued)***

	Ability 1 (N = 1117)			Ability 2 (N = 1010)	
Equation number	*(1) M.A1*	*(2) M.A1*	*(3) M.A1*	*(1) M.A2*	*(2) M.A2*
R^2	0.139	0.152	0.149	0.193	0.201
F	8.40	6.71	5.77	11.24	8.48
College(s) in community					
00 None		...		...	...
13 State college		—0.077*			0.102*
14 Private college		0.021			0.015
15 Teachers college		0.036			—0.038
18 Extension Center		—0.013			—0.048
29 Multiple		0.010			—0.003
49 Madison		0.024			0.098†
39 Milwaukee region A		—0.187*			—0.049
59 Milwaukee region B		—0.093†			—0.023
College(s) within 20 miles					
00 None			...		
13 State college			0.007		
14 Private college			—0.096*		
15 Teachers college			0.032		
18 Extension Center			—0.039		
22 13 + other two-year			—0.096†		
23 14 + other two-year			0.009		
24 13 + 14 + other two-year			—0.009		
25 14 + 14 w/wo two-year			0.040		
27 Multiple two-year			—0.037		
49 Madison			0.026		
39 Milwaukee regions			—0.078*		

* Significant $F_{.01}$ $t_{.05}$ (one-tailed).

† Significant $F_{.01}$ but not $t_{.05}$ (one-tailed).

	Ability 3 (N = 1060)			Ability 4 (N = 1039)		
(3) M.A2	*(1) M.A3*	*(2) M.A3*	*(3) M.A3*	*(1) M.A4*	*(2) M.A4*	*(3) M.A4*
0.207	*0.200*	*0.203*	*0.211*	*0.176*	*0.180*	*0.184*
7.73	*12.38*	*9.06*	*8.31*	*10.32*	*7.66*	*7.07*
. . .		. . .			. . .	
		0.079†			0.061	
		0.015			—0.020	
		0.020			—0.011	
		0.007			0.010	
		—0.019			0.097*	
		0.058			0.001	
		0.002			0.068	
		—0.046			—0.017	
. . .			. . .			. . .
0.139*			—0.024			0.090*
—0.033			—0.108			0.008
0.008			—0.059			0.034
—0.029			0.277*			0.131
0.032			—0.086			—0.066
—0.005			—0.048			0.049
0.069†			—0.038			—0.043
—0.040			—0.178†			—0.155
0.052			—0.043			0.053
0.098†			—0.050			0.000
0.000			—0.115*			—0.000

TABLE 21 ***Regression analysis of college attendance rates of female 1957 Wisconsin high school graduates by ability quarters***

	Ability 1 (N = 1117)			*Ability 2 (N = 1073)*	
Equation number	*(1) F.A1*	*(2) F.A1*	*(3) F.A1*	*(1) F.A2*	*(2) F.A2*
R^2	*0.124*	*0.130*	*0.128*	*0.148*	*0.162*
F	*7.39*	*5.58*	*4.98*	*8.69*	*6.94*
Constant	—0.002	0.003	0.000	0.050	0.017
Father's education					
1. Elementary	. . .	. . .	. . .	. . .	. . .
2. High school 1–3	—0.006	—0.003	—0.006	0.048†	0.049†
3. High school 4	0.030	0.035†	0.032	0.052*	0.056*
4. College 1–3	0.099*	0.103*	0.106*	0.080†	0.079
5. College 4+	0.205*	0.206*	0.208*	0.043	0.019
Mother's education					
1. Elementary	. . .	. . .	. . .	. . .	. . .
2. High school 1–3	0.014	0.010	0.015	0.002	0.003
3. High school 4	0.055*	0.055*	0.056*	0.021	0.018
4. College 1–3	0.202*	0.193*	0.194*	0.097*	0.094*
5. College 4+	0.186*	0.184*	0.181*	0.217*	0.221*
Father's occupation					
1. Farmers	0.041	0.032	0.039	—0.010	0.009
2. Laborers	0.009	0.002	0.011	—0.031	—0.018
3. Private household, service	0.066	0.058	0.070	—0.064	—0.047
4. Operatives	0.006	0.001	0.009	—0.093*	—0.084*
5. Craftsmen	0.022	0.017	0.025	—0.065	—0.061
6. Clerical, sales	. . .	. . .	. . .	. . .	. . .
7. Proprietors	0.068†	0.058	0.069†	0.092†	0.109*
8. Managers, officials	0.119†	0.125*	0.117†	0.167*	0.187*
9. Professionals	0.065	0.057	0.062	—0.029	—0.016
10. Other	—0.042	—0.044	—0.039	—0.063	—0.038
Parental income					
1. Low	. . .	. . .	. . .	. . .	. . .
2.	0.003	0.008	0.004	0.009	0.003
3.	0.005	0.009	0.007	0.055†	0.049†
4. High	0.028	0.036	0.038	0.097*	0.082*
High school program					
1 Vocational	. . .	. . .	. . .	. . .	. . .
2 College preparatory	0.140*	0.139*	0.139*	0.178*	0.177*

	Ability 3 (N = 1098)			*Ability 4 (N = 1047)*		
(3) F.A.2	*(1) F.A3*	*(2) F.A3*	*(3) F.A3*	*(1) F.A4*	*(2) F.A4*	*(3) F.A4*
0.157	*0.261*	*0.266*	*0.270*	*0.221*	*0.229*	*0.233*
5.86	*18.11*	*13.44*	*12.29*	*13.86*	*10.44*	*9.33*
0.017	0.061	0.074	0.043	0.029	0.032	0.065
. . .	. . .	. . .	. . .	. . .	. . .	. . .
0.047†	—0.000	—0.000	0.004	0.062†	0.072†	0.059
0.056*	—0.035	—0.033	—0.033	0.101*	0.105*	0.102*
0.075	0.038	0.040	0.033	0.148*	0.143*	0.146*
0.032	0.077†	0.070	0.078†	0.252*	0.251*	0.252*
. . .	. . .	. . .	. . .	. . .	. . .	. . .
0.004	—0.029	—0.032	—0.029	—0.079*	—0.075†	—0.087*
0.019	0.120*	0.116*	0.119*	—0.006	—0.007	—0.010
0.099*	0.330*	0.326*	0.322*	0.099*	0.096*	0.097*
0.211*	0.310*	0.309*	0.312*	0.086*	0.086*	0.083*
—0.005	0.082*	0.077†	0.083*	0.083†	0.079†	0.090†
—0.020	—0.062	—0.062	—0.056	0.001	—0.004	0.001
—0.057	—0.028	—0.015	—0.008	0.124	0.130	0.169
—0.088*	0.008	0.010	0.013	0.044	0.047	0.051
—0.064	—0.059	—0.050	—0.056	0.051	0.046	0.056
. . .	. . .	. . .	. . .	. . .	. . .	. . .
0.101*	0.157*	0.156*	0.157*	0.023	0.018	0.020
0.174*	0.104†	0.112	0.111†	0.081	0.083	0.091†
—0.010	0.080†	0.083	0.086†	0.051	0.056	0.050
—0.065	—0.015	—0.019	—0.020	0.088	0.074	0.024
. . .	. . .	. . .	. . .	. . .	. . .	. . .
0.010	—0.076*	—0.077*	—0.074*	—0.007	—0.001	—0.012
0.052†	0.008	0.006	0.007	0.056	0.064	0.047
0.086*	0.137*	0.136*	0.135*	0.163*	0.165*	0.161*
. . .	. . .	. . .	. . .	. . .	. . .	. . .
0.180*	0.213*	0.216*	0.213*	0.311*	0.320*	0.312*

TABLE 21 ***(continued)***

	Ability 1 (N = 1117)			Ability 2 (N = 1073)	
Equation number	(1) F.A1	(2) F.A1	(3) F.A1	(1) F.A1	(2) F.A1
R^2	0.124	0.130	0.128	0.148	0.162
F	7.39	5.58	4.98	8.69	6.94
College(s) in community					
00 None		. . .			. . .
13 State college		—0.005			0.087*
14 Private college		—0.045			0.078†
15 Teachers college		0.030			0.087*
18 Extension Center		—0.058†			—0.024
29 Multiple		0.026			—0.002
49 Madison		—0.038			0.170*
39 Milwaukee region A		—0.035			0.094
59 Milwaukee region B		—0.023			0.109*
College(s) within 20 miles					
00 None			. . .		
13 State college			—0.026		
14 Private college			—0.021		
15 Teachers college			0.017		
18 Extension Center			—0.038		
22 13 + other two-year			—0.039		
23 14 + other two-year			—0.008		
24 13 + 14 + other two-year			0.007		
25 14 + 14 w/wo two-year			—0.032		
27 Multiple two-year			—0.001		
49 Madison			—0.016		
39 Milwaukee regions			—0.055†		

* Significant $F_{.01}$ $t_{.05}$ (one-tailed).

† Significant $F_{.01}$ but not $t_{.05}$ (one-tailed).

ing was most important in the top two ability quarters, as was family income. But in those two tables all the parental background traits were put among the independent variables; for example, one could not observe the effect of the mother's education, given the father's schooling. Tables 22 and 23 divide the total sample by father's education, reversing the procedure for ability.

It is useful to begin by emphasizing the fact that no matter what

	Ability 3 (N = 1098)			*Ability 4 (N = 1047)*		
(3) F.A1	*(1) F.A3*	*(2) F.A3*	*(3) F.A3*	*(1) F.A4*	*(2) F.A4*	*(3) F.A4*
0.157	*0.261*	*0.266*	*0.270*	*0.221*	*0.229*	*0.233*
5.86	*18.11*	*13.44*	*12.29*	*13.86*	*10.44*	*9.33*
		. . .			. . .	
		0.020			−0.019	
		−0.063			−0.094†	
		−0.061†			−0.137*	
		−0.063			−0.040	
		−0.046			0.027	
		0.063†			0.042	
		−0.003			−0.033	
		0.002			0.018	
. . .			. . .			. . .
0.030			0.014			0.074
0.103†			0.033			−0.138
0.061†			0.018			−0.103*
−0.030			0.237†			−0.319*
0.043			−0.132†			−0.057
−0.004			−0.016			−0.010
0.013			0.028			−0.009
−0.038			0.049			−0.001
0.009			0.014			−0.071
0.098*			0.136*			−0.016
0.096*			0.000			−0.063

a father's schooling (or the college-accessibility profile), having a mother who had graduated from college substantially increased the likelihood that a girl would attend college. The largest incremental effect of maternal education, however, occurred where fathers had not completed high school or had only begun college. The maximum effect of maternal schooling occurred if she had some college and the father had only elementary schooling or if

(Text continued on p. 106)

TABLE 22 ***Regression analysis of college attendance rates of male 1957 Wisconsin high school graduates by father's education***

	FED 1 (N = 1906)			FED 2 (N = 668)		
Equation number	*(1) M.E1*	*(2) M.E1*	*(3) M.E1*	*(1) M.E2*	*(2) M.E2*	*(3) M.E2*
R^2	*0.218*	*0.220*	*0.224*	*0.250*	*0.257*	*0.270*
F	*26.30*	*18.92*	*16.90*	*10.77*	*7.90*	*7.57*
Constant	−0.023	−0.030	−0.028	−0.054	−0.058	−0.074
Ability						
1. *Low*	...	...	...	...	...	...
2.	0.057*	0.055*	0.057*	0.112*	0.101*	0.097*
3.	0.111*	0.110*	0.109*	0.095*	0.085*	0.087*
4. *High*	0.304*	0.301*	0.303*	0.317*	0.313*	0.306*
Mother's education						
1. *Elementary*	...	...	...	...	...	...
2. *High school 1–3*	−0.006	−0.007	−0.005	0.020	0.015	0.015
3. *High school 4*	0.069*	0.067*	0.069*	0.017	0.016	0.022
4. *College 1–3*	0.113*	0.116*	0.117*	0.235*	0.233*	0.271*
5. *College 4+*	0.089*	0.090*	0.081*	0.190*	0.184*	0.199*
Father's occupation						
1. *Farmer*	−0.008	−0.001	−0.004	0.039	0.053	0.036
2. *Laborers*	−0.020	−0.016	−0.017	−0.013	−0.017	−0.010
3. *Private household, service*	0.013	0.015	0.017	0.230*	0.211†	0.221*
4. *Operatives*	−0.043	−0.040	−0.037	0.011	−0.002	0.000
5. *Craftsmen*	0.044	0.049	0.049	0.070	0.061	0.077
6. *Clerical, sales*	...	...	...	...	...	...
7. *Proprietors*	0.100*	0.105*	0.103*	0.133*	0.127†	0.142*
8. *Managers, officials*	−0.061	−0.052	−0.053	0.189*	0.183*	0.186*
9. *Professionals*	−0.050	−0.040	−0.045	0.198†	0.180†	0.205†
10. *Other*	0.165*	0.169*	0.165*	0.004	−0.016	−0.018
Parental income						
1. *Low*	...	...	...	...	...	...
2.	0.026	0.027	0.027	−0.003	−0.006	−0.020
3.	0.096*	0.097*	0.101*	0.006	−0.010	−0.004
4. *High*	0.130*	0.133*	0.142*	0.071†	0.049	0.050
High school program						
1. *Vocational*	...	...	...	...	...	...
2. *College preparatory*	0.212*	0.213*	0.212*	0.270*	0.273*	0.271*

FED 3 (N = 1073)			*FED 4 (N = 226)*			*FED 5 (N = 353)*		
(1) M.E3	*(2) M.E3*	*(3) M.E3*	*(1) M.E4*	*(2) M.E4*	*(3) M.E4*	*(1) M.E5*	*(2) M.E5*	*(3) M.E5*
0.251	*0.258*	*0.259*	*0.191*	*0.244*	*0.230*	*0.291*	*0.314*	*0.352*
17.64	*12.97*	*11.35*	*2.43*	*2.27*	*1.87*	*6.82*	*5.29*	*5.83*
0.024	0.003	0.058	0.111	0.239	0.255	0.113	0.103	−0.022
...	...	...	...	...	...	...	...	...
0.140*	0.147*	0.148*	0.186*	0.174*	0.173†	−0.011	−0.017	0.029
0.260*	0.270*	0.270*	0.243*	0.260*	0.256*	0.053	0.044	0.115†
0.402*	0.413*	0.412*	0.270*	0.280*	0.270*	0.102	0.090	0.150*
...	...	...	...	...	...	...	...	...
−0.033	−0.038	−0.032	0.014	−0.001	0.007	0.006	−0.002	−0.002
0.040	0.041	0.040	0.044	0.026	0.023	0.118	0.122	0.130†
0.104†	0.099†	0.104†	−0.002	0.002	−0.024	0.294*	0.322*	0.351*
0.148*	0.149*	0.137*	0.143	0.095	0.085	0.212*	0.223*	0.229*
−0.006	0.003	−0.013	0.031	−0.070	−0.007	−0.118	−0.122	−0.185†
−0.085*	−0.085*	−0.091*	−0.126	−0.165†	−0.099	−0.319*	−0.330*	−0.308*
0.017	0.026	0.019	0.458	0.388	0.381	−0.645*	−0.664*	−0.686*
−0.111*	−0.110*	−0.111*	−0.114	−0.149	−0.153	−0.085	−0.060	−0.061
−0.039	−0.043	−0.035	0.057	0.027	0.080	−0.042	−0.035	−0.047
...	...	...	...	...	...	...	...	...
0.106*	0.115*	0.104*	−0.012	−0.067	−0.031	0.034	0.069	0.043
0.041	0.037	0.034	0.183†	0.135	0.193†	0.190*	0.204*	0.186*
0.016	0.010	0.012	−0.021	−0.023	−0.000	0.099†	0.105†	0.091†
−0.342	−0.327	−0.360	0.412	0.345	0.311	0.289	0.268	0.455
...	...	...	...	...	...	...	...	...
0.012	0.008	0.006	−0.042	−0.034	−0.067	0.018	0.012	−0.031
0.041	0.044	0.041	0.110	0.128	0.073	−0.082	−0.100	−0.113
0.104*	0.105*	0.114*	0.156†	0.155†	0.126	0.099	0.079	0.073
...	...	...	...	...	...	...	...	...
0.253*	0.251*	0.247*	0.187*	0.193*	0.214*	0.312*	0.316*	0.276*

TABLE 22 ***(continued)***

	FED 1 (N = 1906)			FED 2 (N = 668)		
Equation number	(1) M.E1	(2) M.E1	(3) M.E1	(1) M.E2	(2) M.E2	(3) M.E2
R^2	0.218	0.220	0.224	0.250	0.257	0.270
F	26.30	18.92	16.90	10.77	7.90	7.57
College(s) in community						
00 None		...			...	
13 State college		0.004			0.053	
14 Private college		0.003			—0.043	
15 Teachers college		0.006			—0.003	
18 Extension Center		0.021			0.067	
29 Multiple		0.045			0.091†	
49 Madison		0.036			0.084	
39 Milwaukee region A		—0.038			0.087	
59 Milwaukee region B		—0.079†			0.133†	
College(s) within 20 miles						
00 None			...			...
13 State college			0.021			0.116*
14 Private college			—0.041			—0.063
15 Teachers college			—0.011			0.065
18 Extension Center			0.178*			0.259
22 13 + other two-year			—0.002			—0.041
23 14 + other two-year			0.004			0.113*
24 13 + 14 + other two-year			0.023			—0.058
25 14 + 14 w/wo two-year			—0.071			—0.172
27 Multiple two-year			0.015			0.030
49 Madison			—0.004			0.074
39 Milwaukee regions			—0.044			0.053

* Significant $F_{.01}$ $t_{.05}$ (one-tailed).
† Significant $F_{.01}$ but not $t_{.05}$ (one-tailed).

she finished high school and the father began but did not finish it. All in all, effects of maternal education were less for boys than for girls except where the father had graduated from college. Having a father who graduated from college and a mother with at least some college work brought the maximum effect. Quite distinctive and complex processes in the determination of educational choice lie back of these rather tangled findings, and some conclud-

FED 3 (N = 1073)			*FED 4 (N = 226)*			*FED 5 (N = 353)*		
(1) M.E3	*(2) M.E3*	*(3) M.E3*	*(1) M.E4*	*(2) M.E4*	*(3) M.E4*	*(1) M.E5*	*(2) M.E5*	*(3) M.E5*
0.251	*0.258*	*0.259*	*0.191*	*0.244*	*0.230*	*0.291*	*0.314*	*0.352*
17.64	*12.97*	*11.35*	*2.43*	*2.27*	*1.87*	*6.82*	*5.29*	*5.83*
	. . .			. . .			. . .	
	0.108*			−0.065			0.003	
	0.020			0.026			0.031	
	0.049			−0.091			0.129†	
	−0.046			−0.346*			−0.038	
	0.045			−0.128			−0.181*	
	0.049			−0.305†			0.130*	
	0.028			−0.205†			0.015	
	−0.061			−0.309†			0.038	
		. . .			. . .			. . .
		0.020			−0.061			0.193*
		−0.143*			0.044			0.177
		−0.039			−0.042			0.281*
		−0.210			. . .			. . .
		−0.088			−0.165			−0.168
		−0.037			−0.122			−0.024
		−0.034			−0.122			−0.215*
		0.073			−0.101			0.120
		−0.036			−0.327			0.168†
		−0.038			−0.226†			0.247*
		−0.114*			−0.190			0.135*

ing interpretations will be offered after data for Illinois and North Carolina have been reviewed in the next chapter.

The effects of parental income upon college attendance rates were almost the reverse of those just described for maternal schooling. Among girls it is where paternal education is highest that income makes the most difference. Among boys, on the other hand, parental income brought the largest effect among sons of relatively

(Text continued on p. 110)

TABLE 23 ***Regression analysis of college attendance rates of female 1957 Wisconsin high school graduates by father's education***

	FED 1 (N = 2042)			FED 2 (N = 724)		
Equation number	*(1) F.E1*	*(2) F.E1*	*(3) F.E1*	*(1) F.E2*	*(2) F.E2*	*(3) F.E2*
R^2	*0.164*	*0.166*	*0.167*	*0.221*	*0.230*	*0.225*
F	*19.79*	*14.32*	*12.56*	*9.95*	*7.41*	*6.49*
Constant	0.053	0.066	0.051	−0.063	−0.072	−0.052
Ability						
1. *Low*	. . .	. . .	. . .	. . .	. . .	. . .
2.	0.013	0.014	0.014	0.055†	0.055†	0.060†
3.	0.077*	0.077*	0.076*	0.074*	0.083*	0.080*
4. *High*	0.111*	0.109*	0.113*	0.166*	0.170*	0.172*
Mother's education						
1. *Elementary*	. . .	. . .	. . .	. . .	. . .	. . .
2. *High school 1–3*	−0.020	−0.022	−0.020	0.039	0.038	0.042
3. *High school 4*	0.018	0.018	0.018	0.131*	0.121*	0.130*
4. *College 1–3*	0.266*	0.266*	0.267*	0.370*	0.365*	0.373*
5. *College 4+*	0.224*	0.224*	0.225*	0.283*	0.278*	0.284*
Father's occupation						
1. *Farmers*	0.003	−0.004	−0.002	0.032	0.035	0.027
2. *Laborers*	−0.049	−0.055†	−0.057†	−0.007	−0.008	−0.008
3. *Private household, service*	0.012	0.009	0.009	0.006	0.012	0.003
4. *Operatives*	−0.022	−0.023	−0.025	−0.018	−0.026	−0.021
5. *Craftsmen*	−0.020	−0.021	−0.023	−0.051	−0.055	−0.048
6. *Clerical, sales*	. . .	. . .	. . .	. . .	. . .	. . .
7. *Proprietors*	0.010	0.005	0.007	0.124*	0.130*	0.128*
8. *Managers, officials*	0.110†	0.111†	0.104†	0.145†	0.135†	0.137†
9. *Professionals*	−0.031	−0.032	−0.037	−0.046	−0.055	−0.045
10. *Other*	−0.162*	−0.166*	−0.170*	−0.130	−0.121	−0.141
Parental income						
1. *Low*	. . .	. . .	. . .	. . .	. . .	. . .
2.	−0.021	−0.019	−0.021	0.002	0.003	0.003
3.	−0.026	−0.023	−0.024	0.093*	0.091*	0.098*
4. *High*	0.092*	0.099*	0.095*	0.151*	0.160*	0.166*
High school program						
1. *Vocational*	. . .	. . .	. . .	. . .	. . .	. . .
2. *College preparatory*	0.185*	0.186*	0.183*	0.173*	0.169*	0.166*

FED 3 (N = 1059)			*FED 4 (N = 208)*			*FED 5 (N = 302)*		
(1) F.E3	*(2) F.E3*	*(3) F.E3*	*(1) F.E4*	*(2) F.E4*	*(3) F.E4*	*(1) F.E5*	*(2) F.E5*	*(3) F.E5*
0.190	*0.196*	*0.199*	*0.272*	*0.309*	*0.209*	*0.303*	*0.327*	*0.333*
12.17	*8.96*	*7.97*	*3.50*	*2.86*	*2.42*	*6.10*	*4.74*	*4.51*
0.031	0.043	0.032	−0.030	−0.090	−0.023	−0.112	−0.120	−0.087
...	...	...	...	...	...	...	...	...
0.040	0.038	0.047	0.040	0.033	0.075	−0.244*	−0.248*	−0.251*
0.052	0.045	0.052	0.097	0.072	0.118	0.039	0.051	0.043
0.181*	0.176*	0.186*	0.162†	0.163†	0.194*	0.089	0.100	0.093
...	...	...	...	...	...	...	...	...
−0.032	−0.034	−0.031	0.083	0.093	0.046	−0.001	−0.010	−0.040
0.035	0.033	0.033	0.100	0.104	0.055	0.074	0.092	0.092
0.041	0.040	0.042	0.139	0.138	0.085	0.161†	0.159†	0.144†
0.141*	0.142*	0.138*	0.256†	0.292†	0.206*	0.148†	0.160*	0.154†
0.057	0.053	0.066	0.276*	0.308*	0.261*	−0.076	−0.068	−0.071
−0.066	−0.071†	−0.070†	0.075	0.099	0.029	0.086	0.082	0.069
0.029	0.021	0.031	−0.470	−0.379	−0.418	−0.299	−0.190	−0.326
−0.082*	−0.081*	−0.083	0.084	0.082	0.063	−0.043	−0.064	−0.056
−0.050	−0.054	−0.056	0.013	0.003	−0.005	0.077	0.101	0.073
...	...	...	...	...	...	...	...	...
0.086*	0.081†	0.093*	−0.052	−0.060	−0.007	0.381*	0.380*	0.387*
0.040	0.037	0.035	0.261*	0.309*	0.252*	0.240*	0.221*	0.229*
−0.001	−0.005	−0.001	0.164†	0.160†	0.158†	0.196*	0.205*	0.205*
0.164	0.172	0.137	0.465*	0.401	0.426	0.152	0.077	0.031
...	...	...	...	...	...	...	...	...
−0.020	−0.020	−0.020	−0.232*	−0.243*	−0.245*	0.171†	0.153†	0.158†
0.055	0.047	0.045	−0.013	−0.057	−0.036	0.218*	0.185*	0.175*
0.116*	0.111*	0.107*	−0.022	−0.085	−0.040	0.284*	0.245*	0.240*
...	...	...	...	...	...	...	...	...
0.252*	0.261*	0.254*	0.335*	0.355*	0.321*	0.299*	0.299*	0.286*

TABLE 23 ***(continued)***

	FED 1 (N = 2042)			FED 2 (N = 724)		
Equation number	(1) F.E1	(2) F.E1	(3) F.E1	(1) F.E2	(2) F.E2	(3) F.E2
R^2	0.164	0.166	0.167	0.221	0.230	0.225
F	19.79	14.32	12.56	9.95	7.41	6.49
Colleges in community						
00 None		. . .			. . .	
13 State college		0.016			0.087†	
14 Private college		−0.051†			0.053	
15 Teachers college		−0.038†			0.018	
18 Extension Center		−0.042			−0.016	
29 Multiple		−0.006			0.058	
49 Madison		−0.012			−0.006	
39 Milwaukee region A		−0.044			−0.142*	
59 Milwaukee region B		−0.031			0.018	
Colleges within 20 miles						
00 None			. . .			. . .
13 State college			0.014			−0.017
14 Private college			0.030			0.016
15 Teachers college			0.001			−0.017
18 Extension Center			0.026			0.014
22 13 + other two-year			−0.045			−0.023
23 14 + other two-year			0.006			−0.003
24 13 + 14 + other two-year			0.015			0.002
25 14 + 14 w/wo other two-year			−0.025			0.072
27 Multiple two-year			0.029			−0.063
49 Madison			−0.017			−0.032
39 Milwaukee regions			−0.047			−0.084†

* Significant $F_{.01}$ $t_{.05}$ (one-tailed).

† Significant $F_{.01}$ but not $t_{.05}$ (one-tailed).

unschooled fathers and of those who began but did not finish college. The pattern, to repeat, is what one might expect if he views going to college as an investment decision among males and a consumption decision among females. The observed influence of income among sons of less-educated fathers surely picks up an effect of exceptional relative ability to meet the burden of financing

FED 3 (N = 1059)			FED 4 (N = 208)			FED 5 (N = 302)		
(1) F.E3	(2) F.E3	(3) F.E3	(1) F.E4	(2) F.E4	(3) F.E4	(1) F.E5	(2) F.E5	(3) F.E5
0.190	0.196	0.199	0.272	0.309	0.209	0.303	0.327	0.333
12.17	8.96	7.97	3.50	2.86	2.42	6.10	4.74	4.51
	. . .			. . .			. . .	
	−0.003			0.165			−0.038	
	−0.025			0.004			−0.075	
	−0.028			0.170†			0.033	
	−0.060			−0.057			−0.132	
	−0.033			0.258*			0.011	
	0.053			0.208†			0.167*	
	0.025			0.181			0.102	
	0.130*			0.113			0.039	
		. . .			. . .			. . .
		0.058			0.038			0.049
		−0.030			0.045			−0.002
		−0.019			0.049			−0.010
		−0.319†			—			—
		−0.051			0.104			0.004
		−0.033			−0.005			−0.008
		−0.001			0.150			−0.071
		−0.111			0.134			0.080
		−0.031			−0.161			−0.230†
		0.074			0.179†			0.184*
		0.067			0.004			0.036

a college education that is less often found where poorly educated men also have low incomes.

After these excursions, we can now ask: Given the controls for ability and parental status, what are the effects of college accessibility upon the likelihood of attending college within each subset of youth as divided by education of father?

1 Among offspring of fathers with only elementary schooling, the rate of continuing into college is little affected by the college-accessibility profiles of the community of residence. Even the modest effects among boys displayed in Table 19 disappear once controls for ability and other traits are used. The only exception is for those living within 20 miles of an Extension Center.

2 Again, residence in Madison is found to stimulate college attendance among boys from modest backgrounds (FED 2 and 3 in this instance).[19] Madison was decidedly favorable for college education of daughters of well-schooled men (again see Table 19).

3 Again, residence in communities with a state college was associated with somewhat higher rates of college going for both sexes within the lower-middle status categories, but the effects were slight.

4 Selective recruitment into Extension Centers of higher-ability men from families with a poorly educated head and a low SES level is strongly indicated (combining evidence from Table 22 with that in Tables 19 and 20).

Overall, we seem to come out with mainly negative, or at least strongly reserved, conclusions, after allowing for the educational level of the head of the family. The major factor in determining level of college attendance among Wisconsin youth had little to do with the college options offered locally. College location would seem to be a weak strategy if one's aim is to induce more youth to undertake college work. The main exception, and an important one, is that Extension Centers do attract boys who come from humble backgrounds but have considerable talent. This proposition will be tested further in the analysis of variance that follows.

Analysis of Variance on a Three-way Matrix

From working with observations of individuals, as in the preceding pages, we turn now to an analysis that uses as observations the proportions of specified subcategories of male or female high school graduates who went on to college. The categories are defined by being in a particular ability quarter, social status (third), and college-accessibility cell of a matrix laid out on these three dimensions. Thus we can consider variations in effects of the local presence of an institution of higher education (or a profile-set of such colleges) upon college attendance rates according to each

[19] To explain this last finding as other than random would entail farfetched speculation, which we forgo.

possible ability-status *combination.* Secondly, by treating these proportions as observations taken on groups instead of on individuals, we can, at little expense, use transforms that allow for the increasing difficulty in changing proportions by any given absolute amount with approach toward the limits of zero or unity. That is, by use of logit transforms we are able to avoid the biases (and ambiguities) inherent in linear least-squares regressions with a dependent variable that has fixed upper and lower limits.[20] The logit transform accommodates the predicted likelihoods to a cumulative sigmoid curve and enables us also to give valid interpretations of coefficients of determination and tests of significance. The bounded [1,0] dependent variable becomes unbounded ($-\infty$, $+\infty$) and the sigmoid distribution of [1,0] responses is thereby transformed into a linear function measured in logits. This of course automatically ensures that no predicted value of proportions attending college could exceed the upper limit of unity or the lower limit of zero. It allows us also to use standard statistical tests of significance in an analysis of variance.

For each sex we carried out such analyses for two matrices. The first was the 24 cells in the first two columns of Table 24; these refer only to residents of noncollege communities or of communities with four-year public colleges (the regional institutions of the system). The second matrix comprises the 24 cells of the first column, which again gives us noncollege communities, but now combined with Extension Center communities. Table 25 gives the net results of the analysis of variance. Immediately one sees that the "main effects" of local access are negligible for both sexes when the comparisons refer to state colleges, and among males when they refer to Extension Centers. Furthermore, interaction effects between access and ability or SES are negligible. The effects of ability and of SES are highly significant in all cases, with ability the stronger among boys and SES among girls. Among girls especially the logit gradients on both the SES and the ability dimensions are steeper for the Extension Center than for those with state colleges though even for towns with the latter they are definitely steeper than in the noncollege towns.

Access did turn out to be highly significant for girls when we

[20] The logit is the logarithm of betters' odds. Where P_c is the proportion attending college, its logit would be the logarithm of $P_c/(1 - p_o)$. For an exceptionally clear discussion of the use of logits, see Theil (1970).

TABLE 24
Selected logit transforms and differentials, Wisconsin, 1957

	Noncollege communities	*State college minus noncollege*	*Extension Centers minus noncollege*
		Males	
Ability 1: SES 1	−1.061	−1.173	−0.698
2	−0.861	−0.882	−1.252
3	−0.294	−0.845	−0.438
Ability 2: SES 1	−0.743	−0.360	−0.602
2	−0.370	−0.389	−0.636
3	−0.151	+0.362	−0.203
Ability 3: SES 1	−0.501	−0.753	−0.448
2	−0.302	+0.026	+0.027
3	+0.226	+0.391	+0.112
Ability 4: SES 1	−0.050	+0.176	+0.000
2	+0.054	+0.570	+0.231
3	+0.562	+0.408	+0.345
		Females	
Ability 1: SES 1	−1.104	−1.495	−1.883*
2	−1.110	−0.662	−1.392
3	−0.423	−1.173	−0.778
Ability 2: SES 1	−1.079	−1.130	−1.337
2	−0.743	−0.302	−0.940
3	−0.430	−0.124	−0.229
Ability 3: SES 1	−0.664	−0.545	−1.227
2	−0.434	−0.276	−0.479
3	−0.040	+0.033	−0.164
Ability 4: SES 1	−0.398	−0.602	−0.653
2	−0.265	−0.124	−0.176
3	+0.222	+0.216	+0.160

$^{*}P = 0.0 \qquad \text{Logit }(P) = \text{Log}\left[\frac{1}{3n}\Big/(1-\frac{1}{3n})\right] = -1.883$

$N = 24$

compared communities with no college and those with Extension Centers, but the significance was in favor of the towns *without* colleges. In this case the interaction between access and SES was also significant (at the .05 level). No one will contend that locating an Extension Center in a community would depress college atten-

TABLE 25 ***Analyses of intercell variance in logits of proportions attending college, Wisconsin, 1957***

MATRIX 1 (Access categories: None and state college)							
				Males		*Females*	
	df	*F*.95	*F*.99	*Sum of squares*	*F*	*Sum of squares*	*F*
Access	1	5.99	13.75	0.0436	0.821	0.0014	0.025
SES	2	5.14	10.92	1.6463	15.501	1.7801	20.698
Ability	3	4.76	9.78	3.9668	24.900	2.4273	18.816
Access/SES	2	5.14	10.92	0.0447	0.420	0.1970	2.291
Access/Ability	3	4.76	9.78	0.2298	1.443	0.1571	1.219
Ability/SES	6	4.28	8.47	0.1740	0.546	0.1424	0.551
Access/Ability/ SES	6			0.3186		0.2584	
TOTAL	23			6.4238		4.9637	
MATRIX 2 (Access categories: none and Extension Centers)							
Access	1	5.99	13.75	0.0002	0.006	0.3119*	21.218
SES	2	5.14	10.92	1.2429	19.006	2.7885	94.850
Ability	3	4.76	9.78	3.0288	30.875	2.8194	63.932
Access/SES	2	5.14	10.92	0.0836	1.278	0.1693	5.762
Access/Ability	3	4.76	9.78	0.0220	0.223	0.1410	3.197
Ability/SES	6	4.28	8.47	0.1750	0.893	0.0705	0.796
Access/Ability/ SES	6			0.1959		0.0883	
TOTAL	23			4.7484		6.3889	

* In favor of communities with no college.

dance—no matter what the statistical significance tests might show. The data are telling us more about communities in which Extension Centers are located than about the effects of those centers on college attendance. It is relevant in this connection to turn back to the evidence in the multiple regressions that suggested more positive college attendance effects of living within 20 miles of an Extension Center than of living next door to it.

In all cases (each sex in each matrix) the analysis of variance presented in Table 25 refers to main effects only. The base distributions that lie back of that analysis provide evidence concerning which ability/SES combinations seem to behave differently according to the particular accessibility situation. Base distributions of college attendance rates (with the *N* for each cell) are shown in Tables 26 and 27 for those accessibility categories having at least

TABLE 26 ***Percentage rates of college attendance by ability/SES categories within selected college-accessibility categories; Wisconsin males, 1957***

	College-access types				
	None	*State college*	*Extension Center*	*Milwaukee*	*Total*
Ability 1: SES 1	8.0 (362)	6.3 (32)	16.7 (18)	12.8 (47)	8.0 (564)
2	12.1 (240)	11.6 (43)	5.3 (19)	12.2 (41)	13.0 (432)
3	33.7 (86)	12.5 (32)	26.7 (15)	20.9 (43)	28.3 (230)
Ability 2: SES 1	15.3 (236)	30.4 (23)	20.0 (20)	17.0 (47)	16.6 (403)
2	29.9 (201)	29.0 (38)	18.8 (32)	22.2 (63)	27.2 (419)
3	41.4 (104)	69.7 (33)	38.5 (26)	44.9 (78)	46.9 (343)
Ability 3: SES 1	24.0 (196)	15.0 (20)	26.3 (19)	36.7 (30)	23.8 (336)
2	33.3 (195)	51.5 (33)	51.6 (31)	47.6 (84)	39.4 (462)
3	62.7 (150)	71.1 (38)	56.4 (39)	64.9 (111)	62.3 (448)
Ability 4: SES 1	47.1 (140)	60.0 (10)	50.0 (16)	50.0 (20)	49.3 (241)
2	53.1 (194)	78.8 (33)	63.0 (27)	75.8 (66)	59.8 (405)
3	78.5 (186)	71.9 (32)	68.9 (45)	83.8 (179)	79.1 (608)

TABLE 27 ***Percentage rates of college attendance by ability/SES categories within selected college-accessibility categories; Wisconsin females, 1957***

	College-access types					
	None	*State college*	*Teachers college*	*Extension Centers*	*Milwaukee*	*Total*
Ability 1: SES 1	7.3 (357)	3.1 (32)	7.1 (56)	0.0 (24)	1.5 (66)	5.9 (609)
2	7.2 (209)	17.9 (28)	15.6 (32)	3.9 (26)	6.9 (72)	7.5 (466)
3	27.4 (73)	6.3 (16)	38.9 (18)	14.3 (14)	20.4 (54)	24.9 (217)
Ability 2: SES 1	7.7 (274)	6.9 (29)	17.7 (34)	4.4 (23)	13.0 (54)	9.4 (488)
2	15.3 (196)	33.3 (21)	21.1 (38)	10.3 (29)	15.2 (92)	18.4 (463)
3	27.1 (107)	42.9 (21)	47.1 (17)	37.1 (27)	29.2 (96)	33.5 (340)
Ability 3: SES 1	17.8 (230)	22.2 (18)	5.6 (36)	5.6 (18)	13.0 (46)	14.8 (393)
2	26.9 (201)	34.6 (26)	14.3 (28)	25.0 (24)	16.3 (86)	21.9 (462)
3	47.7 (132)	51.9 (27)	58.6 (29)	40.7 (27)	55.6 (142)	52.3 (474)
Ability 4: SES 1	28.6 (147)	20.0 (15)	18.8 (16)	18.2 (11)	33.3 (21)	27.2 (250)
2	35.2 (165)	42.9 (21)	28.0 (25)	40.0 (15)	42.0 (69)	36.9 (374)
3	62.5 (176)	62.2 (45)	51.3 (39)	59.1 (44)	65.9 (164)	64.3 (638)

10 observations in every one of the 12 ability/SES cells and for all college-accessibility types combined. The N's in the total columns in each table demonstrate the definite underlying associations between ability quarter of child and SES rank of family; this is seen most dramatically by comparing distributions by SES within the lowest and the highest ability quarters. The sex contrasts for each ability/SES combination are equally obvious. (The first two columns of Table 28 show these differences in percentages and then in logits.) Both versions highlight especially the sex contrasts for all SES categories in the upper quarter of the ability distributions and for SES 2 in the third quarter on ability. The similarities and contrasts over these two columns illustrate also some of the effects of using a linear transform that takes into account the positioning of the segment of a cumulative (sigmoid) distribution spanned by the two rates being compared.

Details of the patterning in percentages entering college as they vary over the cells of Tables 26 and 27 can be examined directly. But for a simple summarization of these results with particular

TABLE 28 ***Analysis of sex differences and of selected accessibility effects on college attendance rates by ability/SES categories; Wisconsin, 1957***

	Male minus female college attendance rates; all communities		*Excess over noncollege communities in percentage rates of college attendance by residents of communities with:*			
			4-Year Public institutions		*Extension Centers*	
	Percentage differences (1)	*Logit differences (2)*	*Males (3)*	*Females (4)*	*Males (5)*	*Females (6)*
Ability 1: SES 1	+ 2.1	+0.14	− 1.7	− 4.2	+ 8.7	− 7.3
2	+ 5.5	+0.27	− 0.5	+10.7	− 6.8	− 3.3
3	+ 3.4	+0.08	−21.2	+21.1	− 7.0	−13.1
Ability 2: SES 1	+ 7.2	+0.20	+15.1	− 0.8	+ 4.7	− 3.3
2	+ 8.8	+0.22	− 0.9	+18.0	−11.1	− 5.0
3	+13.4	+0.24	+28.3	+15.8	− 2.9	+10.0
Ability 3: SES 1	+ 9.0	+0.26	− 9.0	+ 4.4	+ 2.3	−12.2
2	+17.5	+0.37	+18.2	+ 7.7	+18.3	− 1.9
3	+10.0	+0.18	+ 8.4	+ 4.2	− 6.3	− 7.0
Ability 4: SES 1	+22.1	+0.45	+12.9	− 8.6	+ 2.9	−10.4
2	+23.1	+0.41	+25.7	+ 7.7	+ 9.9	+ 4.8
3	+14.8	+0.32	− 6.6	− 0.3	− 9.6	− 3.4

respect to college accessibility, we present in Table 28, for each combination of ability with SES, the differences in college attendance rates by residents of noncollege communities on the one hand, and residents of state college or Extension Center communities on the other. The most striking result is the lack of consistent positive differences—except the negative significance on Matrix 2 for girls. The lack lies behind the insignificance of access in the analysis of variance. Negative differences had appeared earlier (as shown in Table 19) when we examined differences within ability, SES, and paternal education categories separately, but those differences were almost all positive for the state college communities. In Table 28, however, half of the differences in the state college column are negative for each sex. Among girls, there were only two instances with positive differences on Extension Centers (and hence the negatively significant effect of access in this case). There may seem to be some substantial favorable effects of residence in state college communities or in places with Extension Centers for boys from middle-SES levels if they have above-median ability, and quite generally for girls in the middle-SES third in state college communities. If we notice high percentage differences where they seem to fit into reasonable a priori expectations, we will have to be consistent and consider where they do not—most notably in the negative difference in low-ability/high-SES boys and girls in state college towns. Much larger samples and fuller specification of determinants of college-going behavior would be needed to reach really firm positive conclusions concerning the incidence of the benefits of accessibility to college. We do reiterate that inferences concerning positive differences must remain extremely tentative, even when a particular comparison shows up with a tidy and statistically significant positive value.

4. COLLEGE ACCESSIBILITY AND COLLEGE DESTINATIONS

Thus far in this chapter we have discussed the effects of college accessibility on the decision to go to college, paying no attention to the kinds of institution the youth attended, or to their location. But having a college locally accessible may affect the college destinations of youth who would attend some college in any case, quite apart from its overall effect upon the proportion of high school graduates who enter collegiate institutions. Such destination effects relate both to the type of college attended and to the location relative to the home community. It is necessary then to look into locational substitution effects as part of the effort to evaluate how much college attendance (of whom) is raised or lowered (as was done in a preliminary way in Chapter 3). And locational substitution must be examined to find out which and how many youth who would have gone to college somewhere in any case substitute attendance in the vicinity for attendance in more distant environments and in other types of colleges. Problems relating to local substitution effects and their possible societal implications are more complex and also more momentous in those states that are pushing the expansion of rural community colleges and in the large metropolitan conurbations than they are in Wisconsin. We will therefore go further into this problem in Chapter 5. But the destination patterns of college-bound youth are as important for understanding college attendance in the Wisconsin of a decade ago as they are today.

Distance to College and Locational Substitutions

The presence of a college in the immediate vicinity might be expected to draw more youth into college, primarily by inducing them to enter that local institution. It is assumed, that is, that at the "decision margins" some youth who would not go away from home to attend college will enroll in a nearby college. Their reason may be that they can do so at less cost in dollars or because local attendance entails less of a break with familiar experiences, acquaintances, and surroundings. Other individuals would in any case be going to some college but may choose to enroll in the local one—what we term the locational substitution effect. How far each situation prevails will depend on the characteristics of the colleges in the given community for one sort of higher education or another, on the ability to finance further schooling, and on the degree of cultural cosmopolitanism. It is not feasible to work out the relative weight of all these factors at the same time. Accordingly, we start here by picking up the analysis presented simply for college versus noncollege communities (in Table 12), but now we distinguish by ability categories and then by paternal schooling. The basic data are given in Tables 29 and 30; it will be useful to examine these directly before presenting indexes of locational substitution effects.

The effects of ability upon distance to college destinations are best indicated by comparing ability quarters on the proportions of college-bound youth from noncollege towns who travel over 60 miles (including those attending schools out of state). These proportions are given for each sex in Table 29 (last rows). Among boys, these proportions start at just over half in the lowest quarter of

TABLE 29 ***Distance distributions of college attendance of male and female 1957 Wisconsin high school graduates by ability quarters; college and noncollege communities***

Ability quarters	*Ability 1 (Low)*		*Ability 2*	
Colleges in community	*None*	*One or more*	*None*	*One or more*
			Male graduates	
Total number of students	685	406	537	431
Number entering college	80	55	135	141
Percentage entering college	11.7	13.5	25.1	32.7
Distribution of college entrants by distance:				
within community	0.0	30.9	0.0	39.7
within 20 miles	21.3	3.6	17.7	6.4
between 20–60 miles	26.3	5.5	19.2	6.4
greater than 60 miles	40.0	41.8	43.0	30.5
out-of-state	12.4	18.2	20.0	17.0
Sum of percentages beyond 60 miles and out-of-state	52.4	60.0	63.0	47.5
			Female graduates	
Total number of students	634	459	575	469
Number entering college	56	45	85	104
Percentage entering college	8.8	9.8	14.8	22.2
Distribution of college entrants by distance:				
within community	0.0	42.2	0.0	28.8
within 20 miles	16.1	13.3	17.7	5.8
between 20–60 miles	32.2	2.2	27.0	8.6
greater than 60 miles	33.8	26.7	40.0	35.5
out-of-state	17.8	15.5	15.3	21.2
Sum of percentages beyond 60 miles and out-of-state	51.6	42.2	55.3	56.7

ability and rise monotonically to just under three-fourths in the top quarter. Among girls, the proportions run very little above half until we come to the most able quarter, where the ratio exceeds three-fourths. For communities with colleges the patterns are rather different, though the proportions going beyond 60 miles to college are still high. Among boys, these proportions are about three-fifths for the top and bottom quarters in ability but only about 50 percent in the middle half of the ability range. For girls

Ability 3		Ability 4 (High)		Totals	
None	One or more	None	One or more	None	One or more
538	478	518	468	2278	1783
203	216	313	317	731	729
37.7	45.2	60.4	67.7	32.3	40.8
0.0	35.2	0.0	32.5	0.0	34.6
13.3	3.7	11.5	2.4	14.2	3.7
16.7	8.3	14.9	4.1	17.5	5.9
51.7	34.6	53.7	39.5	49.6	36.5
18.2	18.1	19.8	21.5	18.7	19.3
69.9	52.7	73.5	61.0	68.3	55.8
552	487	483	514	2244	1929
147	148	205	258	493	555
26.6	30.4	42.4	50.2	21.9	28.8
0.0	36.5	0.0	29.1	0.0	31.7
17.7	4.7	13.2	4.7	15.6	5.6
27.9	7.4	13.7	5.0	22.3	6.3
33.3	33.8	45.7	40.4	40.7	36.8
21.1	17.6	27.4	20.8	21.3	19.6
54.4	51.4	72.1	61.2	62.3	56.4

(apart from the least able), the pattern for residents of communities with colleges resembles that for boys in communities without a college. Within the 60-mile range, the distributions of distance to college for boys are much the same, irrespective of whether they reside in a college town or not, and irrespective of ability; for girls, the signal feature is the pronounced localism among the less able girls who did go to college.

Turning to Table 30, we may make a similar series of compari-

TABLE 30 ***Distance distributions of college attendance of male and female 1957 Wisconsin high school graduates by father's education; college and noncollege communities***

Father's education	*Elementary*		*High school 1–3*	
Colleges in community	*None*	*One or more*	*None*	*One or more*
				Male graduates
Total number of students	1181	680	329	311
Number entering college	261	184	88	114
Percentage entering college	22.1	27.1	26.7	36.6
Distribution of college entrants by distance:				
within community	0.0	36.5	0.0	33.3
within 20 miles	17.3	3.3	19.3	1.7
between 20–60 miles	20.4	6.5	25.0	6.1
greater than 60 miles	47.6	41.3	41.0	33.3
out-of-state	14.6	12.4	14.7	25.6
Sum of percentages beyond 60 miles and out-of-state	62.2	53.7	55.7	58.9
				Female graduates
Total number of students	1228	772	343	354
Number entering college	194	121	59	88
Percentage entering college	15.8	15.7	17.2	25.7
Distribution of college entrants by distance:				
within community	0.0	39.6	0.0	31.8
within 20 miles	16.5	5.8	17.0	6.8
between 20–60 miles	29.4	10.7	18.6	7.9
greater than 60 miles	36.1	28.2	44.1	34.1
out-of-state	18.0	15.7	20.3	19.3
Sum of percentages beyond 60 miles and out-of-state	54.1	43.9	64.4	53.4

sons in a broad overview, using parental schooling rather than youth's ability as the independent variable. Among college-bound boys from towns without a college, there is a definite jump in proportions going a long distance as between sons of fathers who had not completed high school and of fathers who had at least finished high school. (Notice, however, that sons of college men display no advantage over sons of secondary graduates in likelihood of going to college.) Among girls going to college from noncollege towns, on the other hand, there is a hiatus at the bottom of the scale of paternal schooling and then again when we come to fathers

High school 4		College 1–3		College 4+	
None	One or more	None	One or more	None	One or more
542	482	84	126	140	174
235	232	55	70	92	129
43.3	48.1	65.5	55.6	65.7	74.1
0.0	35.3	0.0	42.9	0.0	27.2
9.4	6.5	16.4	1.4	12.0	2.3
16.1	6.1	9.0	1.4	10.8	6.9
55.3	35.3	43.7	40.0	52.2	32.6
19.2	16.8	30.8	14.3	25.0	31.0
74.5	52.1	74.5	54.3	77.2	63.6
484	530	98	96	92	177
147	170	39	50	54	126
30.4	32.1	39.8	52.6	58.7	71.3
0.0	28.2	0.0	34.0	0.0	28.6
17.8	5.9	7.7	0.0	11.1	6.3
19.7	7.1	15.4	6.0	13.0	0.0
38.8	43.5	69.2	38.0	38.9	36.4
23.7	15.3	7.7	22.0	37.0	28.6
62.5	58.8	76.9	50.0	75.9	65.0

having at least some college education. Among youth who reside in towns possessing colleges, the relationships between paternal schooling and youths' rate of attendance are muted; only the offspring of college graduates display a markedly greater tendency to go longer distances or out of the state to attend college.

Locational substitution effects are summarized in Table 31 using the same procedures as in Table 12; however, now we distinguish first among ability categories and then among categories of paternal schooling. The first column refers only to youth attending college; it summarizes for them how far proportions of graduates from

TABLE 31 ***Indexes of locational substitution and maximum net location effects by ability and father's education; Wisconsin college versus noncollege communities (exclusive of Milwaukee)***

	Indexes of substitution effects			Maximum net location effect
	S_1	S_2	S_3	
Males				
Entire sample	24.1	7.8	5.6	8.5
Ability quarter 1	13.2	1.5	2.4	1.8
2	28.4	7.2	5.4	7.6
3	25.6	9.7	8.4	7.5
4	23.4	14.1	14.7	7.3
FED category 1	22.5	5.0	4.9	5.0
2	15.7	4.2	2.3	9.9
3	32.4	14.0	12.2	4.8
4	27.9	18.3	33.8	(−9.9)
5	17.5	11.5	11.8	8.4
Females				
Entire sample	22.1	4.9	2.2	6.9
Ability quarter 1	39.4	3.5	3.1	1.0
2	16.9	2.5	(−1.0)	7.4
3	23.5	6.3	6.9	3.8
4	20.6	8.7	6.8	7.8
FED category 1	28.9	4.6	6.3	(−0.1)
2	21.6	3.7	(−0.3)	8.5
3	16.3	5.0	7.4	1.7
4	26.3	10.5	5.1	12.8
5	23.8	14.1	7.8	12.6

high schools in college towns who went to college within a radius of 20 miles exceed those for youth from noncollege communities. While these figures almost necessarily must be positive, there is room for considerable variation. This first column displays very little pattern except for the distinctively low substitution effect for males from the lowest quarter of ability. When we use the second index of substitution, systematic relationships do show up. S_2 takes into account not only the college-bound youth but all the graduates from noncollege towns in each category of ability or of paternal education. The scope for S_2 is greater among youth having higher college attendance rates. The index S_3 is more complex; it is larger the greater the proportions of high school graduates from college towns who attend home colleges, but it is reduced by the maximum net location effect, shown in column (4) of Table 31. The latter, it may be recalled, is the difference between youth from college and from noncollege communities in overall rates of college attendance.

College-Accessibility and Destination Types

Behind the figures just discussed, which deal with the distances to colleges attended, there are complex patterns with respect to the differences in locations of various kinds of colleges. We may ask, for example, whether living in a community such as Madison provides at home the cosmopolitan opportunities that might otherwise be sought out in a university elsewhere. Quite another question is to what extent does the presence of a locally oriented college in a rural area divert youth from attending more cosmopolitan colleges? While our data bear only indirectly on some of these questions, it is important to dredge up what clues we can.

We present in the following sets of tables the distributions of types of college attended for each within-community situation of college accessibility; one pair of tables gives the foregoing information by ability quarter for each sex (Tables 32 and 33) and a second pair of tables gives parallel information by paternal education (Tables 34 and 35). Take first the students from noncollege places who attend out of state; as already shown (in Table 29), such students made up about a fifth of all male entrants to college in all but the lowest category of ability (in which they were an eighth). Among girls, the association with ability was somewhat stronger once we pass beyond the small college-bound numbers in the lowest quarter of ability.

Moving abruptly from the noncollege communities to Madison, the pattern in relation to ability becomes quite different. Among Madison boys entering a college, it was the less rather than the more able who went outside the state; the more able (especially those in the top quarter) went overwhelmingly to the university in Madison. Both the many attractions of that university and its selectivity for ability are reflected in these figures. An interesting sex contrast emerges (especially for category 3): Madison girls in this category of ability who do enter college were considerably more likely than were comparable boys to attend private colleges.[21]

[21] No doubt this in part reflects the greater socioeconomic (including income) selectivity in college attendance among girls generally, although other sex-linked factors that have probably changed noticeably over the past decade may have been involved.

TABLE 32 ***Distributions of type of college attended by male 1957 Wisconsin high school graduates by within-community college-accessibility type and ability quarters***

	Within-community college-accessibility type				
		Four-year college only		Teachers college	Extension Center
	None	Public	Private	(county)	(state)
Ability quarter 1					
Percent entering college	11.7	10.3	16.2	13.5	15.4
Number entering college	(80)	(10)	(5)	(15)	(17)
Percentage distribution of college entrants by destinations:					
university (public)	8.7				14.3
public college	61.2	80.0	40.0	40.0	42.9
private college	5.0			20.0	
teachers college	10.0			20.0	
extension center	2.5		20.0	13.3	28.6
out-of-state	12.5	20.0	40.0	6.7	14.3
Ability quarter 2					
Percent entering college	25.1	42.4	39.2	25.3	24.7
Number entering college	(131)	(38)	(18)	(19)	(18)
Percentage distribution of college entrants by destinations:					
university (public)	18.3	2.6	16.7	5.3	16.7
public college	46.5	86.9	33.4	47.3	27.8
private college	8.4		22.2	5.3	22.2
teachers college	4.6			15.9	
extension center	1.5		11.1		22.2
out-of-state	20.6	10.5	16.7	26.3	11.1
Ability quarter 3					
Percent entering college	37.7	51.6	49.1	38.7	48.3
Number entering college	(195)	(47)	(24)	(34)	(43)
Percentage distribution of college entrants by destinations:					
university (public)	16.4	6.4	29.2	17.6	25.6
public college	46.6	66.0	25.0	38.2	11.6
private college	10.2	2.1	25.0	8.8	9.3
teachers college	3.1			11.7	2.3
extension center	4.6	2.1		8.8	32.6
out-of-state	19.0	23.4	20.8	14.7	18.6

		Milwaukee	
Multiple	*Madison*	*City*	*Suburbs*
16.0	23.8	13.7	7.1
(8)	(5)	(17)	(2)
12.5	40.0	58.8	50.0
12.5	20.0	11.8	
	20.0	17.7*	
12.5			
37.5			
25.0	20.0	11.8	50.0
26.2	47.1	29.9	29.7
(17)	(16)	(55)	(11)
17.6	62.5	50.9	54.6
17.6	12.5	5.5	27.3
5.9		19.9*	
35.4			
23.5	25.0	23.6	18.2
38.2	53.5	54.5	35.9
(26)	(23)	(116)	(12)
15.4	69.5	48.2	58.4
19.2	8.7	2.6	25.0
7.7	8.7	29.2*	8.3
34.6			
23.0	13.1	19.8	8.3

TABLE 32 (continued)

	Within-community college-accessibility type				
		Four-year college only		*Teachers college (county)*	*Extension Center (state)*
	None	*Public*	*Private*		
Ability quarter 4					
Percent entering college	60.4	73.3	65.5	61.8	63.6
Number entering college	(306)	(53)	(32)	(45)	(52)
Percentage distribution of college entrants by destinations:					
university (public)	30.6	5.7	40.5	35.5	36.6
public college	38.2	66.0	6.3	22.2	3.8
private college	8.8	1.9	24.9	13.3	11.5
teachers college	0.3			4.4	
extension center	1.6		6.3	4.4	25.0
out-of-state	20.3	26.4	21.8	20.0	23.1

* Includes students at the one private university in Wisconsin; percentages attending that university by ability quarters are 11.8, 12.7, 21.5, and 28.5 respectively.

† Includes students at the one private university in Wisconsin; percentage attending that university is 8.5.

The role of the public four-year state colleges, as complements to the University of Wisconsin system and in part as substitutes for it, shows up clearly in these tables. For males, two facts stand out: the public colleges took in a large fraction of all freshmen from noncollege towns and of the less able individuals from many other towns as well, but few youths from state college towns attended other kinds of institutions. Indeed, regardless of their ability, when boys from such communities went to any institution other than a Wisconsin state college, they enrolled in other states; few, even of the most able, entered the University of Wisconsin. The numbers of low-ability girls from these communities who went to college were few, but within the two upper quarters on ability their patterns are very like those for the men from the state college (now state university) towns. Overall, for both sexes the University of Wisconsin at Madison and the public four-year colleges were the most attractive for youth from the institutions' home communi-

		Milwaukee	
Multiple	*Madison*	*City*	*Suburbs*
71.1	74.5	78.9	65.0
(59)	(38)	(200)	(23)
22.0†	84.2	48.0	56.5
5.1	2.6	1.0	4.3
17.0		31.5*	13.0
22.0			
25.4	13.2	19.5	26.1

ties, and there was relatively little interchange between them, regardless of their attraction of enrollments from other areas.

The diversified private college options available to residents of Milwaukee, together with the presence there of a branch of the university, amply account for the distributions by type in college destinations for that city. At the other extreme, teachers colleges enroll virtually no one from outside the immediate vicinity, and (as has been remarked) these local students are mainly girls of modest ability.

The Extension Centers are of particular interest in several respects. They enrolled a fifth to a third of the boys attending college from communities where they are located (whether other colleges also were present or not). There is no systematic shift in this pattern by ability, once the initial effect of ability on rates of college attendance has been taken into account. Girls make less use of these schools overall; in fact, the most noteworthy charac-

TABLE 33 ***Distributions of type of college attended by female 1957 Wisconsin high school graduates by within-community college-accessibility type and ability quarters***

	Within-community college-accessibility type				
		Four-year college only		Teachers college	Extension Center
	None	Public	Private	(county)	(state)
Ability quarter 1					
Percent entering college	8.8	9.2	7.8	14.3	4.7
Number entering college	(54)	(7)	(5)	(14)	(3)
Percentage distribution of college entrants by destinations:					
university (public)	3.7		20.0		
public college	48.1	71.3	20.0	21.4	66.6
private college	3.7			7.1	
teachers college	25.9	14.3		71.3	
extension center			20.0		
out-of-state	18.5	14.3	40.0		33.3
Ability quarter 2					
Percent entering college	14.8	25.4	23.7	24.7	17.7
Number entering college	(82)	(17)	(13)	(21)	(14)
Percentage distribution of college entrants by destinations:					
university (public)	9.8		53.9	14.3	14.2
public college	45.2	58.8	15.3	47.6	28.4
private college	7.3		7.7	4.7	7.2
teachers college	18.3		23.1	14.3	7.2
extension center	3.6				21.5
out-of-state	15.9	41.2		19.0	21.5
Ability quarter 3					
Percent entering college	26.6	36.2	26.9	24.7	26.1
Number entering college	(141)	(25)	(16)	(23)	(17)
Percentage distribution of college entrants by destinations:					
university (public)	10.4		18.8	17.3	23.6
public college	43.2	88.0	31.2	34.8	23.6
private college	9.6	4.0	31.2	8.7	17.3
teachers college	14.7			17.3	5.9
extension center			6.3		
out-of-state	22.0	8.0	12.4	21.8	29.4

		Milwaukee	
Multiple	*Madison*	*City*	*Suburbs*
12.0	11.4	12.0	3.1
(10)	(4)	(15)	(1)
	75.0	39.9	
10.0	25.0	20.0	
10.0		13.3*	†
40.0		6.6	
20.0			
20.0		20.0	100.0
17.3	38.5	18.9	24.4
(18)	(10)	(45)	(10)
5.5	50.0	57.8	60.0
27.8		2.2	
5.5	20.0	24.4*	30.0†
22.2			
16.7			
22.2	30.0	15.5	10.0
30.2	45.2	33.2	31.7
(31)	(19)	(85)	(13)
22.5	52.6	44.7	53.9
19.3	10.5	4.7	30.8
6.4	21.0	35.3*	7.7†
3.2			
22.5			
25.8	15.8	15.4	7.7

TABLE 33 (continued)

	Within-community college-accessibility type				
		Four-year college only			
	None	Public	Private	Teachers college (county)	Extension Center (state)
Ability quarter 4					
Percent entering college	42.4	49.4	45.8	37.5	47.8
Number entering college	(199)	(40)	(27)	(30)	(32)
Percentage distribution of college entrants by destinations:					
university (public)	28.6	7.5	33.3	29.9	15.6
public college	35.2	65.0	11.1	29.9	34.4
private college	6.0	2.5	11.1	16.6	18.7
teachers college	4.0			6.6	
extension center	0.5		7.4		12.5
out-of-state	25.6	25.0	37.0	16.6	18.7

* Includes students at the one private university in Wisconsin; percentages attending that university by ability quarters are 0.0, 20.0, 0.0, and 11.1.

† Includes students at the one private university in Wisconsin; percentages attending that university by ability quarters are 0.0, 11.1, 18.8, and 21.8.

teristic of the distributions of destinations by type of college among youth residing in places with an Extension Center only is their diversity; the patterns are very like those for noncollege communities except for the substitution (mainly among boys) of attendance at the local Extension Centers for attendance at the public four-year state colleges.

Tables 34 and 35 present type-of-college destination patterns for categories based on paternal education. Setting aside the erratic results for offspring of men who had some but not four years of college, the patterns can be allowed to speak for themselves.

5. POST-SECONDARY OPTIONS AND THE STUDENT MIX

While the main thrust of this project is toward identification of effects (if any) of geographic proximity of a college upon rates and patterns of college attendance, two related topics demand some attention before we complete our analysis of the data for Wisconsin. We need to find out how many individuals make use of the institutions of vocational, technical, and adult education; most of these have been regarded as noncollegiate, though today this placement

		Milwaukee	
Multiple	*Madison*	*City*	*Suburbs*
52.5	64.3	53.2	55.1
(59)	(35)	(124)	(27)
28.8	79.9	40.3	55.5
15.2	2.8	3.2	3.7
10.0	2.8	37.9*	29.6†
6.8			
13.6			3.7
25.4	14.3	18.5	7.4

may be changing. We need also to compare the characteristics of students in these sorts of schools and in various main types of colleges.

The Importance of Postsecondary Vocational Schools

The main characteristics of the system of higher education in Wisconsin and its development over the past decade were set forth in the opening part of this chapter. However, longitudinal data on enrollments in vocational and technical schools and in adult education centers are lacking. Seldom, indeed, have those schools been given any careful scrutiny as destinations for recent high school graduates. These are important postsecondary schools, nevertheless, and fortunately the data for Wisconsin give us some indication of their attractiveness to the 1957 high school graduates. When those young people were interviewed in 1964, 12 percent of the males reported that they had attended vocational or community institutions and 16 percent of the females had done so. Such schools accounted for two-fifths of the girls who had any kind of postsecondary schooling, but for less than one-fourth of the boys

(Text continued on p. 142)

TABLE 34 Distributions of type of college attended by male 1957 Wisconsin high school graduates by within-community college-accessibility type and father's education

	Within-community college-accessibility type				
		Four-year college only		*Teachers college*	*Extension Center*
	None	*Public*	*Private*	*(county)*	*(state)*
FED: elementary					
Percent entering college	22.1	28.3	31.1	20.3	31.4
Number entering college	(256)	(36)	(20)	(33)	(32)
Percentage distribution of college entrants by destinations:					
university (public)	19.9	5.6	35.0	12.1	34.4
public college	51.5	80.4	10.0	33.4	9.4
private college	5.9	2.8	35.0	3.0	18.7
teachers college	3.5			21.2	
extension center	4.3		5.0	6.0	31.2
out-of-state	14.8	11.2	15.0	24.2	6.2
FED: high school 1–3					
Percent entering college	26.7	37.5	25.0	28.6	39.4
Number entering college	(85)	(27)	(8)	(18)	(25)
Percentage distribution of college entrants by destinations:					
university (public)	14.1		12.5	16.7	20.0
public college	55.1	70.2	37.5	27.7	20.0
private college	7.1		25.0	22.2	10.0
teachers college	4.7			16.7	
extension center	3.5				24.0
out-of-state	15.3	29.6	25.0	16.7	26.0
FED: high school 4					
Percentage entering college	43.3	47.1	49.0	50.0	44.7
Number entering college	(227)	(46)	(24)	(36)	(40)
Percentage distribution of college entrants by destinations:					
university (public)	26.4	6.5	20.8	16.7	20.0
public college	43.6	74.0	25.0	41.6	12.5
private college	7.1		16.7	13.8	12.5
teachers college	1.8			2.8	2.5
extension center	1.3		16.7	11.1	35.0
out-of-state	19.8	19.5	20.8	13.8	17.5

		Milwaukee	
Multiple	*Madison*	*City*	*Suburbs*
31.2	30.8	31.2	18.8
(33)	(12)	(77)	(6)
18.2	75.0	49.4	33.3
18.2	12.5	6.5	50.0†
18.2		36.4*	
36.4			
9.1	12.5	7.8	16.6
41.9	38.9	43.4	37.0
(18)	(11)	(50)	(10)
22.2	57.4	60.0	50.0
16.7		2.0	30.0
11.1		26.0*	†
5.6			
22.2			
22.2	42.6	12.0	20.0
49.4	61.0	56.9	39.5
(37)	(25)	(139)	(16)
24.3	92.0	51.8	81.3
5.4	4.0	2.1	6.2
8.1		28.0*	6.2†
29.7			
32.4	4.0	17.9	6.2

TABLE 34
(continued)

	Within-community college-accessibility type				
		Four-year college only		*Teachers college*	*Extension Center*
	None	*Public*	*Private*	*(county)*	*(state)*
FED: college 1–3					
Percentage entering college	65.5	61.0	78.6	55.6	37.5
Number entering college	(53)	(25)	(8)	(9)	(6)
Percentage distribution of college entrants by destinations:					
university (public)	18.9	4.0	62.5	44.4	33.3
public college	32.1	72.0	12.5	33.3	16.6
private college	18.9		25.0	11.1	
teachers college	1.9				
extension center		4.0			16.6
out-of-state	28.3	20.0		11.1	33.3
FED: college 4+					
Percentage entering college	65.7	71.4	81.5	68.0	71.4
Number entering college	(89)	(14)	(18)	(26)	(31)
Percentage distribution of college entrants by destinations:					
university (public)	26.9	7.1	22.2	7.6	32.2
public college	25.8	50.0	16.6	42.2	6.5
private college	16.9	7.1	22.2	3.8	19.4
teachers college	3.4			23.1	
extension center	1.1			11.5	25.7
out-of-state	25.8	35.7	38.8	11.5	16.1

* Includes students at the one private university in Wisconsin; percentages attending that university by father's education are 31.2, 24.0, 23.7, 14.7, and 19.3.

† Includes students at the one private university in Wisconsin; percentages attending that university by father's education are 0.0, 0.0, 6.2, 0.0, and 0.0.

		Milwaukee	
Multiple	*Madison*	*City*	*Suburbs*
60.0	42.9	60.7	37.5
(8)	(6)	(34)	(3)
25.0	66.7	50.0	100.0
	16.6	2.9	
25.0		23.5*	†
37.5			
12.5	16.6	23.5	
50.0	86.5	80.4	77.8
(9)	(32)	(88)	(13)
	65.6	37.4	30.7
11.1	6.2		
	9.4	26.1	23.1†
11.1			
77.7	18.7	36.3	46.2

TABLE 35 ***Distributions of type of college attended by female 1957 Wisconsin high school graduates by within-community college-accessibility type and father's education***

	Within-community college-accessibility type				
		Four-year college only		*Teachers college (county)*	*Extension Center (state)*
	None	*Public*	*Private*		
FED: elementary					
Percent entering college	15.8	19.0	13.6	13.7	15.1
Number entering college	(189)	(23)	(13)	(24)	(13)
Percentage distribution of college entrants by destinations:					
university (public)	10.6	4.3	23.1	8.3	15.4
public college	41.7	82.6	7.7	29.2	38.5
private college	8.5	4.3	15.4		15.4
teachers college	20.1	4.3	23.1	50.0	
extension center	0.5				15.4
out-of-state	18.6	4.3	30.8	12.5	15.4
FED: high school 1–3					
Percent entering college	17.2	30.9	25.0	27.0	17.2
Number entering college	(57)	(17)	(9)	(17)	(10)
Percentage distribution of college entrants by destinations:					
university (public)	19.3		44.4	11.8	20.0
public college	42.1	82.5	22.2	58.8	20.0
private college	3.5		11.1		20.0
teachers college	10.5			5.9	10.0
extension center	3.5		11.1		
out-of-state	21.0	17.5	11.1	23.5	30.0
FED: high school 4					
Percent entering college	30.4	32.5	29.3	30.1	30.8
Number entering college	(139)	(25)	(20)	(25)	(28)
Percentage distribution of college entrants by destinations:					
university (public)	17.2		25.0	28.0	21.4
public college	45.2	72.0	40.0	24.0	28.5
private college	4.5		20.0	28.0	17.7
teachers college	7.9			16.0	3.6
extension center			5.0		14.3
out-of-state	25.2	28.0	10.0	4.0	14.3

		Milwaukee	
Multiple	*Madison*	*City*	*Suburbs*
17.0	19.1	16.0	13.3
(25)	(9)	(49)	(6)
8.0	77.7	38.8	50.0
24.0		6.1	16.6
8.0	11.1	38.8*	16.6†
8.0			
24.0			
28.0	11.1	16.3	16.6
28.9	16.0	20.6	20.6
(23)	(4)	(37)	(7)
8.7	25.0	51.1	57.2
17.4		5.4	28.6
8.7	50.0	35.1	14.3†
21.8			
21.8			
21.8	25.0	8.1	
31.7	39.5	33.5	37.5
(39)	(15)	(84)	(15)
30.7	66.6	48.8	52.3
10.3	13.3	3.6	7.6
10.3	20.0	35.7	20.0
12.8			
12.8			
23.0		11.9	20.0

TABLE 35
(continued)

	Within-community college-accessibility type				
		Four-year college only		*Teachers college (county)*	*Extension Center (state)*
	None	*Public*	*Private*		
FED: college 1–3					
Percent entering college	39.8	50.0	33.3	52.9	45.5
Number entering college	(36)	(8)	(3)	(9)	(5)
Percentage distribution of college entrants by destinations:					
university (public)	38.8	25.0	33.3	11.1	20.0
public college	44.5	37.5		33.3	20.0
private college	2.8		33.3	11.1	20.0
teachers college	5.6			11.1	
extension center					20.0
out-of-state	8.3	37.5	33.3	33.3	20.0
FED: college 4+					
Percent entering college	58.7	64.0	61.5	63.6	60.0
Number entering college	(53)	(16)	(16)	(13)	(9)
Percentage distribution of college entrants by destinations:					
university (public)	24.5		43.7	30.8	
public college	18.9	56.3		30.8	22.2
private college	17.0	6.2	6.2	15.4	22.2
teachers college	1.9				
extension center			12.5		
out-of-state	37.8	37.5	37.5	23.1	55.5

* Includes students at the one private university in Wisconsin; percentages attending that university by father's education are 26.6, 16.2, 17.3, 24.8, and 17.0.

† Includes students at the one private university in Wisconsin; percentages attending that university by father's education are 0.0, 0.0, 20.0, 0.0, and 6.3.

‡ Includes students at the one private university in Wisconsin; percentage attending that university is 13.1.

		Milwaukee	
Multiple	*Madison*	*City*	*Suburbs*
55.0	69.2	51.6	50.0
(11)	(8)	(33)	(6)
36.4	75.0	60.6	20.0
45.5	12.5	3.0	
9.1		24.2	60.0
9.1	12.5	12.1	20.0
67.6	88.9	60.2	84.2
(23)	(32)	(65)	(16)
21.7	68.6	32.3	75.0
8.7	3.1	3.1	
17.4‡	3.1	33.9*	18.7†
4.4			
17.4			
30.4	25.0	30.8	6.2

who took some kind of training after high school. How these proportions compare with entrants to collegiate institutions can be discerned readily from the last row of Table 36.

Whereas there are marked relationships between college attendance rates and parental status or youth's ability, there is only a loose relationship between these attributes and enrollment in vocational courses of one kind or another at the subcollegiate level. A few moderate relationships merit attention. In particular, among lower-ability youth (especially among girls) there is a definite and positive association with SES. In the top quarter of ability, however, this relationship is reversed.

Place of residence and the equipment of colleges to be found there had little discernible relationship with the proportion of high school graduates who went to these "practical" schools (Table 37).

TABLE 36 ***Percentage distributions of postsecondary school destinations by ability/SES categories; Wisconsin, 1957***

	Males				*Females*			
	No post-secondary school training	*Non-collegiate*	*College*	*Total*	*No post-secondary school training*	*Non-collegiate*	*College*	*Total*
Ability 1								
SES 1	80	12	8	100	82	12	6	100
2	73	14	13	100	78	14	8	100
3	56	16	28	100	54	21	25	100
Ability 2								
SES 1	68	15	17	100	76	15	9	100
2	59	14	27	100	65	17	18	100
3	39	14	47	100	47	20	33	100
Ability 3								
SES 1	59	17	24	100	71	14	15	100
2	46	14	40	100	60	18	22	100
3	27	10	63	100	36	11	53	100
Ability 4								
SES 1	38	12	50	100	56	17	27	100
2	30	10	60	100	45	18	37	100
3	18	3	79	100	26	10	64	100
All categories	49	12	39	100	62	16	22	100

TABLE 37 ***Proportions of high school graduates attending postsecondary vocational and community schools by ability/SES category; selected home-community types, Wisconsin 1957***

	College-access types			
	None	*State college*	*Extension Centers*	*Milwaukee*
		Males		
Ability 1				
SES 1	10	9	11	30
2	14	14	10	22
3	19	19	13	16
Ability 2				
SES 1	11	9	10	32
2	14	8	6	21
3	13	6	8	18
Ability 3				
SES 1	16	10	26	13
2	16	9	10	23
3	11	11	13	7
Ability 4				
SES 1	12	20	13	15
2	12	6	7	9
3	4	6	2	3
		Females		
Ability 1				
SES 1	12	13	17	12
2	18	11	12	15
3	21	25	29	22
Ability 2				
SES 1	17	3	13	15
2	17	19	14	17
3	21	14	26	19
Ability 3				
SES 1	16	11	6	11
2	20	8	8	16
3	14	22	18	9
Ability 4				
SES 1	16	20	9	9
2	18	24	13	14
3	14	9	14	7

There is a striking exception: the less able half of boys were much more likely to take postsecondary vocational training if they lived in Milwaukee rather than elsewhere.

School Types and Student Mix

Turning the data around, we may answer for this sample a question that is of central interest for understanding how these various institutions differ from each other. Whom do they serve and what are the clusterings of students and peer-group experiences among youth who enter these schools? The data are organized from this perspective in Tables 38 and 39.

A decade ago, at least, the University of Wisconsin drew half or more of its freshmen from the upper quarter of the ability distribution; only a fifth came from below the median in ability. The distribution of entrants' ability for the private colleges was virtually the same as for the university. The state colleges, by contrast, were relatively open, which partially accounts for their rapid expansion in recent years and their strong pull among youth residing in the regions they serve. Over a third of the entrants to these state colleges were below the median in ability and only a third came from the top quarter. We have remarked several times that the Extension Centers are branches of the university more than they are "free access" junior colleges. Their intermediate position for ability of entrants between the university and the state colleges bears out that contention. The basically negative selection of girls into the county teachers colleges is unmistakable; while by now this observation should not cause surprise, it raises some embarrassing questions about what may have been happening—or perhaps not happening—in rural elementary and even secondary schools. (The main differences in selectivity indexes between males and females in Table 38 are due to inclusion of the teachers colleges in the analysis for girls.)

The ability distribution for boys in vocational schools (column (2) of Table 39) looks very like that for girls in teachers colleges (Table 38); the bias is against the most able, yet a sixth are from the top quarter in ability. Among girls, the representation in vocational school matches the ability distribution for the total population. For both sexes these schools clearly occupy a middle ground between the college-bound and those who had no formal postsecondary training in schools.

The distributions of enrollees by thirds in the ranking on parental SES are quite similar to those by ability, with which of course they are positively correlated.

TABLE 38 ***Percentage distributions of ability by type of institution, Wisconsin freshmen, Fall 1957***

	Males			
	Public university	*State college*	*Private college or university*	*Extension Center*
Total in sample	619	540	249	97
Percentage by ability quarter				
1 Low	4	14	6	11
2	16	23	16	14
3	26	30	31	38
4 High	54	33	47	37
	100	100	100	100
*Selectivity ratios**				
Ability quarter				
1 Low	0.5	1.8	0.8	1.4
2	0.8	1.2	0.8	0.7
3	0.9	1.0	1.1	1.3
4 High	1.2	0.8	1.1	0.8

	Females				
	Public university	*State college*	*Private college or university*	*Extension Center*	*Teachers college*
Total in sample	352	362	259	35	102
Percentage by ability quarter					
1 Low	5	11	5	8	28
2	17	19	15	26	26
3	28	32	33	23	27
4 High	50	38	47	43	19
	100	100	100	100	100
*Selectivity ratios**					
Ability quarter					
1 Low	0.5	1.1	0.5	0.8	2.8
2	0.9	1.0	0.8	1.4	1.4
3	1.0	1.1	1.1	0.8	0.9
4 High	1.2	0.9	1.1	1.0	0.5

* Notice that here as elsewhere "quarters" on ability refer to all high school graduates. However, the ratios to expectancy are computed using the frequencies for all those attending college; this raises ratios for low-ability and reduces those for the high-ability students compared to the ratios that would be obtained if youth not attending college had been included in the totals.

TABLE 39 ***Ability and SES distributions among youth with postsecondary school experience***

	No postsecondary training	*Postsecondary vocational courses*	*Collegiate institutions*
Number of males	2407	596	1893
Number of females	3004	775	1048
Ability quarters		*Males*	
1 Low	37	28	9
2	27	28	19
3	22	28	28
4 High	13	16	44
	99	100	100
		Females	
1 Low	32	24	10
2	28	28	18
3	24	25	28
4 High	16	23	44
	100	100	100
SES categories		*Males*	
1 Low	42	36	16
2	37	39	32
3 High	21	25	52
	100	100	100
		Females	
1 Low	43	32	15
2	37	38	26
3 High	20	30	59
	100	100	100

6. SOME CONCLUSIONS FROM THE WISCONSIN DATA

Wisconsin has long been one of the leading states in the proportion of youth who complete secondary school. In 1963 it tied Minnesota for first place with a ratio of secondary graduates to 18-year-olds of 0.87, compared to the national average of 0.71. It was just average, however, in the ratio of college freshmen to 18-year-olds and thus below average in the proportion of high school graduates who went directly to degree-credit collegiate institutions (either two-year or four-year) in both 1963 and 1968. But it is not at all clear how we should compare these rates of college going across states with different systems of educational provision for the postsecondary years. For even today, and even more in 1957, Wisconsin has no system of *collegiate* free access colleges as respects selection for ability. Moreover, the four-year state colleges came closer to being open door for ability than did the two-year Extension Centers of the university, as is probably still the case. On the other hand, Wisconsin possesses a considerable array of community institutions of vocational, technical, and adult education offering a wide gamut of programs; and most of these courses do not carry academic degree credit. There is no unambiguous way to take such data into account in comparisons with other states, or with the performance in California in particular. So we are constrained in our interpretations of the Wisconsin data by the structure of postsecondary schools and colleges that the state possessed a dozen years ago.

Several broad findings do emerge clearly, along with a multitude of questions.

1 No matter what else is considered, the ability of high school graduates and the status of their parents have strong effects upon the likelihood that they will go on to collegiate institutions. The inclusion of a set of variables for the college-access profile of the high school community had no effect on the regression coefficients for ability or status. These relationships sometimes differed for the two sexes, however. Other things being equal, generally college attendance rates for boys exceeded those for girls. In addition, the gradients of attendance rates with ability were definitely steeper for boys than for girls. They were only slightly steeper in raw percentages over the quarters of SES; moreover, this sex difference in gradient with SES disappeared with transformation of the percentages into logit form. When the background variable was father's schooling rather than the composite SES index, it became apparent that for girls it was of special importance to have a father with college experience. On the whole these patterns are quite unrelated to location, being repeated usually for each college-access classification.

2 It is clear that information concerning college-accessibility profiles has little overall explanatory power. Even giving the dummy set for college accessibility full play, without introducing other variables in a regression on college attendance, we got very little predictive effect. These results recurred within subpopulations classified by ability and by father's schooling. However, interpretation of results from regressions using a dichotomous dependent variable is ambiguous. In order to check on these results we manipulated the data another way. The data were classified into cells showing percentage rates of college going in each ability-SES-access category. For this analysis, access was taken as each of the profiles for within-community college-access type. The negative findings of the earlier cruder regressions were confirmed: access proved to be quite insignificant. This outcome outlines unambiguously the confounding effects from other characteristics of the community upon rates of college attendance. Study of these data surely must shake any faith in the likely impact of college accessibility as such upon rates of college going. The increase in rates of entry to college among residents of noncollege compared with other communities over the years after 1957 further supports our skeptical and negative finding.

3 Some types of college accessibility may make a difference for some categories of ability or social status even when overall main effects are negligible. In simple cross-tabulations by ability quarters and from regressions run within each ability quarter we reached the following tentative conclusions:

- Among youth in the lowest quarter of ability, college-access type had little or no effect upon attendance rates, except for girls going to teachers colleges. Those schools were definitely negatively selective for ability and they were located in communities such that the total effect was to dampen observed rates of college attendance of the most able youth. In other words, these were not education-prone communities, and the encouragement that teachers colleges gave to *low-ability* girls seems to have been substantial, though probably of questionable social benefit.
- Living in Madison, home of the state university and seat of the state government, seems to encourage university attendance, especially among both boys and girls in the middle- and middle-low–ability range but with relatively good socioeconomic status. The apparently strong effects of residence in Madison otherwise reflect the composition of that city's population.
- The four-year state colleges and universities (next to Madison) seemed to have the broadest impact on college attendance, judging from simple cross-tabulations against ability. For boys in all but the lowest quarter of ability, this generally was still the case after controlling for parental status (despite some variation by SES within categories of ability). For

girls, however, introduction of the index of parental status wipes out any effect of residence in a state college community, regardless of the youth's level of ability.

- Residence near Extension Centers seems clearly to have had a net positive effect on college going among boys in the lowest status categories generally, and especially among the more able boys from the middle-status homes.
- Overall, it is the young men in the middle half of the ability range and the young women in the top quarter for ability who appear to have been the most responsive—when there was a response—to the presence of a college in the community (teachers colleges excepted).
- Relationships between responsiveness (or its absence) in attendance at college and paternal schooling suggest that going to college is primarily an investment decision among males, but more nearly a consumption decision, at the margins at least, among girls.

4 The most important effects attributable to college-access profiles lie not in rates of overall college going, but in where youth go to school and the sorts of schools they choose to enter. Teachers colleges aside, in Wisconsin this has meant primarily that young people residing in state college communities attend those institutions when they do not go out of the state. Young people living in Madison go to the university unless they fail to qualify, in which case they are more likely to leave the state to attend private or open public institutions elsewhere. Youth from communities with Extension Centers are scattered widely in their college destinations, but students at those centers tend to come from nearby. Attending these centers seems to bring an important saving in costs for the first one or two years of college. But broadly, location has little effect on whether youth will leave the state to attend a college. The substitution effects of the presence of a college in the immediate vicinity were far greater throughout than the overall net effects on attendance rates. If this is true also where the junior college plays an important part in the collegiate system, it may be a matter of very great importance, with repercussions that would not occur in the Wisconsin setting.

5. High School to College: A Cross-State Comparison

The SCOPE survey sampled 1966 high school seniors in four states: California, Illinois, Massachusetts, and North Carolina. These four states are dissimilar, and the history and present structure of their systems of higher education are quite unlike in several respects. Before trying to generalize our very mixed batches of evidence, we have tc scrutinize the structure of the SCOPE samples and give readers some information about the contextual variety among the four systems.

The first part of this chapter compares certain basic elements of these four collegiate systems and also contrasts them with Wisconsin. Then (in Section 2) we portray the college-accessibility profiles of each state in their spatial features and comment briefly on each of the samples, presenting for three states a preliminary comparison of rates of college going by ability and by paternal schooling. Particular attention is paid to contrasts between residents of noncollege and of two-year college communities. For Illinois (Section 3) and North Carolina (Section 4) that analysis is pursued in greater detail. We then return to an interstate comparison of three of the SCOPE states, and, with data from Medsker and Trent, use the three-way matrices of ability, family status, and college-access profiles to assess factors in college attendance rates. Finally, patterns of college destinations are compared across states.

1. SYSTEMS OF HIGHER EDUCATION: INTERSTATE COMPARISONS

Neither intellectuals generally nor academicians in particular are free from the influence of fashion in their work. Both groups also share with other spokesmen a tendency to suppose that what one state deems to be a successful program could and should be transplanted to others. Even when the transfer could be successful, anyone concerned with improvement of higher education (in this instance) must regret the casual neglect of an opportunity to innovate. As has been observed often, the temptation to take this paternalistic viewpoint is especially strong when the proposal entails public intervention and responsibility along with a large degree of centralized planning. In fact, if we are thinking of what warrantably can be called higher education, any strong admixture of centralized planning is mainly an anomaly. Today we hear few proposals to imitate the Massachusetts system of higher education, although in an earlier era that was done with the midwestern University of Chicago. In more recent years it is the California system that has been lauded around the world as the twentieth-century model. Except when used to defend entrenched interests against any change, questions as to what may be the basic common and divergent circumstances affecting the vitality of a present, new, or transformed system of higher education receive short shrift. Obviously, to treat such questions adequately would require much more scrupulous attention to details than there is space for in this condensed bit of educational history.

Past and Present, Public and Private

Among the four SCOPE states, as of 1963, the ratios of new entrants in degree-credit courses to 18-year-olds ranged from 0.62 for California down to 0.22 for North Carolina. For all 50 states the median was 0.35 (which is quite near the rate for Wisconsin), while the minimum was somewhat lower than the rate for North Carolina. Expressed as proportions of high school graduates, the rates would be generally higher; among the states with which we are concerned, the effect of shifting the denominator for rates in this way would be greatest for North Carolina, and for 1968 (Table 40). But any interpretation of the contrasts among these aggregative rates of entry to college is confounded by the varying mixture of two-year and four-year colleges—to measure the effects of which is one of our main tasks. The next two rows divide the 1968 rates between free-access schools and others. Free-access schools are defined as having annual tuition and fees (for 1968) not over $400, admitting at least a third of their entrants from below the median of all secondary school graduates, and having no special emphasis (as on one sex or a religious denomination). In California a clear majority of college freshmen (three-fifths of the high school graduates) entered free-access colleges; since total entrants were three-fourths of secondary graduates, only 15 percent entered some other kind of college. In Massachusetts, by contrast, only 11 percent of secondary graduates entered free-access colleges, while over half entered colleges that were more selective either for financial capability or for academic ability. This selectivity for ability also appears in the data for Wisconsin. North Carolina has more nearly the emphasis of Massachusetts on private schools and on ability—more nearly like Wisconsin—but against a very different historical background. Illinois is intermediate between California and Massachusetts in the structure and composition of its system, though these three states were all in the upper quarter for rates of entry to college in 1963 and in the upper fifth in 1968 (see lines 6–8). Among these three states, overall rates of entry in California were only about a tenth greater and that came about mainly by taking in more lower-ability youth.

A glimpse of long-term developments can be obtained by comparing the ratios of college students to population in 1890 and 1958, together with shifts in ranking over the seven decades. The top-ranking states in 1890 were mainly in New England and in the Far West (where California fell behind Oregon and Nevada despite its rank of twelfth). By the time the era of mass higher education opened after World War II, California had caught up with its immediate neighbors, and the Mountain and Southwestern states had reached parity with most of the nation west of the Mississippi River. Meanwhile, New England declined markedly in relative position, as did much of the Southeast. Ranking the states in order of net favorable change in rank, California comes out eighteenth, Wisconsin and Illinois shifted downward a little (twenty-sixth and twenty-seventh places in shift), while Massachusetts and North Carolina underwent more decided downward relative shifts. Still, for ratio of students to population Massachusetts remained in the upper third among states in 1958 and has been picking up again recently. Perhaps the main lesson to derive from this historical review is a sense of the broad forces operating over whole regions of the country, and not only with respect to higher education. The educational scenario has changed along with the massive but nonrandom shifts in population and the changes in economic activity, which have brought new levels and geographic patterns in the public and private provisions for higher learning and in college-going behavior.

Patterns in the choice to attend public or private colleges within the state or to attend (mainly at private colleges) in other states repeat, less dramatically, the counterpoint between free-access and

TABLE 40 ***Interstate comparisons of college attendance rates over time; attendance at and migrations to public and private institutions***

	California	Illinois	Massachusetts
Ratio of college freshmen 1 *to all 18-year-olds, 1963*[a]	0.63	0.47	0.43
Ratio of college freshmen to all high school graduates[a]			
2 *1963: total*	0.80	0.63	0.56
3 *1968: total*	0.75	0.68	0.66
4 *To free-access institutions*	0.60	0.33	0.11
5 *To other institutions*	0.15	0.35	0.55
Ranks among states in:			
Ratio of college freshmen to 6 *18-year-olds, 1963*	1	3½	12½
Ratio of college freshmen to high school graduates:			
7 *1963*	1	3½	12
8 *1968*	2	7	9
Ratio of college attendance to total population[b]			
9 *1890*	12	18	4
10 *1958*	6	24½	15
11 *Gain in rank*	6	(− 6½)	(−11)
12 *Rank in gain in rank*	18	27½	32½
Distribution of college-bound 1968 high school graduates by destinations[c]			
13 *To public institutions in state*	0.66	0.43	0.24
14 *To private institutions in state*	0.05	0.11	0.28
15 *Outside of state*	0.04	0.14	0.14
Interstate migrations of undergraduates			
Out-migration rates, 1963[d]			
16 *Public*	2.6	14.9	18.3
17 *Private*	23.3	30.5	23.2
In-migration rates, 1963[e]			
18 *Public*	3.2	3.3	2.5
19 *Private*	19.0	21.3	39.9
Net migration matrix, 1963[f]			
20 *Public*	39	14	3
21 *Private*	26	25	42

[a] From Willingham, 1970, Table E, pp. 202–203.

[b] From Bowman, 1962.

[c] From Willingham, Table F, pp. 203–204.

North Carolina	Wisconsin	Maximum	Median	Minimum
0.22	0.36	0.63	0.35	0.19
0.36	0.41	0.80	0.48	0.31
0.41	0.48	0.97	0.56	0.34
0.14	0.16			
0.27	0.32			
45½	24			
44	41			
45	36			
32	20			
43	26			
(−11)	(− 6)			
32½	26			
0.25	0.38	0.88	0.38	0.15
0.12	0.05	0.28	0.07	0.00
0.04	0.05	0.30	0.08	0.03
7.0	5.2	47.7		2.6
17.4	36.8	100.0		14.5
15.1	12.4	41.5		0.9
37.9	38.2	86.4		0.0
31	28	47		0
43	28	44		0

[d] From Gossman et al., 1968, public p. 32, private p. 63.

[e] Ibid., public p. 34, private p. 65.

[f] Ibid., public p. 116, private p. 124.

other kinds of schools already discussed, and shown in rows (4) and (5). The evidence for California is particularly dramatic: out of 75 college-bound youth from each hundred secondary graduates, 66 entered a public college in the state. That proportion was exceeded only in Arizona, though Wisconsin is as low as California in proportions entering private colleges or going out of state. Massachusetts is distinctive in that more young people enter private than public colleges. (The states most resembling Massachusetts were New York and Rhode Island, with 19 and 18 percent at in-state private colleges and 18 and 14 percent going out of state.) The large proportions leaving their home state, however, were for youth from New Jersey and from Connecticut; these states are located near dense concentrations of population and associated colleges or universities. Illinois and North Carolina hold intermediate positions with respect to the public-private balance of college going, with the stronger tendency toward private colleges among the youth of North Carolina.

When we look at the migratory propensities of students (as in the last section of Table 40) more light is thrown also on the public-private balance. Most of those youth of the five states who attend a public college do so within their home state—even in Massachusetts. Whichever type of college, North Carolina youth usually attend within their state. There are four states, nevertheless, that send more than half of their public college entrants out of state, and in 37 states a fifth or more of those attending public colleges did so in another state.

In the SCOPE states there is another side to the home pattern for public college attendance: immigration of students to public colleges is low, especially in Massachusetts, California, and Illinois, despite the strong weight of the public sector in the latter two states. For the state of California this situation partly reflects distance from other major population concentrations and, in addition, is affected strongly by the prominence of junior colleges. Those colleges are local in the double sense that they may restrict attendance (but on grounds not included in Willingham's definition) and that they are comparatively invisible except to individuals who have come through the local secondary schools. These colleges tend also to be terminal rather than to serve as avenues to upper-division work in a four-year college, though there are many exceptions. North Carolina and Wisconsin are in a quite different situation, mainly because their quality institutions are so prominent within the total system of public colleges.

What we call "net migration matrix scores" are shown in the last two lines of Table 40; they are given separately for student migrations to public and to private colleges. These scores are simply the numbers of instances in which a state imports more college youth than it sends out to attend college in the given other state. The effects of population size on gross migration streams, so conspicuous in crude gravity models, are eliminated by the pairing of each state with all others to obtain the net migration scores. (The District of Columbia is included, but Alaska and Hawaii are not; hence if a state imported from all other states in greater numbers than it exported, its score would be 48, and of course the minimum possible score is zero.) For public colleges in 1963, Arizona had the highest score (47); Maine had the highest possible score for private colleges (48). California ranked seventh for public colleges, North Carolina fifteenth, Wisconsin twentieth, Illinois thirty-sixth, and Massachusetts was forty-sixth (only New York and New Jersey being lower). For private colleges the District of Columbia came first; Utah, North Carolina, and Massachusetts took second, third, and fourth places; Wisconsin ranked eighteenth, California nineteenth, and Illinois tied four other states just after California.

The Two-Year Colleges

There is no need for us to document the explosive spread of two-year colleges during recent years. In our comments on Table 40 and earlier it was emphasized that the five states differ in the extent to which they have been sponsoring an expansion in this segment of higher education. The part played by junior colleges in the system of each state is made clearer by the indicators displayed in Table 41. The first four rows of the table again highlight the contrast between California and Massachusetts and the very large role played by junior colleges in California. The first row gives the two-year enrollment as a proportion of *all* who attend within the state; the third row shows the entering two-year students as a proportion of new entrants who come from in-state high schools. In North Carolina these two percentages are about the same and in Massachusetts they are reversed (but not greatly different in size); in California and Wisconsin, by contrast, the gaps are wide. (Massachusetts also has the large cluster of in-migrant graduate students attending colleges in the Boston area.) One line that we did not pursue is to investigate the obviously large differences among states in the proportion of college starters who will obtain at least a baccalaureate degree.

TABLE 41 ***Interstate comparisons of roles of two-year and free-access institutions***

	California	*Illinois*	*Massachusetts*	*North Carolina*	*Wisconsin*
*Undergraduates enrolled in two-year colleges and on two-year branch campuses, 1968**					
Proportion of all undergraduates	61	35	18	28	18
Rank in proportions of undergraduates	1	6	25	13	27
FTE (First-time enrollments) who were in free-access institutions, 1968†					
Proportions of all FTE	80	48	17	33	34
Rank in proportions of all FTE	3	19½	42½	32	30½
Two-year public institutions according to Willingham					
Total public 1968	86	40	15	26	22
Free-access:					
Total 1968	86	39	12	25	17
New 1958–68	31	26	10	24	4
Other		1	3	1	5
Two-year institutions in 1968 according to Medsker and Tillery					
Total public (+ specialized)	86	42	14 (+1)	16 (+28)	27 (+4)
Community	86	42	14	13	15
Branches				3	12
Total private (+ specialized)	2 (+2)	14 (+2)	23 (+2)	15 (+1)	4
Distributions of junior college students by ability class; SCOPE samples (public and private)					
Ability 1 (Low quarter)	18 } 50	12 } 40	11 } 43	22 } 59	
2	32	28	32	37	
3	29	31	38	31	
4 (High quarter)	21	29	20	11	

* Medsker and Tillery, 1971, Table 2, pp. 24–25.

† Willingham, 1970; Table G, pp. 205–206.

California was not the inventor of the junior college that has become so widely disseminated there. Setting aside the earliest two-year colleges and finishing schools, Illinois pioneered the development of colleges that were "junior" in a world of senior colleges.[1] Today, however, California indisputably leads in number of schools, their age, and their size. In 1968 there were 642 public two-year colleges in the nation; 339 had been established in the previous decade and 303 were at least 10 years old. Of these 303 oldest schools, 55 (or 18 percent) were in California. The others were widely scattered: Texas had 26, New York 24, and Illinois 16. If the Wisconsin Extension Centers are counted, that state matched New York, though it is a much less populous state. During the decade of 1958–1968, California built 31 additional junior colleges, Illinois 26, North Carolina 24, and Florida 21. These figures show that the SCOPE sample was drawn disproportionately from states that had been most actively founding junior colleges; that sample includes none of the 25 states that built or added fewer than 10 junior colleges between 1958 and 1968. One of the problems inherent in these cross-state comparisons is highlighted by the figures for North Carolina. In that state most of the public junior colleges are quite new and many are specialized technical schools, while most of the older junior colleges in the state are private. In Massachusetts the private schools are even more important relatively among the two-year colleges.

The last section of Table 41 is taken from Medsker and Tillery's report. They used SCOPE data for their estimates, combining public and private junior colleges. The allocation to ability quarters refers to the graduates from high schools for all four states combined; one effect is to place a smaller proportion of California than of North Carolina youth in the lowest quarter.[2] Nonetheless, students from the lowest-ability quarter (or even all below the median) make up a larger fraction of the California junior college entrants than among entrants in Illinois or Massachusetts. The junior colleges in Illinois enroll a distinctively larger proportion of

[1] For that history, see Griffith and Blackstone (1945).

[2] This fact underlines also the importance of both cultural effects and rates of high school completion on test performance. The SCOPE research team is well aware of this, and the SCOPE survey included ninth graders as well as twelfth graders. For an initial report of their research, including comments on some of these problems, see Tillery, Donovan, and Sherman (1966).

top-quarter students, while the schools in North Carolina have a distinctively small representation of such youth. These contrasts are important—whatever our political or other preferences—as to the part that junior colleges should play in a system of higher education.

2. A PREVIEW ACROSS THE SCOPE STATES

Whether a college of any kind is close at hand, and what sorts of colleges are to be found in a community, obviously will depend upon the total pattern of higher education in a state. The data presented thus far, however, say little directly about the geography of college accessibility or about its relationship to the distribution of population over one state as compared to another. Efforts to attack these questions involve the use of certain sets of data (in our case the SCOPE sample), and the adequacy of these data cannot go unscrutinized.

College-Access Profiles and the Samples

Because junior colleges are so thickly scattered over the landscape in California, we have not included that state for cross-community analysis, though geographic distributions of the population of colleges and of the SCOPE sample of high schools in California are shown in Figures 8, 9, and 10. As respects local access to college in California, the most important questions relate to urban ecology, and the SCOPE data (supplemented by other information which would have been very expensive to collect) might have been used for an intra-urban analysis of that state; but the venture was beyond our resources. Unfortunately, the utility of analyses applying the tools of urban ecology with respect to questions about access to schools has been too little appreciated, and not only for California. One can understand why so many writers are advocating a still further expansion of junior colleges in California, especially if we scan Willingham's estimates of populations residing within commuting distance of a free-access college. Statewide, Connecticut is at the top on this index (87 percent), followed by North Carolina (68 percent), Mississippi (65 percent), Florida (64 percent), and in fifth place California (60 percent). Similar figures for sections of metropolitan areas show that California provides less adequate access to college in central cities than in fringe or suburban areas. In most other states, by contrast, it is the inner city (as in Chicago) that is more adequately served by free-access colleges—whether or not youth who could attend them do so. When Willingham's estimates of proportions of youth within commuting distance of a college are

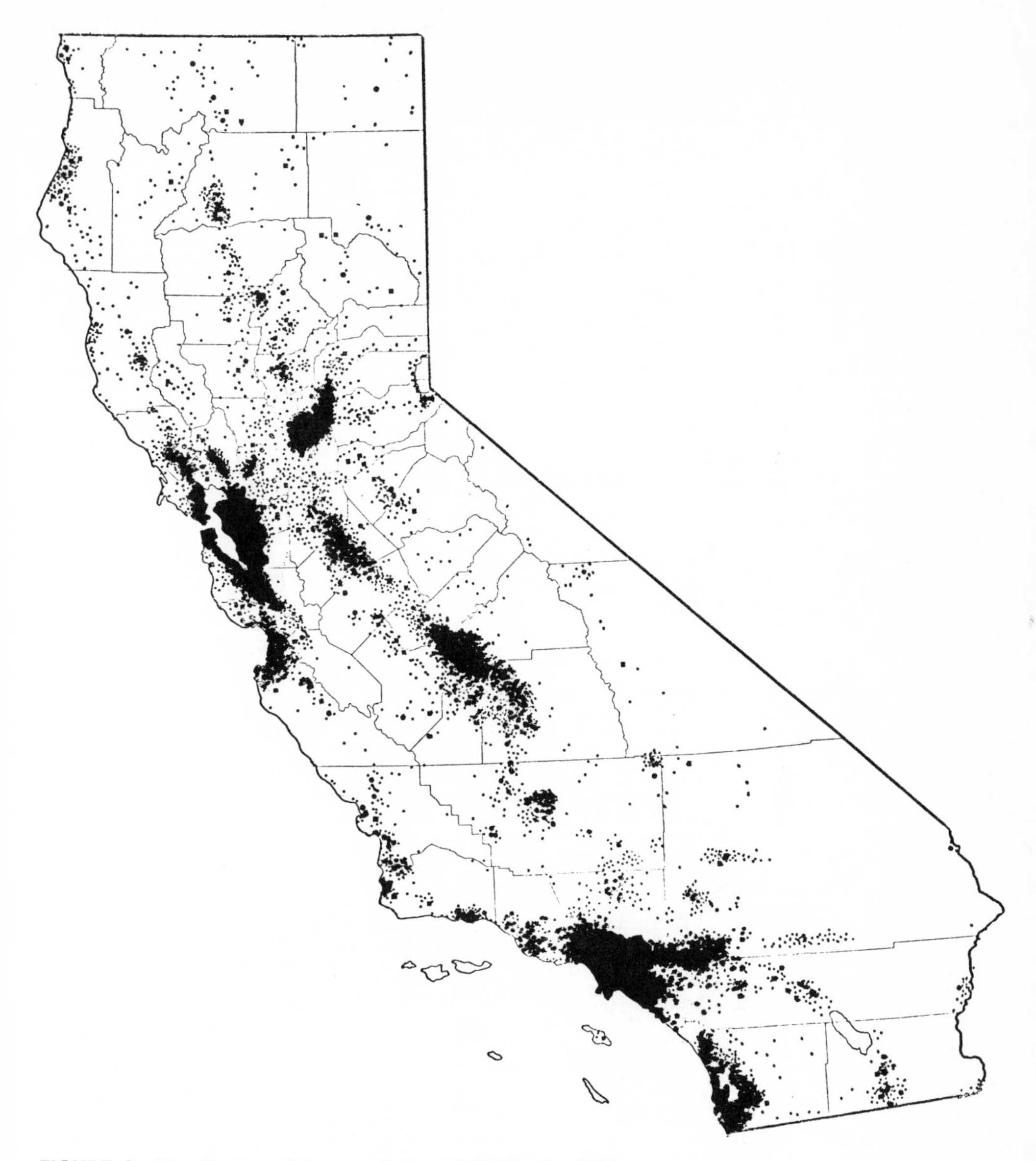

FIGURE 8 ***Distribution of the population of California, 1960***

taken into consideration, the pattern in California seems impressive less for the number of colleges than for their scale and the use that is made of them. With a 1968 average of 2,538 students per junior college in California, we have typically twice as large a college as in other states (except Arizona, 2,369, Florida 1,700, and Washington 1,675). The median for all states was about 800 students.

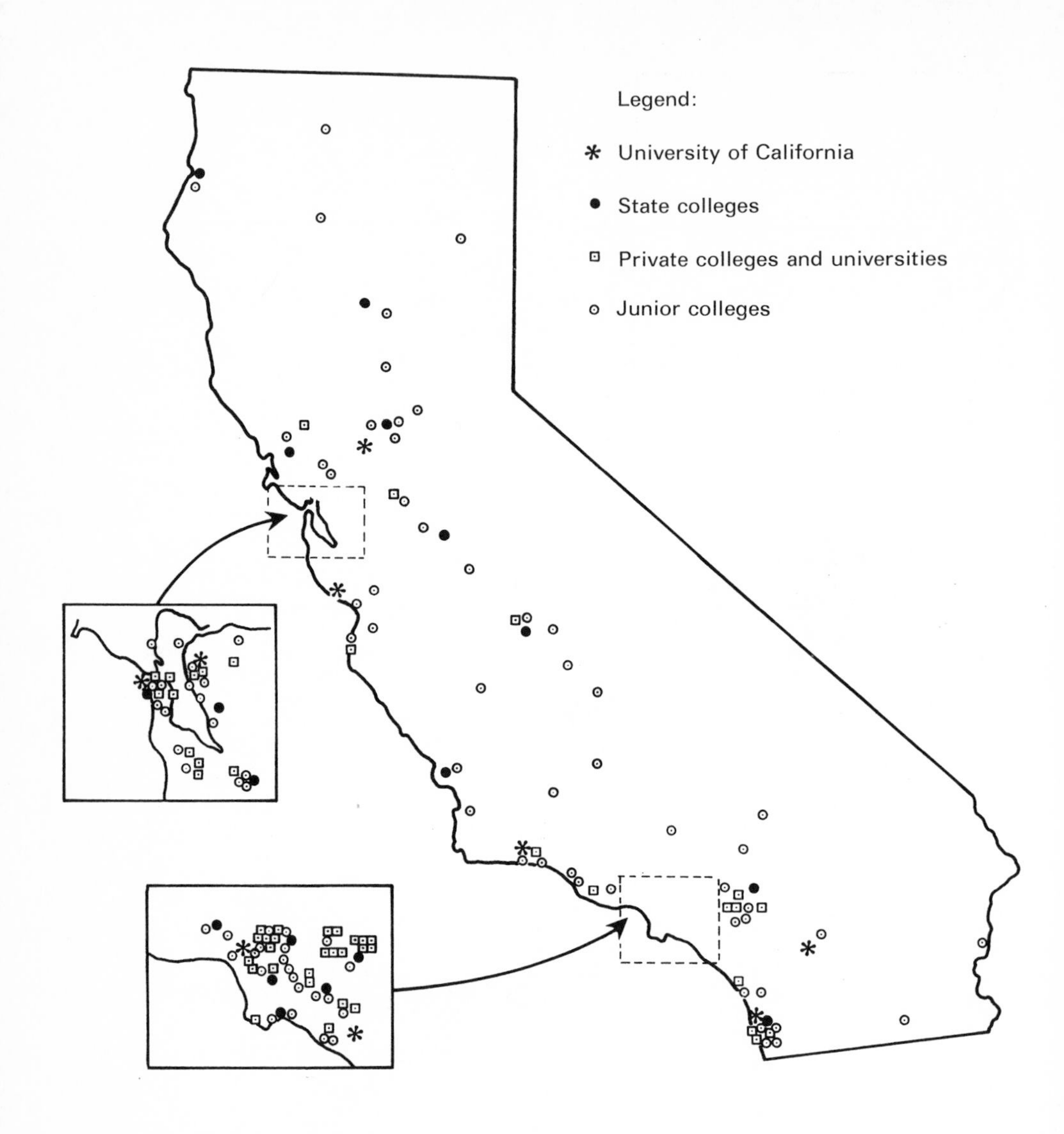

FIGURE 9 ***College and university campuses in California***

The renowned University of California is huge and academically very selective, but it accounts for only a tiny fraction of college freshmen in the whole state. Even if we add to that fraction the freshmen in the four-year state colleges, the combined figure is less than a sixth of the state's freshmen. The most interesting question lies beyond the scope of this inquiry: to what degree has the junior college system served to protect an intellectually elitist university system against being inundated, even while extending

FIGURE 10 ***SCOPE sample of California high schools, 1966***

other varieties of postsecondary schooling to a wider spectrum of the youth in the state?[3]

[3] Willingham (1970, p. 55) concluded his remarks about California with these words: "But ironically, the critical current problem in California is inadequate space in the senior institutions to handle new students and junior college transfers. At the close of the sixties—which many would call California's decade in higher education—some state colleges were rejecting 9 out of 10 applicants for admission (*San Francisco Chronicle,* 1969). If California is a bellwether, it is surely to signal problems as well as progress."

FIGURE 11
Distribution of the population of Massachusetts, 1960

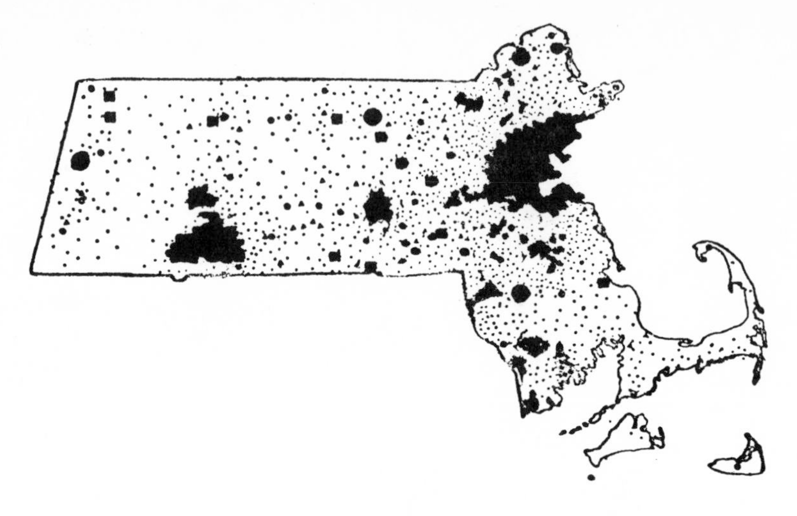

Though the SCOPE sample is less adequate for Massachusetts than for California, it nevertheless provides somewhat clearer internal contrasts in profiles of college accessibility by location (see the maps in Figures 11 and 12). The clustering of outstanding private colleges and universities in the Boston area is well known, but private schools with national reputations are not confined to that area and the main public colleges are also in other parts of the state. Outside the Boston area, however, too many of the sampled high schools in college towns appear to have been confined to one sex or the other. The main exception, and an important one, is the few communities with junior colleges only. Given these limitations of the SCOPE sample for Massachusetts, we will use those data selectively and bypass comment on the well-known historical background of higher education in that state. Worthy of notice, however, is the recent gain in the prestige and quality of the state's public colleges, along with the establishment of some junior colleges.

Some historical background of the higher education systems in Illinois and North Carolina will be filled in when we relate college attendance to accessibility in those states. Figures 13 and 14 show the geographic distribution of the population of Illinois and of colleges and sampled high schools in that state. SCOPE sampled high schools (not individuals, as in the Wisconsin study), and in Illinois the schools were unrepresentative, as was pointed out earlier (in Chapter 1).

(Text continued on p. 168)

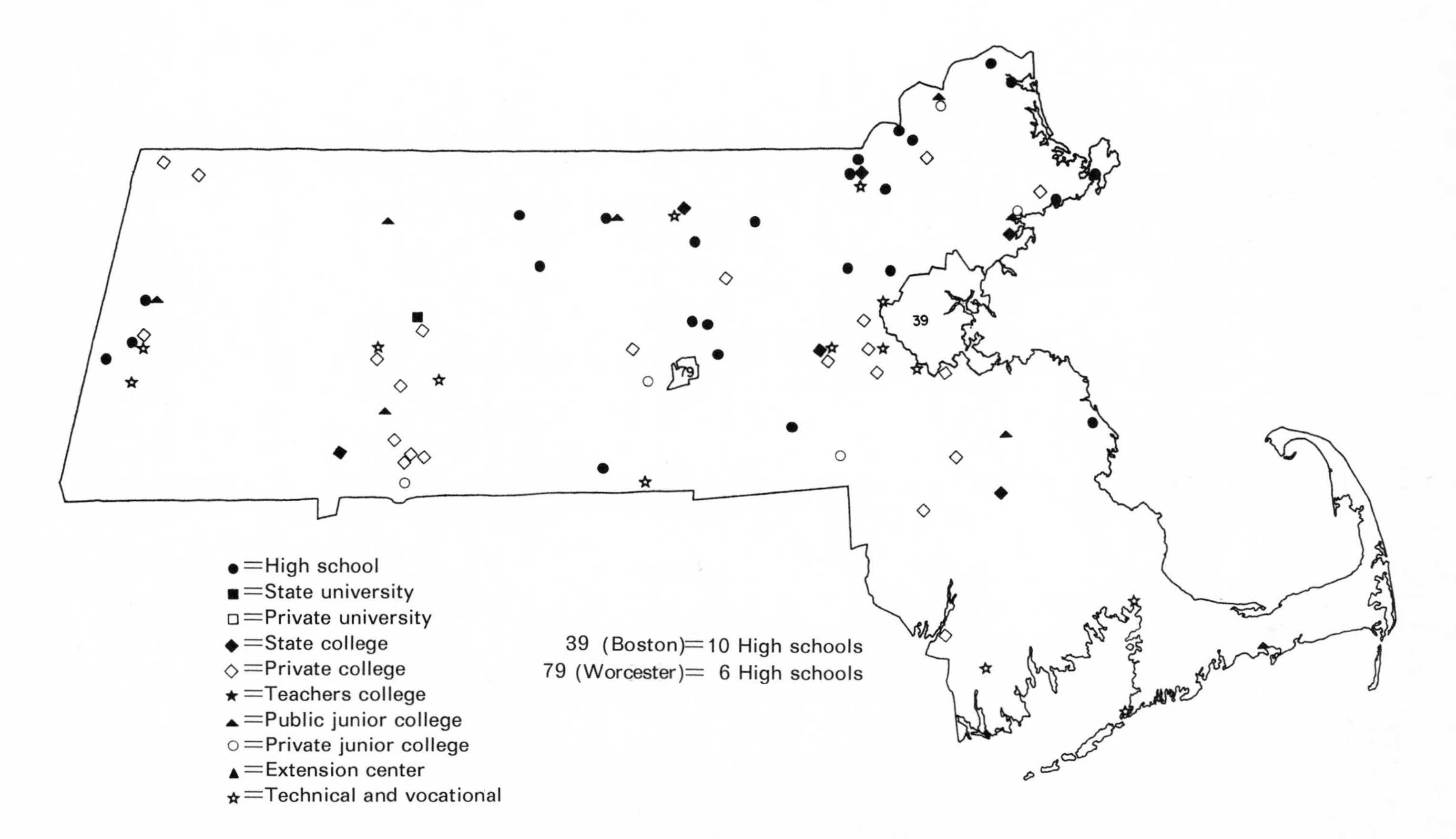

FIGURE 12 ***Colleges and universities in Massachusetts and the SCOPE sample of high schools, 1966***

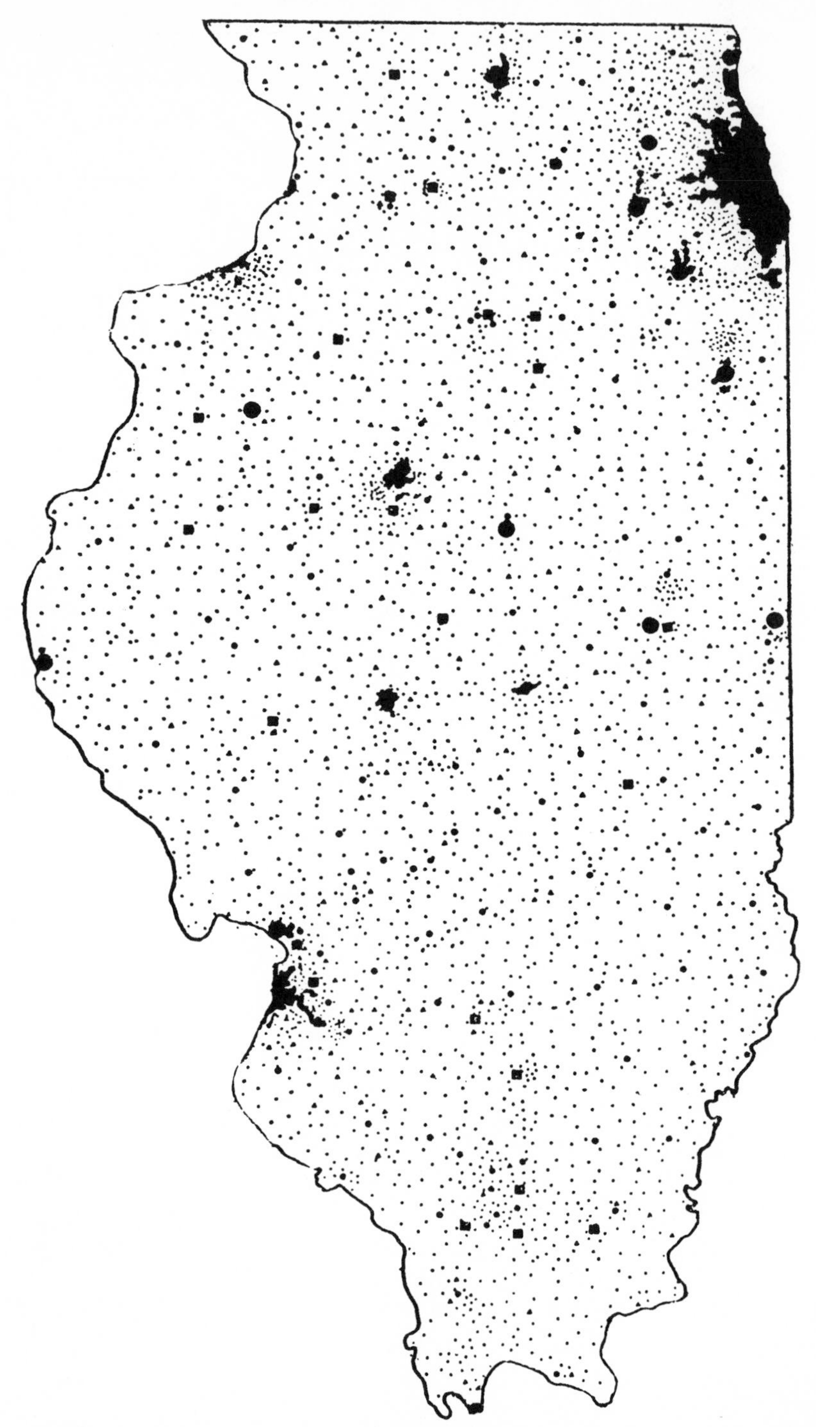

FIGURE 13 ***Distribution of the population of Illinois, 1960***

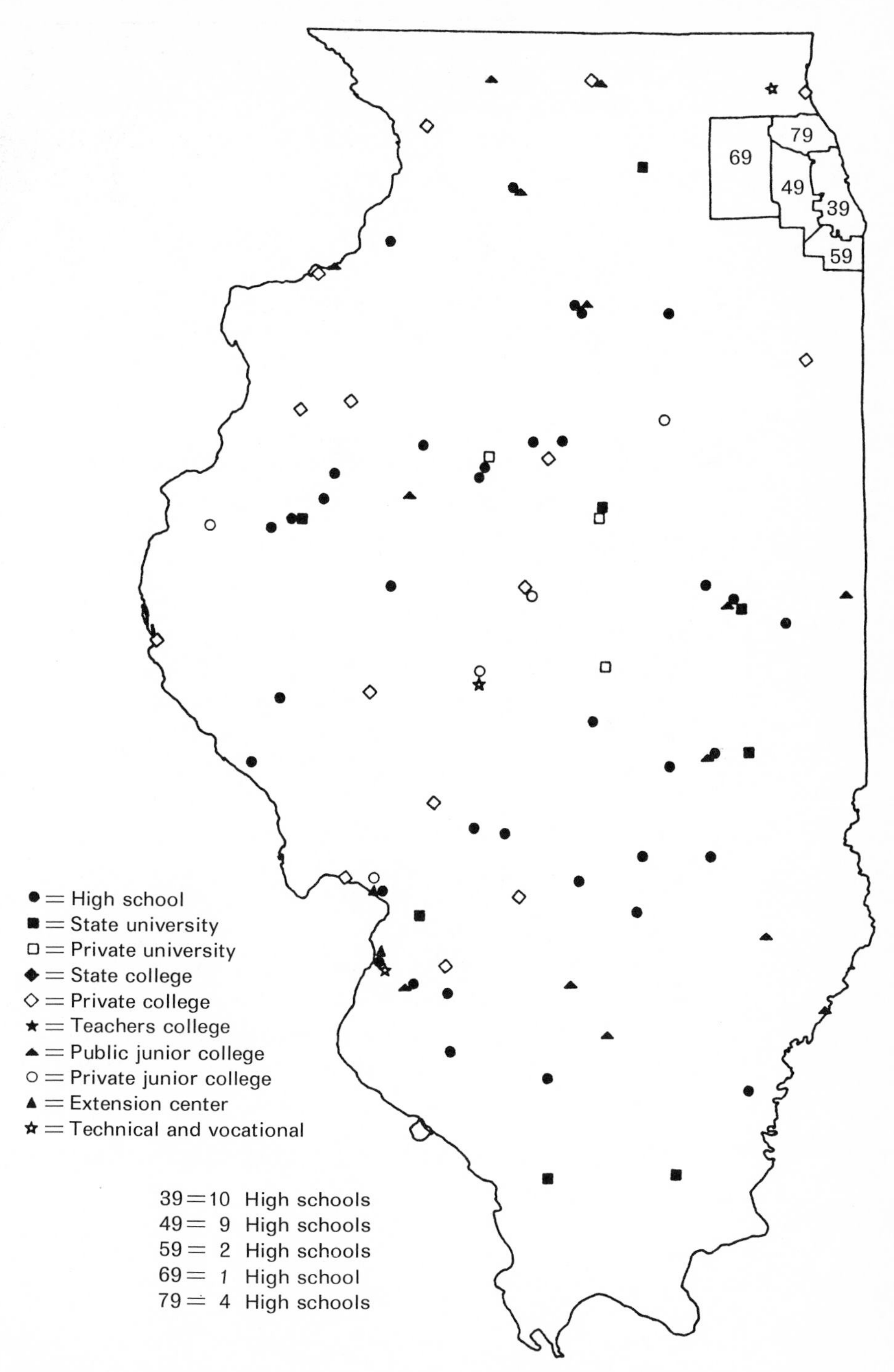

FIGURE 14 ***Colleges and universities in Illinois and the SCOPE sample of high schools, 1966***

These defects in the sample kept us from going as far as we had hoped with comments about communities or with multivariate analysis using logit transforms. However, for Illinois as elsewhere, the SCOPE samples for noncollege towns and for towns with only public junior colleges appear to be adequate—fortunately for our main aims. The North Carolina sample was better than that for either Illinois or Massachusetts (see Figures 15 and 16). The communities in these several states have quite diverse populations in socioeconomic features, as do the youth in the secondary schools; this naturally reflects the characteristics of the states and the history of college founding. Such diversity among communities, even without sample biases, must underline the importance of using controls for ability of youth and for their parental status in any study of how college-accessibility profiles affect rates of attendance at college. The summary comparisons presented in Chapters 2 and 3 did not allow for those factors.

Population and College-Access Profiles

As in Wisconsin, there is, of course, in Illinois and North Carolina an association between size of community and the profile of colleges accessible to its youth (Table 42). The Illinois SCOPE sample was actually extreme in this respect: All 26 high schools were in noncollege places but none of the other 30 secondary schools in the sample were in communities with fewer than 10,000 inhabitants. Many more high schools were included in the North Carolina sample and some of the towns with colleges were small. But even for this state there is a problem in sorting out possible effects of community size versus college accessibility on rates of college going, a problem that stands out when we compare the rows for noncollege with those for college communities in Table 43.[4] However, there was also considerable variation across access types within community-size categories, and gradients by size of community were modest. Furthermore, as will be shown later, variations in rates of attendance at college by size of community could be explained largely (or even overexplained) by associated variations in parental backgrounds and measures of ability of the high school graduates.

(Text continued on p. 172)

[4] In the regressions, size classes have been altered to give a better distribution of observations than in Table 42.

TABLE 42 Distribution of community samples by community size and college-accessibility profile; Illinois and North Carolina

College-accessibility profiles	Community size: Under 2,500	2,500–4,999	5,000–9,999	10,000–19,999	20,000–49,999	50,000–99,999	100,000 and over
Number of high schools in Illinois sample:							
Noncollege	19	3	4				
Public two-year only				3	3		
Extension					2		
All others (including multiple)				2		1	19
Number of high schools in North Carolina sample							
Noncollege	60	7	6	7			
Public two-year only	1	1	1				
Private two-year only	2				5		
All others (including multiple)	3				8		14

TABLE 43 Community size and college-going rates among high school graduates in SCOPE samples for noncollege and college towns; Illinois and North Carolina

Sample and college-access type	Community size: Under 1,000	1,000–2,999	3,000–19,999	20,000–99,999	100,000 and over
Illinois males					
Noncollege	41.8	51.2	47.6		
College			63.7	43.7	69.7*
Illinois females					
Noncollege	44.3	43.1	39.0		
College			57.7	42.3	42.7
North Carolina males					
Noncollege	33.6	42.7	45.2	40.6	
College	12.5	27.2	46.5	45.0	48.3
North Carolina females					
Noncollege	33.2	38.9	43.1	25.0	
College	34.8	37.4	38.0	48.5	45.8

* This reflects extremely biased samples in both the Chicago area and East St. Louis.

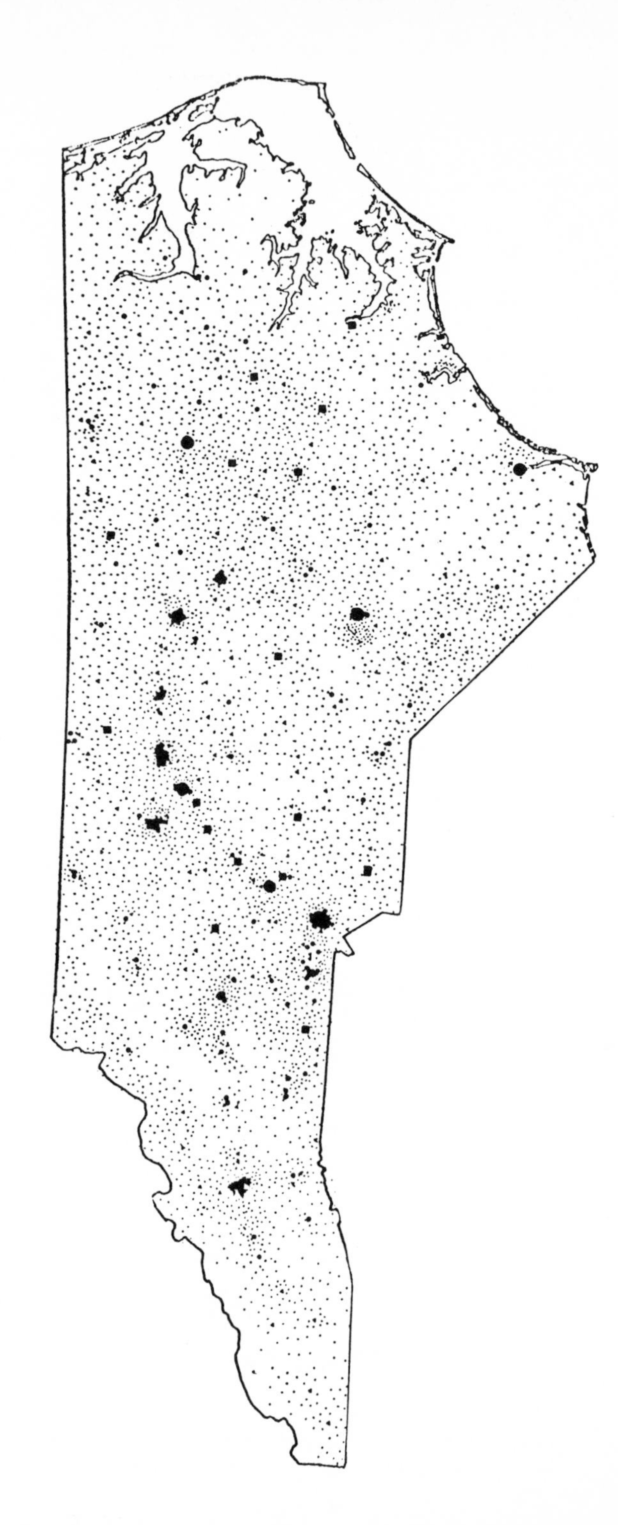

FIGURE 15 ***Distribution of the population of North Carolina, 1960***

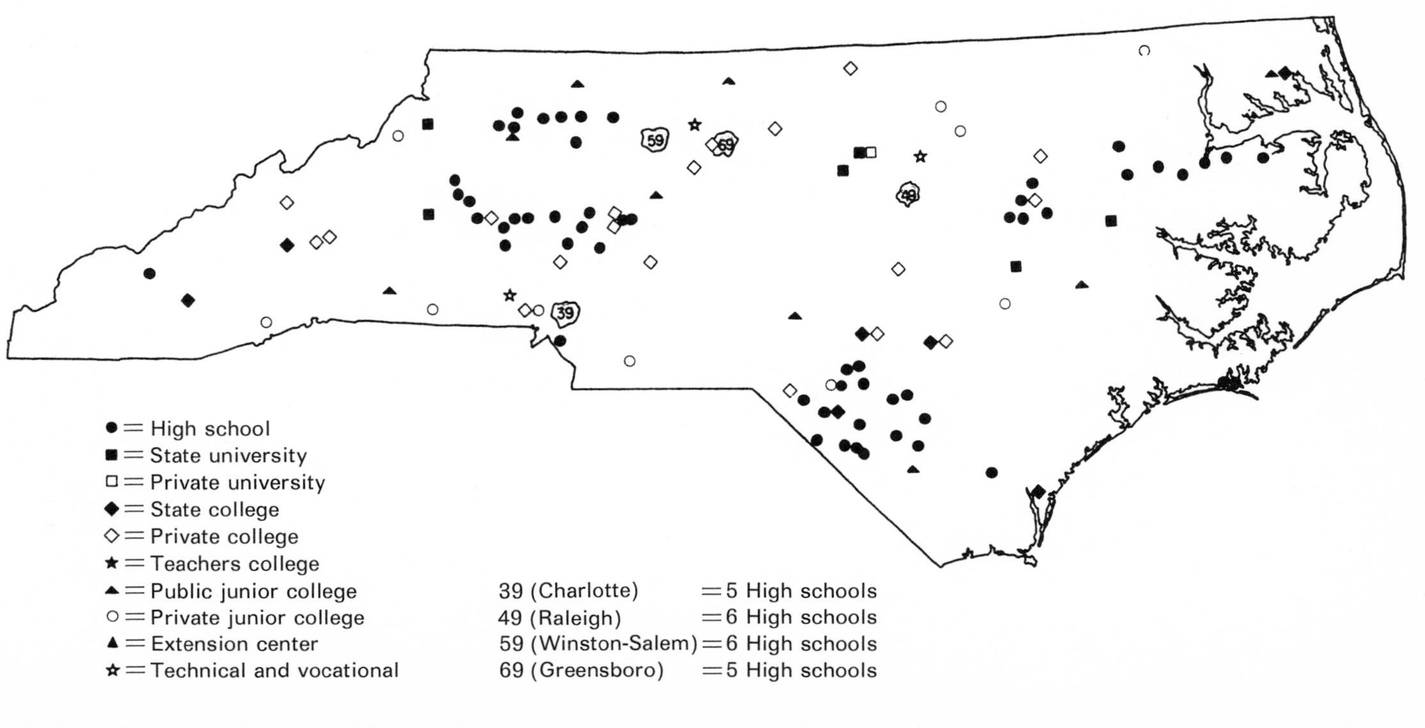

FIGURE 16 ***Colleges and universities in North Carolina and the SCOPE sample of high schools, 1966***

Interstate Comparisons of College Attendance by Ability

Overall contrasts in rates of college attendance among high school graduates from college and noncollege communities are shown for Wisconsin and the three SCOPE states at the bottom of Table 44. Consistently there is a larger attendance from communities with a college, but among boys the differences in the 1966 SCOPE data are smaller than in the 1957 Wisconsin data—despite the tendency for the SCOPE biases generally to run in favor of college communities. For girls, the differences in the 1966 SCOPE samples for Illinois and North Carolina match that for Wisconsin in 1957, at 7 to 8 percent. The low differential for girls in Massachusetts is congruent with the socioeconomic patterns of settlement in that state; we do not have to take recourse to sample biases favoring suburban areas. Note that in Massachusetts virtually all the sample from noncollege towns comes from places within 20 miles of a college—a sufficient reason for giving less attention to the data for this state than to those for Illinois and North Carolina.

We can obtain a better clue to the gross effects of the presence of a college (regardless of its type) by dividing the samples by ability quarters, as has been done for Table 44.[5] Two features of that table that have no direct connection with college accessibility deserve comment first. One of these is the fact that, controlling for measured ability, girls of 1966 in Massachusetts, Illinois, and North Carolina were at least as likely as boys to continue into college. This parity sharply contrasts with the finding for Wisconsin a decade earlier. While the sex difference in Wisconsin has declined, Table 44 nevertheless reflects a persisting high level of college going among able girls in both Massachusetts and North Carolina that has not been matched in the upper Midwest.

The other point to be stressed is the very large ability differentials in rates of college attendance in all the SCOPE samples for both college and noncollege communities. Rates of college entry among youth in the lowest quarter of ability have remained small for both boys and girls, but in the three SCOPE states those rates are over 80 percent for youth in the top quarter of ability. Large as they were, the percentage-point differences among ability quarters for Wisconsin in 1957 seem modest when placed against those for the other three states in 1966.

[5] The ability measure used by SCOPE was the new Academic Ability Test (AAT) developed by the Educational Testing Service. It gives verbal, mathematical, and total scores, and is easily administered within a class period. Scores correlate very closely with those on the School and College Ability Test (SCAT). For comments concerning this and other features of the SCOPE study, see Tillery et al. (1966).

Controlling for youths' ability, those from college communities do not consistently display greater propensity to attend college. That pattern appears only for the Wisconsin sample for both sexes and the North Carolina sample for girls. Indeed, the latter difference turns to negative when the comparison is between college towns and communities more than 20 miles from a college. For Illinois the data give us a strong suggestion that the less able half of the males are more likely to attend college if they dwell in a community with a college. But overall the main inference to be drawn from these data must be that in Illinois, and especially in North Carolina,

TABLE 44 ***Interstate comparisons of college attendance rates of high school graduates by ability quarters; youth from college communities, from all noncollege communities, and from communities with no colleges within 20 miles***

	Percentage rates of college attendance			*Differences in percentage rates of attendance*	
		Noncollege communities			
	College communities (1)	*All (2)*	*No college within 20 miles (3)*	*Column (1)— Column (2)*	*Column (1)— Column (3)*
			Males		
Wisconsin					
Ability 1	13.6	11.7	10.6	+ 1.9	+ 3.0
2	31.8	25.1	22.2	+ 6.7	+ 9.6
3	48.2	37.7	40.0	+10.5	+ 8.2
4	71.7	60.4	59.0	+11.3	+12.7
Massachusetts					
Ability 1	17.4	20.9	*	− 3.5	*
2	35.1	33.8	*	+ 1.3	*
3	54.3	57.2	*	− 2.9	*
4	82.2	89.0	*	− 6.8	*
Illinois					
Ability 1	19.2	8.9	6.1†	+10.3	(+13.1)†
2	38.1	28.6	31.5	+ 9.5	+ 6.6
3	60.1	62.0	67.2	− 1.9	− 7.1
4	83.9	81.9	87.3	+ 1.9	− 3.7
North Carolina					
Ability 1	15.8	12.5	8.1	+ 3.3	+ 7.7
2	34.9	35.3	40.2	− 0.4	− 5.3
3	61.7	63.0	64.3	− 1.3	− 2.6
4	82.7	82.7	77.2	0.0	+ 5.5

TABLE 44 (continued)

	Percentage rates of college attendance			Differences in percentage rates of attendance	
		Noncollege communities			
	College communities (1)	All (2)	No college within 20 miles (3)	Column (1)— Column (2)	Column (1)— Column (3)
			Females		
Wisconsin					
Ability 1	9.2	8.8	8.7	+ 0.4	+ 0.5
2	21.3	14.8	15.0	+ 6.5	+ 6.3
3	31.4	26.6	27.0	+ 4.8	+ 4.4
4	50.9	42.4	49.0	+ 8.5	+ 1.9
Massachusetts					
Ability 1	12.9†	18.6	*	— 5.7	*
2	31.5	37.5	*	— 6.0	*
3	62.2	67.1	*	— 4.9	*
4	86.2	89.5	*	— 3.3	*
Illinois					
Ability 1	16.6	11.7	16.9	+ 4.9	— 0.3
2	32.3	32.9	35.1	— 0.6	— 2.8
3	58.2	52.0	47.3	+ 6.2	+ 9.9
4	82.6	86.3	89.4	— 3.7	— 6.8
North Carolina					
Ability 1	20.2	17.6	23.9	+ 2.6	— 3.7
2	41.2	36.4	45.8	+ 4.8	— 4.6
3	65.6	61.0	67.5	+ 4.6	— 1.9
4	84.4	83.6	87.8†	+ 0.8	(+ 3.4)
All ability categories combined					
Males:					
Wisconsin	43.7	32.1	30.2	+11.6	+13.5
Massachusetts	60.5	58.4	*	+ 2.1	*
Illinois	57.3	48.5	48.3	+ 8.8	+ 9.0
North Carolina	46.0	40.4	34.0	+ 5.6	+12.0
Females:					
Wisconsin	29.0	21.9	23.8	+ 7.1	+ 5.2
Massachusetts	52.9	54.0	(48.7)†	— 1.1	(+ 4.2)†
Illinois	48.8	41.1	43.4	+ 7.7	+ 5.4
North Carolina	45.2	37.7	41.5	+ 7.5	+ 3.7

* No samples of male students from communities more than 20 miles from a college. One small girls' school was in such a community; it had no students in the top ability quarter.

† 20 to 49 cases in denominator (or in one of the relevant denominators).

the high school senior classes in college communities contain mixes of ability that are quite different from comparable classes in noncollege communities. Such necessarily is the case given the relatively strong positive differentials for the total samples and the mixed or even negative differentials within quarters on ability.

The best representations in the SCOPE samples were for the nonmetropolitan communities without colleges or with two-year institutions only. Table 45 permits us to compare college-going rates for communities having one or another type of two-year college with those for communities lacking any college. For boys, the advantage of dwelling in a community possessing some sort of two-year college occurs almost solely below the median in ability; moreover, all differentials for boys in the lowest quarter of ability are positive (higher if the community has a college). The generally weak or negative differentials for public junior colleges in North Carolina may be owing to the fact that the public (not the private) junior colleges in that state were new and that some have deliberately been sited in localities with lagging college attendance. Aside from Wisconsin, it is the positive rather than the negative differentials for the least able boys that may be the more puzzling, especially in view of the preponderantly negative differentials for boys above median ability—though the negative differences were in most cases small. The Wisconsin Extension Centers stand out for their positive impact among boys from the upper half of the ability distribution, though the differential is small for the most able quarter of the boys.

The contrast between girls and boys in Wisconsin towns with Extension Centers was discussed at some length in Chapter 4. Generally, the differentials among girls were small (and even negative, after controlling for ability and SES). In Massachusetts also, girls of similar ability and living in noncollege towns or in towns with public junior colleges were very alike in their propensities to go on to college. In Illinois, by contrast, girls in all but the top quarter on ability (where the differential was negative) were more likely to attend college when they lived in communities with a public junior college than otherwise. North Carolina is distinctive, especially for the contrasting sex patterns with respect to enrollment from communities with public and private junior colleges. Among girls in that state, the differentials run progressively more against college attendance from communities with public junior colleges as we move from the lowest to the third quarter of ability;

(Text continued on p. 178)

TABLE 45 ***Interstate comparisons of college attendance rates of high school graduates from communities with two-year colleges, by ability quarters***

	Males			
	Wisconsin	*Massachusetts*	*Illinois*	*North Carolina*
Ability 1 (Lowest quarter)				
Noncollege community: percentage to college	11.7	20.9	8.9	12.5
Differential percentages to college by access type				
Public two-year		+ 3.2	+ 9.2	+10.4
Private two-year				+ 7.8
Extension center	+ 3.4		+ 2.2	
Ability 2				
Noncollege community: percentage to college	25.1	33.8	28.6	35.3
Differential percentages to college by access type				
Public two-year		+12.5	+ 6.1	− 2.0
Private two-year				+18.7
Extension center	− 0.4		− 3.4	
Ability 3				
Noncollege community: percentage to college	37.7	57.2	62.0	63.0
Differential percentages to college by access type				
Public two-year		− 1.2	−14.5	− 6.9
Private two-year				0.0
Extension center	+ 9.6		− 9.9	
Ability 4				
Noncollege community: percentage to college	60.4	89.0	81.9	82.7
Differential percentages to college by access type				
Public two-year		− 4.0	− 4.3	− 0.6
Private two-year				− 3.6
Extension center	+ 3.2		− 8.6	

Females			
Wisconsin	*Massachusetts*	*Illinois*	*North Carolina*
8.8	18.6	11.7	17.6
	− 2.1	+ 8.4	+ 4.0
			+ 3.8
− 4.1		− 1.3	
14.8	37.5	32.9	36.4
	− 1.2	+ 3.8	− 9.7
			+ 2.5
+ 2.9		− 4.7	
26.6	67.1	52.0	61.0
	− 1.1	+11.1	−25.7
			+20.5
− 0.5		+ 5.1	
42.4	89.5	86.3	83.6
	− 0.1	− 7.1	−15.4
			+ 8.5
+ 5.4		− 0.4	

the difference remains negative, but not so large among the most able girls. At the same time, for North Carolina girls the largest positive differential between communities with private junior colleges and with no college was in the third quarter on ability; living in a town with a private junior college was unrelated to college attendance among boys. The long history of private versus public institutions in North Carolina and the tradition of the finishing school for ladies may both be reflected in these figures.

Interstate Comparisons of College Attendance by Father's Education

In each of the three SCOPE states for which the data were analyzed, we observe the expected monotonic relationship between paternal schooling and rates of college going within each sex. Generally girls lag behind boys at the lower levels of father's education, but catch up to or excel boys if the fathers are college men. The gradient of college going with paternal education is modified slightly in the noncollege towns of Massachusetts, where remarkably high rates of college entry appear among sons of the least educated fathers.[6]

The differences in college attendance rates between communities with and without colleges are on the whole small and erratic within categories of paternal education (Table 46), as they were within quarters of ability (Table 44). The exception is the positive differentials of 6 to 9 percent among sons and daughters of men who had not completed high school. Comparing Table 46 with Table 44, we infer that the positive differentials reflect responses primarily of low-ability boys distributed across the categories of paternal education.

Differences at the lower FED levels take on quite another pattern in comparisons of towns having two-year institutions with those having no college (Table 47). Differences are consistently positive across FED categories for North Carolina men in communities with public two-year institutions, but negative for Illinois boys from communities with public junior colleges or extension centers if we except sons of men with elementary schooling only. Among North Carolina girls there are consistently positive differentials at all levels of paternal education for communities with private but not with public two-year colleges. These results raise more questions than they begin to answer. Evidently the Illinois and the North Carolina evidence needs further scrutiny, particularly with reference to the intermingling of factors underlying college attendance.

[6] The figure for daughters of college graduates is clearly out of line, which accounts also for the large positive differentials on public junior colleges and extension centers in that FED category for Illinois females.

3. THE ILLINOIS EVIDENCE FURTHER CONSIDERED

Postsecondary education in Illinois has been marked from one period to another by shifting emphases between private and public provision. Private higher education in Illinois, as in Ohio and Indiana, was at one time the residue of a bitter rivalry among denominational programs. That denominational concern, during

(Text continued on p. 182)

TABLE 46 ***Interstate comparisons of college attendance rates of high school graduates by father's education; youth from college communities, from all noncollege communities, and from communities with no colleges within 20 miles***

	Percentage rates of college attendance			*Differences in percentage rates of college attendance*	
	College communities	*Noncollege communities*			
		All	*No college within 20 miles*	*Column (1)— Column (2)*	*Column (1)— Column (3)*
	(1)	*(2)*	*(3)*		
Males					
Massachusetts					
FED 1 (Elementary)	42.2	45.0	*	− 2.8	*
FED 2 (HS 1–3)	58.4	53.7	*	+ 4.7	*
FED 3 (HS 4)	60.8	59.5	*	+ 1.3	*
FED 4 (College 1–3)	66.8	71.5	*	− 4.7	*
FED 5a (College 4)	72.3	72.5	*	− 0.2	*
FED 5b (College 5+)	80.2	79.3	*	+ 0.9	*
Illinois					
FED 1	41.1	34.5	35.1	+ 6.6	+ 6.0
2	48.7	40.4	42.7	+ 8.3	+ 6.0
3	55.2	57.5	56.8	− 2.3	− 1.6
4	70.3	66.1	63.0†	+ 4.2	(+ 7.3)†
5a	78.9	75.6	83.3‡	+ 3.3	(− 4.4)‡
5b	81.4	84.8	§	− 3.4	§
North Carolina					
FED 1	28.5	28.2	20.5	+ 0.3	+ 8.0
2	38.2	37.0	30.5	+ 1.2	+ 7.7
3	51.8	55.9	49.5	− 4.1	+ 2.3
4	65.3	67.8	72.7†	− 2.5	(− 7.4)†
5a	76.6	73.6	66.7†	+ 3.0	(+ 9.9)†
5b	74.5	65.2	§	+ 9.3	§

TABLE 46 ***(continued)***

	Percentage rates of college attendance				
	College communities	Noncollege communities		Differences in percentage rates of college attendance	
		All	No college within 20 miles	Column (1)— Column (2)	Column (1)— Column (3)
	(1)	(2)	(3)		
Females					
Massachusetts					
FED 1	34.5	32.4	*	+ 2.1	*
2	43.2	47.3	*	− 4.1	*
3	50.4	54.3	*	− 3.9	*
4	67.3	67.8	*	− 0.5	*
5a	77.1	76.4	*	+ 0.7	*
5b	89.2	88.4	*	+ 0.8	*
Illinois					
FED 1	31.5	25.0	35.5	+ 6.5	− 4.0
2	38.2	29.4	37.0	+ 8.8	+ 1.2
3	48.0	51.7	52.0	− 3.7	− 4.0
4	61.7	63.4	78.3†	− 1.7	(−16.6)†
5a	76.9	59.0†	§	(+17.9)†	§
5b	85.0	88.5†	§	(− 3.5)†	§
North Carolina					
FED 1	26.9	28.0	37.7	− 1.1	− 1.1
2	35.7	35.0	38.6	+ 0.7	− 2.9
3	52.1	52.3	53.6	− 0.2	− 1.3
4	62.8	65.4	67.2	− 2.6	− 4.4
5a	77.4	71.6	63.6‡	+ 5.8	(+13.8)‡
5b	80.2	83.8†	§	− 3.6	§

* No such communities are in the sample.

† 20 to 49 cases in the denominator.

‡ 10 to 19 cases in the denominator.

§ Fewer than 10 cases in the denominator (or in one of the relevant denominators).

TABLE 47 ***Interstate comparisons of college attendance rates of high school graduates from communities with two-year colleges, by father's education***

	Males			*Females*		
	Massachusetts	*Illinois*	*North Carolina*	*Massachusetts*	*Illinois*	*North Carolina*
FED 1, Elementary						
Noncollege community; percentage to college	45.0	34.5	28.2	32.4	25.0	28.0
Differential percentages to college by access type						
Public two-year	− 1.9	+ 2.4	+ 5.1	+ 4.8	+ 7.6	− 8.8
Private two-year			− 0.2			+ 5.3
Extension center		+ 0.6			− 1.9	
FED 2, (HS 1–3)						
Noncollege community; percentage to college	53.7	40.4	37.0	47.3	29.4	35.0
Differential percentages to college by access type						
Public two-year	+ 4.8	− 1.5	+13.0	− 7.5	+ 8.2	+13.5
Private two-year			+20.8			+ 2.7
Extension center		−10.1			+ 8.1	
FED 3, (HS 4)						
Noncollege community; percentage to college	59.5	57.5	55.9	54.3	51.7	52.3
Differential percentages to college by access type						
Public two-year	+10.2	− 8.9	+ 6.6	+ 1.5	+ 0.4	− 5.9
Private two-year			+ 5.5			+19.1
Extension center		−13.4			−11.0	
FED 4, (College 1–3)						
Noncollege community; percentage to college	71.5	66.1	67.8	67.8	63.4	65.4
Differential percentages to college by access type						
Public two-year	− 0.7	− 1.9	+ 4.4	+ 3.4	− 0.7	+ 1.3
Private two-year			− 5.9			+ 9.6
Extension center		− 7.6			− 9.3	

TABLE 47 ***(continued)***

	Males			Females		
	Massa-chusetts	*Illinois*	*North Carolina*	*Massa-chusetts*	*Illinois*	*North Carolina*
FED 5, (College 4)						
Noncollege community; percentage to college	72.5	75.6*	73.6	76.4	59.0*	71.6
Differential percentages to college by access type						
Public two-year	− 1.1	(−10.2)*	+ 8.1	+10.9	(+14.8)*	†
Private two-year			− 0.3			+ 8.4
Extension center		(− 6.4)*			(+16.9)*	
FED 6, (College 5+)						
Noncollege community; percentage to college	79.3	84.8*	65.2	88.4	88.5*	83.8
Differential percentages to college by access type						
Public two-year	+ 2.5	−11.3	†	− 0.9	(− 7.9)*	†
Private two-year			†			− 0.5
Extension center		−14.4			(+ 6.7)*	

* 20 to 49 cases in denominator (or in one of the relevant denominators).

† Under 10 cases in denominator (or in one of the relevant denominators).

its height in the later half of the nineteenth century, produced such institutions as the University of Chicago, Northwestern University, and Loyola University. Only Pennsylvania, Massachusetts, and New York today have more private colleges than does Illinois.[7]

The surge of public contributions to the number and size of colleges in Illinois has occurred more recently, and the patterns of enrollment today are quite different from what they were a half-century ago. Despite the University of Illinois at Champaign and early state concern for normal schools, public investment in higher education has come about in Illinois mainly since 1945. Public institutions accounted for only 36 percent of all enrollments in higher education in Illinois in 1939, but today four-fifths of all Illinois youth attending colleges in their own state are enrolled in state-supported four- or two-year colleges. Over two-thirds of all

[7] California has the same number, but they account for a much smaller fraction of college students in that state.

the public junior colleges in Illinois have been opened within the last decade—even though public junior colleges have been associated with high school districts since 1902, when the first public college in the country opened in Joliet.

This diversity of the Illinois system of higher education would justify an intensive analysis of college going in relation to the spatial arrangement of colleges if only we had a considerably larger and more representative sample available. The SCOPE sample is adequate enough with respect to noncollege communities and for public two-year schools. In other college-access categories, however, samples are small or they pick up populations with characteristics that might be expected to mislead us about the effects of accessibility upon attendance. Because of socioeconomic selectivity in residence patterns and sample distortions in representation of high schools, some way of controlling for ability or parental background must be applied if we are to draw any inferences for Illinois about the effects of accessibility upon college attendance. In the immediately preceding cross-state comparisons, a first step was taken in this direction; data were presented by ability quarter or by level of paternal schooling. Using multiple regressions, that analysis is now pushed another step. First, however, an important digression on community size is interpolated.

Community Size and College Attendance

Rather than substituting size of community for type of college access (as was done in some of the regressions for Wisconsin), in the analysis for Illinois and North Carolina a differentiation by community size was incorporated into the noncollege category. The results can be read off the multiple regressions for the entire Illinois sample (Table 48), the regressions within ability categories (Tables 49 and 50), and those within categories of paternal education (Tables 51 and 52).[8] Whether we look at males or females, in most cases the smallest noncollege communities had relatively high college attendance rates. Since this was the omitted dummy of the accessibility-population set, it tended to push most of the coefficients of that set into the negative range.[9] The smallest towns

[8] For a discussion of the methodology, including some caveats, see Chapter 4, pp. 74–76 and 112–115.

[9] We chose to take the smallest communities as the omitted dummy variable in the expectation that these communities would have the lowest college attendance rates. On the whole, this was true within the class "noncollege town" for North Carolina; but in the Illinois sample, the smallest towns had high

(Footnote continued on p. 185)

TABLE 48 ***Regression analysis of college attendance rates of male and female 1966 Illinois high school graduates***

	Male (4273)		Female (4413)	
Equation number	*(1) M*	*(2) M*	*(1) F*	*(2) F*
R^2	.286	.302	.299	.301
F	77.22	55.68	85.15	57.21
Constant	.106	.122	.074	.131
Ability quarters				
1. *Low*	. . .	. . .	. . .	. . .
2.	.155*	.154*	.132*	.132*
3.	.389*	.384*	.340*	.339*
4. *High*	.582*	.573*	.552*	.551*
NA.	.320*	.319*	.117*	.114*
Father's education				
1. *Elementary*	. . .	. . .	. . .	. . .
2,3. *High school*	.057*	.053*	.067*	.066*
4. *College 1–3*	.128*	.121*	.130*	.131*
5a. *College graduate*	.153*	.141*	.143*	.144*
5b. *Postgraduate*	.149*	.137*	.235*	.238*
NA.	—.012	—.023	—.059†	—.059*
Mother's education				
1. *Elementary*	. . .	. . .	. . .	. . .
2,3. *High school*	.031†	.030†	.032*	.033*
4. *College 1–3*	.111*	.110*	.174*	.175*
5a. *College graduate*	.075*	.076*	.179*	.184*
5b. *Postgraduate*	.084†	.061†	.192*	.195*
NA.	—.028	—.024	.018	.017
Father's occupation				
0. *Workman, service, machine operator*	.007	—.005	—.030*	—.030†
1. *Skilled craftsman, technician*	.032	—.026	—.010	—.011
2. *Clerical, sales*	. . .	. . .	. . .	. . .
3. *Farm operator*	.028	.051†	.121*	.112*
4. *Business proprietor*	.074*	.074*	.064*	.062*
5. *Artist, entertainer*	.016	.015	.053	.054
6. *Manager, official, executive*	.047*	.062*	.082*	.085*
7. *Professional*	.017	.023	.010	.010
8. *NA*	—.066*	—.059*	—.017	—.019

	Male (4273)		Female (4413)	
Equation number	(1) M	(2) M	(1) F	(2) F
R^2	.286	.302	.299	.301
F	77.22	55.68	85.15	57.21
Accessibility within community				
00 None: population 0–999		. . .		. . .
01 None: population 1,000–2,499		—.017		—.073†
02 None: population 2,500–9,999		—.050		—.071†
11 University (state)		—.031		—.048
12 University (private)		.176*		§
16 Junior college (public)		—.059		—.029
18 Extension center		—.088*		—.078*
19 Technical, vocational, religious		—.108‡		.004
29 Multiple two-year		§		—.061
39 Chicago		.086*		—.068†
49 Chicago suburb (west)		§		—.014
59 Chicago suburb (south)		—.003		—.065†
79 Chicago suburb (north)		—.018		—.077*

* Significant $F_{.01}$, $t_{.05}$ (one-tailed).
† Significant $F_{.01}$, but not $t_{.05}$ (one-tailed).
‡ Includes 10 to 20 cases.
§ Includes no cases.

uniformly rated high in regressions for the entire sample (with ability, father's education, and so on treated as control but not as design variables).[10] There were exceptions, however, among the regressions run within ability or paternal education categories as design variables.

attendance rates. Unfortunately, this complicates the reading of the regression equations for Illinois, making most of the regression coefficients on other categories negative.

[10] The terms "design variable" and "moderator variable" have the same meaning in this context: we refer to variables that are used to subdivide a sample population before continuing with the analysis. Thus, the "design" of the regression analysis in the present case is to separate ability categories and examine patterns of relationships within each, and similarly to treat father's education as a design variable. Both the ability and the father's education categories are also used simply as control variables, along with other independent variables, whereas sex is a design variable throughout; all regressions are run separately for males and for females.

TABLE 49 ***Regression analysis of college attendance rates of male 1966 Illinois high school graduates by ability quarters***

	Ability 1 (681)		*Ability 2 (1018)*	
Equation number	*(1) M.A1*	*(2) M.A1*	*(1) M.A2*	*(2) M.A2*
R^2	*.060*	*.110*	*.053*	*.087*
F	*2.34*	*2.78*	*3.27*	*3.48*
Constant	.153	.046	.233	.257
Father's education				
1. Elementary	. . .	. . .	. . .	. . .
2,3. High school	.043	.051†	.064†	.075*
4. College 1–3	.108*	.088†	.126*	.134*
5a. College graduate	.138*	.128†	.273*	.294*
5b. Postgraduate	.073	.036	.278	.265
NA.	.005	—.014	.007	.007
Mother's education				
1. Elementary	. . .	. . .	. . .	. . .
2,3. High school	.045	.046	.030	.025
4. College 1–3	.090†	.074	.083†	.072
5a. College graduate	.111	.091	.160†	.156†
5b. Postgraduate	.063‡	.077‡	.306*§	.257*§
NA.	—.018	—.010	—.007	—.001
Father's occupation				
0. Workman, service, machine operator	—.059	—.062	.010	.032
1. Skilled craftsman, technician	—.048	—.054	—.013	.015
2. Clerical, sales	. . .	. . .	. . .	. . .
3. Farm operator	—.159*	—.100	—.034	.009
4. Business proprietor	.095	.096	.088	.108†
5. Artist, entertainer	—.307‡	—.304‡	¶	¶
6. Manager, official, executive	.062	.067	.111†	.139*
7. Professional	—.004	.030	—.023	.015
8. NA	—.165*	—.162*	—.064	—.058
Accessibility within community				
00 None: population 0–999		. . .		. . .
01 None: population 1,000–2,499		.061		—.053
02 None: population 2,500–9,999		.036		—.135†
11 University (state)		—.068§		—.036

Ability 3 (1053)		*Ability 4 (1494)*	
(1) M.A3	*(2) M.A3*	*(1) M.A4*	*(2) M.A4*
.055	*.101*	*.051*	*.068*
3.34	*4.09*	*4.40*	*3.83*
.484	.582	.747	.734
. . .	. . .	. . .	. . .
.069†	.053	.024	.024
.146*	.138*	.094*	.090*
.103†	.081	.121*	.108*
.211*	.189*	.092*	.077†
—.060	—.062	—.072	—.088
. . .	. . .	. . .	. . .
.058	.046	—.012	—.013
.190*	.199*	.060†	.056†
.096	.095	.022	.019
.072	.018	.003	—.006
—.003	—.001	—.141*	—.145*
—.040	—.036	.012	.014
—.079†	—.064	—.012	—.006
. . .	. . .	. . .	. . .
.117†	.127†	.077†	.109*
.021	.030	.096*	.092*
.146‡	.168‡	.005‡	—.016‡
.029	.076	.043	.050†
—.040	—.036	.055*	.066*
—.067	—.052	.014	.022
	. . .		. . .
	—.031		—.042
	—.111		.027
	—.221†§		.069

TABLE 49 (continued)

	Ability 1 (681)		Ability 2 (1018)	
Equation number	(1) M.A1	(2) M.A1	(1) M.A2	(2) M.A2
R^2	.060	.110	.053	.087
F	2.34	2.78	3.27	3.48
Accessibility within community (cont.):				
12 University (private)		.187†		.235*
16 Junior college (public)		.122†		—.045
18 Extension center		.044		—.140†
19 Technical, vocational, religious		—.106‡		—.341†‡
39 Chicago		.279*		.050
49 Chicago suburb (west)		¶		¶
59 Chicago suburb (south)		.077		—.018
79 Chicago suburb (north)		.123		—.138

* Significant $F_{.01}$, $t_{.05}$ (one-tailed).
† Significant $F_{.01}$, but not $t_{.05}$ (one-tailed).
‡ Includes fewer than 10 cases.
§ Includes 10 to 19 cases.
¶ Includes no cases.

TABLE 50 Regression analysis of college attendance rates of female 1966 Illinois high school graduates by ability quarters

	Ability 1 (880)		Ability 2 (1329)	
Equation number	(1) F.A1	(2) F.A1	(1) F.A2	(2) F.A2
R^2	.087	.101	.108	.113
F	4.58	3.29	8.78	5.72
Constant	.107	.250	.195	.301
Father's education				
1. Elementary	. . .	. . .	. . .	. . .
2,3. High school	.058*	.058*	.048*	.050†
4. College 1–3	.244*	.254*	.095†	.102*
5a. College graduate	.141*	.149*	.037	.040
5b. Postgraduate	.144‡	.149‡	.354*	.358*
NA.	.007	.013	—.119*	—.119
Mother's education				
1. Elementary	. . .	. . .	. . .	. . .
2,3. High school	.023	.026	.042	.041
4. College 1–3	.133*	.136*	.277*	.277*
5a. College graduate	.162*‡	.165*‡	.354*	.355*
5b. Postgraduate	.187	.203§	.175†‡	.161‡
NA.	—.038	—.030	.096	.096

Ability 3 (1053)		Ability 4 (1494)	
(1) M.A3	(2) M.A3	(1) M.A4	(2) M.A4
.055	.101	.051	.068
3.34	4.09	4.40	3.83
.164†		.103	
—.223*		—.035	
—.142†		—.078	
—.013‡		.195‡	
.044		.072	
¶		¶	
—.061		.014	
—.114		.031	

Ability 3 (1130)		Ability 4 (1034)	
(1) F.A3	(2) F.A3	(1) F.A4	(2) F.A4
.102	.110	.064	.078
7.02	4.70	3.87	2.94
.378	.262	.660	.739
. . .	. . .	. . .	. . .
.096*	.085*	.067*	.056†
.150*	.137*	.103*	.096*
.181*	.159*	.153*	.154*
.301*	.278*	.129*	.137*
—.098	—.114	.038	.023
. . .	. . .	. . .	. . .
—.012	—.020	.082*	.090*
.143*	.136*	.145*	.149*
.152*	.158*	.158*	.172*
.191†‡	.184†‡	.224*	.245*
.068	.057	—.249*‡	—.213*‡

TABLE 50
(continued)

	Ability 1 (880)		*Ability 2 (1329)*	
Equation number	*(1) F.A1*	*(2) F.A1*	*(1) F.A2*	*(2) F.A2*
R^2	*.087*	*.101*	*.108*	*.113*
F	*4.58*	*3.29*	*8.78*	*5.72*
Father's occupation				
0. *Workman, service, machine operator*	—.062	—.073†	—.021	—.024
1. *Skilled craftsman, technician*	—.010	—.022	—.032	—.032
2. *Clerical, sales*	. . .	. . .	. . .	. . .
3. *Farm operator*	.014	.015	.209*	.170*
4. *Business proprietor*	.033	.020	.062	.053
5. *Artist, entertainer*	.143§	.144§	.142§	.183§
6. *Manager, official, executive*	.039	.034	.134*	.138*
7. *Professional*	—.110†	—.120†	—.024	—.026
8. *NA*	—.104*	—.099†	.002	—.010
Accessibility within community				
00 *None: population 0–999*		. . .		. . .
01 *None: population 1,000–2,499*		—.181*		—.094
02 *None: population 2,500–9,999*		—.174*		—.112†
11 *University (state)*		—.119‡		.001
16 *Junior college (public)*		—.110†		—.078
18 *Extension center*		—.186*		—.150*
19 *Technical, vocational, religious*		—.223*‡		—.054§
29 *Multiple two-year*		—.143†		—.107
39 *Chicago*		—.111†		—.095
49 *Chicago suburb (west)*		—.172*		—.080
59 *Chicago suburb (south)*		—.109†		—.147*
69 *Chicago suburb (far west)*		¶		¶
79 *Chicago suburb (north)*		—.202†		—.146*

* Significant $F_{.01}$, $t_{.05}$ (one-tailed).

† Significant $F_{.01}$, but not $t_{.05}$ (one-tailed).

‡ Includes 10 to 19 cases.

§ Includes fewer than 10 cases.

¶ Includes no cases.

Ability 3 (1130)		*Ability 4 (1034)*	
(1) F.A3	*(2) F.A3*	*(1) F.A4*	*(2) F.A4*
.102	*.110*	*.064*	*.078*
7.02	*4.70*	*3.87*	*2.94*
.001	.005	—.040	—.048
.034	.040	—.033	—.033
. . .	. . .	. . .	. . .
.144*	.186*	.065	.033
.112*	.126*	.039	.041
.105§	.117§	—.305§	—.325§
.208*	.203*	—.027	—.022
.080	.086	—.012	—.013
.075	.077	—.020	—.002
	. . .		. . .
	.076		—.062
	.092		—.031
	.078		—.103
	.180*		—.113†
	.128		—.061
	.388*§		.142§
	.071		—.052
	.130		—.154*
	.172†		—.016
	.072		—.043
	¶		¶
	.137†		—.096

TABLE 51 ***Regression analysis of college attendance rates of male 1966 Illinois high school graduates by father's education***

	FED 1 (N = 782)		FED 2 (N = 761)	
Equation number	*(1) M.E1*	*(2) M.E1*	*(1) M.E2*	*(2) M.E2*
R^2	.248	.272	.222	.258
F	14.84	10.45	12.47	9.46
Constant	.166	.104	.179	.137
Ability quarters				
1. Low	. . .	. . .	. . .	. . .
2.	.143*	.130*	.104*	.108*
3.	.389*	.387*	.360*	.346*
4. High	.636*	.617*	.514*	.498*
NA.	.200‡	.202‡	—.176‡	—.145‡
Mother's education				
1. Elementary	. . .	. . .	. . .	. . .
2. High school 1–3	.028	.031	.067	.059
3. High school 4	.026	.022	.074	.063
4. College 1–3	.063	.056	.279*	.267*
5. College 4	—.243§	—.255§	.217*	.195*
6. College 5+	.344‡	.594‡	—.064‡	—.125‡
NA.	—.028	—.024	—.032§	—.031§
Father's occupation				
0. Workman, service, machine operator	—.059	—.078	—.056	—.042
1. Skilled craftsman, technician	—.091	—.095	—.075	—.067
2. Clerical, sales	. . .	. . .	. . .	. . .
3. Farm operator	—.049	—.028	—.075	—.014
4. Business proprietor	—.029	—.036	—.006	—.008
5. Artist, entertainer	¶	¶	¶	¶
6. Manager, official, executive	—.135§	—.130¶	.010	.046
7. Professional	.030§	.051§	—.232‡	—.216‡
8. NA	—.129	—.146	—.192*	—.177*
Accessibility within community				
00 None: population 0–999		. . .		. . .
01 None: population 1,000–2,499		.134†		.068
02 None: population 2,500–9,999		.009		—.039
11 University (state)		.127‡		.042§

FED 3 (N = 1105)		*FED 4 (N = 738)*		*FED 5 (N = 331)*	
(1) M.E3	*(2) M.E3*	*(1) M.E4*	*(2) M.E4*	*(1) M.E5*	*(2) M.E5*
.232	*.255*	*.232*	*.245*	*.258*	*.293*
18.19	*12.66*	*12.04*	*8.52*	*6.41*	*4.64*
.200	.256	.236	.391	.163	.458
. . .	. . .	. . .	. . .	. . .	. . .
.191*	.193*	.153*	.160*	.229*	.248*
.434*	.423*	.428*	.428*	.285*	.297*
.627*	.621*	.600*	.596*	.538*	.549*
.682‡	.687‡	.711‡	.693‡	—.531‡	—.628‡
. . .	. . .	. . .	. . .	. . .	. . .
—.040	—.032	—.073	—.052	.016	.021
—.023	—.028	.039	.046	.156	.153
.047	.048	.076	.085	.201†	.207†
—.022	—.035	.045	.059	.197†	.215†
—.155‡	—.164‡	.060§	.073§	.293*	.248†
—.031	—.058	—.155§	—.153§	¶	¶
—.030	—.022	.057	.059	.008§	.058§
—.036	—.025	—.056	—.053	.167§	.184§
. . .	. . .	. . .	. . .	. . .	. . .
.102	.118	.018	.054	.143‡	.135‡
.128*	.130*	.047	.039	.132†	.133
—.338‡	—.334‡	.071‡	.058‡	.143‡	.061‡
.067	.088	.048	.052	.095†	.099†
—.029	—.013	.001	.008	.022	.019
—.020	—.004	—.019	—.021	—.090§	—.064§
	. . .		‡		‡
	—.076		—.297*		—.265
	—.057		—.137		—.367†
	—.137		—.148§		—.311‡

TABLE 51 ***(continued)***

	FED 1 (N = 782)		FED 2 (N = 761)	
Equation number	*(1) M.E1*	*(2) M.E1*	*(1) M.E2*	*(2) M.E2*
R^2	.248	.272	.222	.258
F	14.84	10.45	12.47	9.46
Accessibility within community (cont.):				
12 *University (private)*		.357*		.268*
16 *Junior college (public)*		.061		—.023*
18 *Extension center*		.026		—.061
19 *Technical, vocational, religious*		—.671‡		.017‡
39 *Chicago*		.175*		.208*
59 *Chicago suburb (south)*		.090		.064
79 *Chicago suburb (north)*		.004		.029

* Significant $F_{.01}$, $t_{.05}$ (one-tailed).

† Significant $F_{.01}$, but not $t_{.05}$ (one-tailed).

‡ Under 10 cases.

§ 10 to 20 cases.

¶ No cases.

NOTE: Performance on tests of significance is not shown when there are fewer than 20 cases.

TABLE 52 ***Regression analysis of college attendance rates of female 1966 Illinois high school graduates by father's education***

	FED 1 (N = 824)		FED 2 (N = 811)	
Equation number	*(1) F.E1*	*(2) F.E1*	*(1) F.E2*	*(2) F.E2*
R^2	.215	.230	.183	.193
F	12.95	8.48	9.88	6.44
Constant	.127	.213	.067	.198
Ability quarters				
1. *Low*	. . .	. . .	. . .	. . .
2.	.149*	.147*	.139*	.137*
3.	.325*	.319*	.321*	.318*
4. *High*	.601*	.591*	.568*	.564*
NA.	.172‡	.160‡	.212‡	.200‡
Mother's education				
1. *Elementary*	. . .	. . .	. . .	. . .
2. *High school 1–3*	—.008	—.016	.013	.003
3. *High school 4*	.021	.018	.061	.064
4. *College 1–3*	.102*	.087†	.090†	.090†
5. *College 4*	.171§	.194§	.225‡	.248‡
6. *College 5+*	¶	¶	.646‡	.595‡
NA.	.003‡	—.016‡	—.023‡	—.049‡

FED 3 (N = 1105)		FED 4 (N = 738)		FED 5 (N = 331)	
(1) M.E3	(2) M.E3	(1) M.E4	(2) M.E4	(1) M.E5	(2) M.E5
.232	.255	.232	.245	.258	.293
18.19	12.66	12.04	8.52	6.41	4.64
	.137		—.026		—.228§
	—.114		—.190		—.434§
	—.153		—.236†		—.375*
	—.294‡		¶		.038‡
	.057		—.142		—.222
	—.049		—.148		—.272
	—.087		—.155		—.318

FED 3 (N = 1100)		FED 4 (N = 830)		FED 5 (N = 338)	
(1) F.E3	(2) F.E3	(1) F.E4	(2) F.E4	(1) F.E5	(2) F.E5
.248	.257	.218	.226	.366	.385
19.85	12.78	12.56	8.06	10.23	6.66
.175	.278	.182	.172	.071	.099
...	...	...	...	...	...
.140*	.132*	.023	.033	.119†	.119†
.373*	.369*	.226*	.229*	.374*	.361*
.619*	.613*	.420*	.423*	.532*	.536*
—.104§	—.091§	—.051‡	—.075‡	.516‡	.541‡
...	...	...	...	...‡	...‡
—.017	—.028	.040	.026	—.014	—.054
.046	.040	.147*	.121*	.221†	.210†
.173*	.164*	.293*	.267*	.346*	.341*
.015	.002	.335*	.306*	.422*	.419*
.250‡	.252‡	.335§	.295§	.317‡	.277‡
—.130§	—.152§	.157‡	.168‡	—.358‡	—.477‡

TABLE 52
(continued)

	FED 1 (N = 824)		FED 2 (N = 811)	
Equation number	(1) F.E1	(2) F.E1	(1) F.E2	(2) F.E2
R^2	.215	.230	.183	.193
F	12.95	8.48	9.88	6.44
Father's occupation				
0. Workman, service, machine operator	—.069	—.086	.004	—.003
1. Skilled craftsman, technician	—.057	—.078	.067	.063
2. Clerical, sales	. . .	. . .	. . .	. . .
3. Farm operator	.072	.068	.082	.069
4. Business proprietor	—.048	—.057	.140†	.131†
5. Artist, entertainer	—.212‡	—.219‡	.704‡	,715‡
6. Manager, official, executive	—.019§	—.028§	.134	.129
7. Professional	.144§	.153§	.070§	.081§
8. NA	—.030	—.047	.107	.103
Accessibility within community				
00 None: population 0–999		. . .		§
01 None: population 1,000–2,499		—.064		—.212†
02 None: population 2,500–9,999		—.163*		—.165
11 University (state)		—.024§		.061§
16 Junior college (public)		—.026		—.102
18 Extension center		—.112†		—.127
19 Technical, vocational, religious		—.136‡		.087‡
29 Multiple two-year		—.131		—.111
39 Chicago		—.041		—.100
49 Chicago suburb (west)		—.020		—.083
59 Chicago suburb (south)		—.000		—.141
79 Chicago suburb (north)		—.114		—.172

* Significant $F_{.01}$, $t_{.05}$ (one-tailed).
† Significant $F_{.01}$, but not $t_{.05}$ (one-tailed).
‡ Includes fewer than 10 cases.
§ Includes 10 to 20 cases.
¶ Includes no cases.

FED 3 (N = 1100)		FED 4 (N = 830)		FED 5 (N = 338)	
(1) F.E3	(2) F.E3	(1) F.E4	(2) F.E4	(1) F.E5	(2) F.E5
.248	.257	.218	.226	.366	.385
19.85	12.78	12.56	8.06	10.23	6.66
—.047	—.047	.074	.071	—.095§	—.117§
—.045	—.043	.031	.035	—.114	—.142
. . .	. . .	. . .	. . .	. . .	. . .
.060	.041	.368*	.373*	.033‡	.030‡
.037	.023	.114*	.122*	—.005	—.059
.510‡	.491‡	—.176‡	—.229‡	—.791‡	—.748‡
.015	.001	.118*	.115*	.038	.035
—.051	—.047	—.050	—.055	.023	—.001
—.039	—.042	—.013	—.018	—.092§	—.095§
	. . .		§		‡
	—.115		.047		—.063§
	—.022		.002		—.045§
	—.130		.094		—.076‡
	—.050		.056		.012
	—.108		—.016		.071
	.076‡		.237†		.296‡
	—.126		.009§		—.214‡
	—.169*		—.018		.059
	—.104		.102		.137
	—.107		—.055		.006§
	—.085		.044		—.053

Among boys, community size was associated in an interesting way with parental education, after controlling on other parental traits and for the youth's ability. Sons of poorly educated fathers were less likely to go to college if living in very small communities, whereas the sons of better-educated men in such communities displayed high college attendance rates. (Though muted, that pattern is almost reversed among the girls.) Among boys, the coefficients on farmers in the father's occupation set are consistently positive where the smallest communities display high rates of college going and vice versa; there seems to be no serious multicollinearity problem here. What these patterns may reflect or portend with respect to urbanization of farming areas is suggestive, though interpretations must be cautious. Whatever the policy for locating colleges, we would expect the particular features of the rural community to have a major effect on the likelihood that youth will attend college: rich versus poor areas, farming versus coal communities, and so on.

Specific Effects of Accessibility on College Attendance

In the Illinois as in the Wisconsin regressions for all male and for all female youth, personal ability and parental background manifested stable impacts on rates of college attendance. That is, the addition of a set of categorical variables for college-access types did not affect the coefficients linked to ability or parental background. On the other hand, in both Wisconsin and Illinois the coefficients on accessibility categories were highly sensitive to the inclusion of ability and background variables. (The first of these findings is displayed clearly in a comparison of the two equations for each sex in Table 48.) What remains to be explained by access types when these are introduced in an equation with controls for ability and parental background is almost totally summed up for girls in the generally higher rates of college attendance from the smallest noncollege localities.

Among the boys, two positively deviant cases still stand out: the sample for private universities and that for the city of Chicago. The former reflects the particular sample from East St. Louis; after controlling for ability and parental background, we are apparently observing a school-selectivity effect and possibly an effect of classroom composition on college going beyond what might be predicted on the basis of the ability and status of the individual students in that subsample. School-selectivity and composition effects are not so manifest for Chicago; the sample included vocational along with elite schools and reveals different patterns for boys and girls. Some unraveling of these puzzles will emerge when we examine the regressions within ability (or paternal schooling) categories, for we will be able to examine interaction effects that are concealed in Table 48.

Interaction Effects on College Attendance for Illinois

Looking first at the multiple regressions within ability quarters for the separate sexes, we may ask two general questions. What patterns can we discern within each ability category in the relationships between parental background and college attendance? Controlling for parental background in order to avoid some of the effects of biased samples, what effects of accessibility on college attendance emerge for each ability category?

Among males, the most dramatic effects of parental background occur in the second quarter for ability (Table 49: the coefficients ascend steeply and regularly with education of either parent except for a leveling off when father's schooling exceeded college completion). Among girls, the effects of both father's and mother's education appear to be substantial for all ability ranks (but especially for father's schooling among girls in the lowest category of ability). These patterns have little in common with what we observed for Wisconsin, except for the consistently strong contrasts between sons and daughters of less- and of better-educated parents even when those variables are entered in the same equations (which might have introduced severe distortions on account of multicollinearities).

Contrasting college-accessibility types within ability categories, strong positive coefficients reappear for males in the private university category. This holds across all four sets of equations, though most strongly in the second quarter of ability; given the nature of the sample, perhaps this was to be expected. Results for Chicago are something else. For males, the important contrast between rates of college attendance from Chicago high schools versus high schools in noncollege towns occurs in the lowest quarter on ability. The Chicago sample is not distinctive among girls in any of the within-ability regressions, with their controls for parental background.

The regression coefficients for public junior college and extension center access types in Tables 49 and 50 may be compared with the differentials of Table 47. However, it must be kept in mind that the base for comparison in Table 47 was all noncollege towns, whereas the omitted dummy variable in the access set in the regressions was the smallest category of noncollege places. Hence, we should consider the regression coefficients on public junior colleges not only as they are shown directly but also in relation to (as they differ from) the coefficients on the noncollege towns with populations of 1,000–2,499 and 2,500–9,999. When this is done, the introduction of controls for family background (Table 49) alters the relative position of communities with public junior colleges very little. Among boys of lowest ability, the coefficient for public junior colleges is significantly positive as compared with small noncollege towns and is moderately above the coefficients on other noncollege communities and communities with extension centers. Among boys in the upper half of the ability distribution (and particularly among those in category 3), the coefficients on communities with public junior colleges are strongly negative, as are those for towns with extension centers. Among the least able girls, the coefficient on communities with public junior colleges is higher (less negative) than for noncollege communities with over a thousand population or for communities with an extension center, though it is negative compared with the country villages. The most able girls living in towns with public junior colleges turn out again (as in Table 47) to attend college relatively seldom. As in Table 47, but in contrast to the boys, it is among girls in the next to top quarter that we found the highest positive coefficients associated with residence in a community possessing a public junior college, even after controlling for parental background. Overall, when we sum up the evidence presented in Tables 47 through 50, there is remarkably little in common between the male and female patterns on the college-accessibility variables.

Multiple regressions within separate categories of father's education are set forth in Tables 51 and 52. The coefficients of determination here are consistently higher than in the regressions previously shown within categories of ability because the latter is a better predictor of college attendance rates than is either family background or college-access type. Thus, notice the consistently monotonic patterns of the regression coefficients by ability. As for Wisconsin, we now are in a position also to identify interactive effects of mother's education on college attendance rates within each category of paternal education, though in some instances cases are so few as to constrain inference. The category for fathers with postcollege education has been omitted as a design variable because it constituted too small a subsample for such treatment.

Among boys, maternal schooling made relatively little difference given father's education, with the notable exception of sons of men with 1–3 years of high school and (in lesser degree) sons of college graduates. There was a definite break (for both boys and girls) at Some College among mothers when fathers were in the categories High School 1–3 or College 4, and among boys the highest MED coefficients were at College 1–3 for other FED categories as well (if we exclude erratic small subsamples). For girls, but not for boys, coefficients rose monotonically up through mother's completion of college when fathers had some college or had completed it.

In Tables 51 and 52 the access category, "university, private," turns up again with the favorable coefficients we should by now expect, and for boys, the city of Chicago comes in next. Within categories of paternal schooling, the communities with junior colleges lose their positive coefficients for boys as they did in the simple cross-tabulations. And as in Table 47, negative coefficients are found for extension centers. Among girls whose fathers are in the lower categories on schooling, the maximum contrast across college-access categories is entirely within the noncollege set, across subcategories by community size; in none of the subsamples for father's education were there significant differences between the regression coefficients on any accessibility category in the college set and rates of attendance from noncollege communities, with the exception of the negative differential for the Chicago sample of daughters of high school graduates. In the Illinois samples, although it looks at first sight as if the proximity of public junior colleges might be encouraging college attendance (at least among youth of lower measured ability), we may instead be seeing the effects of community or high school differences in socioeconomic composition.

4. THE NORTH CAROLINA EVIDENCE FURTHER CONSIDERED

As in the rest of the South, denominational participation in higher education together with steeply stratified relationships within and between the races found expression in the North Carolina system of higher education. There was strong denominational control over collegiate education during the nineteenth century, laggard participation in land-grant development, and many private two-year colleges—with low rates of persistence through, and especially beyond, high school. Furthermore, as in other states of Appalachia, there are wide cultural distances between remote mountain communities and the richer agricultural areas and urban centers. Whereas private junior colleges were socially elite schools located in the economically favored parts of the state (though not in its main urban centers), public two-year colleges are of recent origin and have been sited mainly in poorer towns or more isolated rural sections.

As in Illinois, the shift of dominance within the system of higher education from private denominational to public colleges came only during this century. The prestige of small private colleges has persisted in North Carolina, which continues to have one of the highest percentages of college enrollment in private institutions outside of southern New England. In 1968, of all students attending college in the state, a third were in the private sector, making North Carolina seventh among the states for proportion attending private colleges. Massachusetts was the highest at two-thirds—in contrast to the nationwide average of just under one-fifth.

Though North Carolina was among the first to charter a state university, private schools predominated through most of the nineteenth century; the prevailing influence happened to be Presbyterian, though such well-known colleges as Wake Forest (Baptist, 1838) and Duke (originally Methodist Trinity, 1852) were founded, together with many small two-year colleges, often for girls only. The expansion of public higher education was stimulated by the Morrill Act, but response was sluggish. Gradually the older normal schools became state colleges and, more recently, branches of the University of North Carolina. Despite increasingly heavy investment in public higher education, North Carolina still has one of the lowest transition rates from secondary school to college. In 1963, that state was exactly at the Southern mean of .60 in ratio of high school graduates to 18-year-olds. But with only 36 percent of secondary graduates entering college, it stood below the Southern average of 47 percent and the national one of 51 percent. Thus, out of the 18-year-old age cohort, North Carolina was sending 22 percent to college compared to a Southern average of 28 and a national average of 36 percent. In 1968, North Carolina held about the same relative position; 41 percent of high school graduates entered college as compared to 57 percent for the nation as a whole.[11]

The map of colleges within North Carolina still reflects the early antipathy of towns to nearby colleges. Indeed the charter of the university in 1789 "provided that it could not be located within five miles of any seat of government or any place where law or equity courts met." Private institutions are also widely scattered. More recently new public junior colleges (with special emphasis on collegiate two-year technical education) have been systematically placed to reach into all parts of the state. Seen against this socio-historical background, some of the contrasts between Illinois and North Carolina with respect to college-access patterns and attendance become more comprehensible. Thus, when examining some of the regressions it will prove useful to consider the "within 20 miles" besides the "within community" profiles only, as was done for Wisconsin. First, however, we turn to a special 1961 study for an analysis of counties as sites for colleges.

5. COUNTY CHARACTERISTICS AND COLLEGE ATTENDANCE, 1961

It would have been possible to carry out extensive explorations of the effects of county characteristics upon rates of college going in many states. Resources for this project, however, would not have covered such inquiries in addition to the analyses that took individuals as the unit of observation. Given the seemingly distinctive spatial pattern of accessibility to college in North Carolina and the historical attitudes just mentioned, 1961 county rates of continuation into college by high school graduates were classified separately by county median incomes and by proportions of adults with at least some college education (Table 53). Without differentiating the counties, total rates of continuation range from 31 percent in noncollege counties to 45 percent in counties having more than one college or university. Among counties having no college or no more than a single public college, those with the lowest median family incomes have definitely lower continuation rates than do those with higher median incomes; however, above the $2,500 line there is no further association between levels of income

[11] These figures are all taken from the summary tables and the analysis for each state in Willingham (1970).

and attendance, and the one distinction mentioned does not entail more than about a 5-point difference in percentage of attendance. Only one county with a private institution (in this case a junior college) fell in the lowest category for median incomes, and none with multiple institutions was in that category. This explains in part the finding that, taking all counties with colleges as a set (next to last line Table 53), it is those with highest family incomes that stand out, though again only by 5 percent. There is some correlation between college-access type and county-income median, and possibly some interaction between such categories and college attendance rates by youth from the several counties, but on the whole, classification by median family incomes leaves unaffected the differentials in county college attendance rates across college-access types.

When we classify counties by level of adult schooling we find relationships rather different from those based on classification by median income. Indeed, if we look only at counties with inter-

TABLE 53 ***County college attendance rates among 1961 North Carolina high school graduates by selected county characteristics***

	Median family income (1959)		
	(0–2,499) *Low*	*(2,500–3,999)* *Middle*	*(Above 4,000)* *High*
College accessibility within county	*Percentage of high school graduates entering college (numbers of counties), 1961*		
No college	28.6 (20)	31.5 (36)	32.4 (9)
Public college or university	27.0 (2)	42.2 (3)	41.9 (1)
Private college or university		33.4 (5)	39.3 (5)
Private junior college	35.3 (3)	32.4 (5)	36.1 (2)
Multiple colleges and/or universities		46.8 (2)	44.5 (7)
Mean of college-county percentages	36.0 (5)	36.6 (15)	41.5 (15)
Mean of all county percentages	30.1 (25)	33.0 (51)	38.1 (24)

SOURCE: Data on college or university characteristics are from Hamilton, 1962, pp. 237–238. Data on median incomes and on education are from the 1960 U.S. Census of Population. Data on rates of continuation into college are from Hamilton, 1962, pp. 28, 243–246.

mediate levels of adult schooling, the variations by college-access types in proportions of youth attending college are negligible. Among counties with the best-schooled adults, the noncollege counties match those with private junior colleges, but it is those with public colleges or with more than one college that have the distinctively high rates of college going.

The measures used in this brief intercounty overview are very crude indexes of characteristics that may operate especially among the marginal decision makers with respect to college attendance. Nevertheless, they point once again to the importance both of seeking sensitive indicators for counties and of taking account of individual characteristics that affect college-going behavior generally, or responsiveness to accessibility of a college, or both.

Effects of Community Size

Presumably the spatial gradients in communication and in modernization are steeper in North Carolina than in any of the other SCOPE states or in Wisconsin. To specify those gradients would

Percent of persons in county 25 yrs. or older who had some college			
(Under 9.0) Low	*(9.0–12.0) Middle*	*(Above 12.0) High*	*Totals*
28.6 (39)	33.3 (18)	35.4 (8)	30.7 (65)
	34.2 (2)	43.5 (4)	40.4 (6)
29.9 (1)	35.8 (6)	39.8 (3)	38.3 (10)
42.9 (1)	32.0 (6)	35.6 (3)	34.0 (10)
	39.1 (2)	45.6 (7)	44.9 (9)
36.4 (2)	34.6 (16)	42.3 (17)	39.1 (35)
29.0 (41)	33.9 (34)	36.1 (25)	33.6 (100)

require a more detailed categorization of data within the county groupings used in Table 53.[12] Unfortunately, data on community size that were used in specifying noncollege-access categories for the regressions do not meet the stipulations, although for North Carolina the coefficients by population size do relate to college-going behavior more, as one would expect a priori, than in the sample for Illinois.[13] Whichever subsample or regression equation is examined, the (omitted dummy) smallest noncollege communities in North Carolina displayed either lower rates of entry to college than in other noncollege communities or merely negligible reverse differentials (Tables 54 through 58).[14] Even allowing for ability and family background, there is for males a monotonic size effect on college going from the communities without colleges (equation (2)*M* in Table 54); the regression coefficients rise slowly but steadily with size of community up to 10,000 and then jump to .106 for the largest towns. Among girls, there is no parallel pattern. This sex contrast is partially reflected in the behavior of the constant or intercept in the equations. Specifically, the equations predict that among girl high school graduates who are low in ability, who have relatively uneducated parents, whose fathers are employed in clerical jobs, and who reside in small communities without colleges, a sixth will enter college; among comparable boys the predicted proportion is only half as large.

The favorable effect of residing in the largest noncollege towns recurs among boys within each ability range, though especially in the high-medium category (Table 55). In the regressions separating subsamples by father's education rather than youth's ability (not shown), this effect of community size occurs mainly at the elementary and high school 4 levels of father's education, where observations also are most numerous. Among girls, a damped repetition of this relationship between size of noncollege community and college attendance rates shows up in the regressions for the subsample in ability quarter 2 and for the subsamples of girls whose fathers had at least finished high school (Tables 56 and 58). Among daughters of the least-educated parents, the figures are

[12] Some of these problems are a primary concern in Plunkett and Bowman (1972).

[13] Illinois college attendance rates may have been misleadingly high in the smallest noncollege communities, given the small number of cases in such communities and the lack of representation from the southern part of the state.

[14] Because the range in sizes of communities without colleges was greater in North Carolina than in the Illinois samples (despite the very wide scattering of colleges across North Carolina), the specifications by population size include an extra size class, from 10,000 to 20,000, within the noncollege set in the regressions for North Carolina.

erratic; if anything, such girls, if they live in a larger noncollege town, are less likely to enter college than those living in smaller communities.

Specific Effects of Accessibility on College Attendance

As we have seen, for both Wisconsin and Illinois the regression coefficients on ability and on paternal education for both sexes were stable. This stability is repeated for North Carolina (Table 54). However, the coefficients for accessibility were less sensitive to inclusion of ability and parental-status variables than in the data for Illinois. To be sure, residence in Charlotte clearly fostered college attendance in the raw comparisons, but this town shifted to a comparatively unfavorable position in the regression equation of Table 54. And among girls, residence in a town with a state college became a favorable indicator only after introducing controls for ability and parental background. On the other hand, among communities with colleges, those having private junior colleges had the largest proportions of boys going on to college in both the raw comparisons and the regressions. Among girls, first and second place went to the multiple-college towns and the towns with private junior colleges, with or without the introduction of ability and status controls.

Little of this picture carries over when we deal with classifications of accessibility in the wider 20-mile zone. The main import of comparison between equations (3)*M* and (2)*M* appears to be the advantage of living near to, but not in, towns with a state college or university as compared with any other locality.[15] In view of the pattern among coefficients for the within-community access types, it is surprising that we find negative coefficients on the categories for "private junior colleges" and "private four-year and junior college" situations within 20 miles. Perhaps even more striking is the fact that among girls the highest rates of continuation into college are for those who finished high school in communities more than 20 miles from the nearest college. Anyone who would claim that the data for North Carolina manifest a clear effect of college accessibility upon attendance—rather than manifesting effects of other community traits—will have to work hard to make out his case.

Interaction Effects on College Attendance

The confusing or even contradictory picture that has just been sketched is not cleared up greatly by examining further the regressions run within categories of ability (Tables 55 and 56) or of

(Text continued on p. 222)

[15] This fact will not surprise those who know the socioeconomic map of these North Carolina locations, though it is not so clear why this pattern comes through even with controls for parental backgrounds.

TABLE 54 ***Regression analysis of college attendance rates of male and female 1966 North Carolina high school graduates***

	Male (N = 5481)			*Female (N = 5896)*		
Equation number	*(1) M*	*(2) M*	*(3) M*	*(1) F*	*(2) F*	*(3) F*
R^2	*.321*	*.324*	*.326*	*.288*	*.293*	*.297*
F	*117.31*	*84.25*	*72.99*	*107.98*	*78.39*	*65.01*
Constant	.076	.068	.066	.169	.182	.250
Ability quarters						
1. *Low*	. . .	. . .	. . .	. . .	. . .	. . .
2.	.175*	.172*	.173*	.134*	.132*	.139*
3.	.401*	.399*	.401*	.328*	.325*	.331*
4. *High*	.560*	.558*	.561*	.478*	.478*	.486*
NA.	.137*	.141*	.142*	.060	.063	.060
Father's education						
1. *Elementary*	. . .	. . .	. . .	. . .	. . .	. . .
2,3. *High school*	.062*	.064*	.067*	.044*	.049*	.048*
4. *College 1–3*	.103*	.106*	.108*	.079*	.086*	.085*
5a. *College graduate*	.107*	.114*	.115*	.112*	.121*	.122*
5b. *Postgraduate*	.040	.044	.047	.139*	.150*	.148*
NA.	.007	.007	.012	—.057*	—.055*	—.058*
Mother's education						
1. *Elementary*	. . .	. . .	. . .	. . .	. . .	. . .
2,3. *High school*	.087*	.089*	.094*	.085*	.084*	.082*
4. *College 1–3*	.163*	.167*	.172*	.251*	.247*	.243*
5a. *College graduate*	.213*	.213*	.221*	.302*	.300*	.295*
5b. *Postgraduate*	.205*	.209*	.216*	.317*	.311*	.300*
NA.	—.001	.004	.004	.046*	.044†	.044†
Father's occupation						
0. *Workman, service,*	. . .	. . .	. . .	. . .	. . .	. . .
machine operator	—.045*	—.050	—.053	—.090*	—.102*	—.101*
1. *Skilled craftsman, technician*	—.042*	—.046	—.046	—.061*	—.070*	—.069*
2. *Clerical, sales*	. . .	. . .	. . .	. . .	. . .	. . .
3. *Farm operator*	.017	.009	—.007	—.002	—.016	—.024
4. *Business proprietor*	.029	.024	.023	—.002	—.010	—.008
5. *Artist, entertainer*	.057‡	.063‡	.063‡	.080‡	.061‡	.067‡
6. *Manager, official, executive*	.022	.022	.024	—.008	.005	.007
7. *Professional*	.084*	.083*	.081*	—.060*	—.069*	—.070*
8. *NA*	—.004	—.007	—.008	—.086*	—.096*	—.096*
Accessibility within community						
00 *None: population 0–999*		. . .			. . .	
01 *None: population 1,000–2,499*		.019			—.009	

	Male (N = 5481)			Female (N = 5896)		
Equation number	*(1) M*	*(2) M*	*(3) M*	*(1) F*	*(2) F*	*(3) F*
R^2	.321	.324	.326	.288	.293	.297
F	117.31	84.25	72.99	107.98	78.39	65.01
Accessibility within community (cont.):						
02 *None: population 2,500–9,999*		.028†			.031†	
03 *None: population 10,000–20,000*		.106*			.015	
13 *State college*		—.082†			.050	
14 *Private college*		.006			—.017	
16 *Junior college (public)*		.034			—.063*	
17 *Junior college (private)*		.059*			.041†	
26 *Multiple*		—.004			.087*	
39 *Charlotte*		—.017			—.041*	
Accessibility within 20 miles						
00 *None*			. . .			. . .
11 *State university*			.098*			—.006
13 *State college*			.079*			—.064*
14 *Private college*			.029			—.149*
16 *Junior college (public)*			.041†			—.119*
17 *Junior college (private)*			—.052			—.139*
21 *Multiple junior colleges*			.076*			—.041
22 *Private college + junior college (public)*			.027			—.123*
23 *Private college + junior college (private)*			—.056*			—.086*
24 *State college + junior college*						—.029
25 *State college + private college*			.022			—.051
26 *Multiple private colleges*			—.003			—.079*
27 *Multiple private colleges + junior college*			.053†			—.027
28 *Multiple four-year colleges*			.001			—.038†
30 *Multiple two-year and four-year colleges*						—.009
39 *Charlotte*			—.021			—.107*
59 *Winston-Salem*			—.023			—.090*

* Significant $F_{.01}$, $t_{.05}$ (one-tailed).

† Significant $F_{.01}$, but not $t_{.05}$ (one-tailed).

‡ Includes fewer than 10 cases.

TABLE 55 ***Regression analysis of college attendance rates of male 1966 North Carolina high school graduates by ability quarters***

	Ability 1 (N = 1806)		*Ability 2 (N = 1396)*	
Equation number	*(1) M.A1*	*(2) M.A1*	*(1) M.A2*	*(2) M.A2*
R^2	.040	.049	.079	.093
F	4.15	3.41	6.52	5.22
Constant	.110	.092	.218	.205
Father's education				
1. *Elementary*	. . .	. . .	. . .	. . .
2,3. *High school*	.028†	.028†	.087*	.091*
4. *College 1–3+*	.095*	.095*	.176*	.187*
5a. *College graduate*	.095†	.088†	.127*	.152*
5b. *Postgraduate*	.027‡	.045‡	—.046	—.043
NA.	—.015	—.013	.003	.002
Mother's education				
1. *Elementary*	. . .	. . .	. . .	. . .
2,3. *High school*	.048*	.047*	.122*	.120*
4. *College 1–3+*	.075*	.072*	.166*	.171*
5a. *College graduate*	.178*	.173*	.367*	.350*
5b. *Postgraduate*	.109‡	.100‡	.319*	.315*
NA.	.013	.013	.032	.041
Father's occupation				
0. *Workman, service, machine operator*	—.036	—.035	—.046	—.042
1. *Skilled craftsman, technician*	.002	.006	—.191*	—.092*
2. *Clerical, sales*	. . .	. . .	. . .	. . .
3. *Farm operator*	—.034	—.024	.000	.008
4. *Business proprietor*	.034	.037	—.018	—.018
5. *Artist, entertainer*	§	§	§	§
6. *Manager, official, executive*	.008	.008	.006	.005
7. *Professional*	.214*	.222*	.099	.110†
8. *NA*	—.025	—.021	.040	.036
Accessibility within community				
00 *None: population 0–999*		. . .		. . .
01 *None: population 1,000–2,499*		.018		.003
02 *None: population 2,500–9,999*		—.017		.072*
03 *None: population 10,000–20,000*		.097*		.098†

Ability 3 (N = 1044)		*Ability 4 (N = 1127)*	
(1) M.A3	*(2) M.A3*	*(1) M.A4*	*(2) M.A4*
.076	*.083*	*.075*	*.087*
4.69	*3.38*	*5.02*	*3.90*
.454	.429	.586	.572
. . .	. . .	. . .	. . .
.050	.052	.109*	.116*
.035	.043	.139*	.147*
.070	.077	.146*	.158*
.033	.043	.091†	.104†
.056	.056	.025	.029
. . .	. . .	. . .	. . .
.085*	.097*	.150*	.156*
.186*	.196*	.209*	.217*
.222*	.236*	.188*	.198*
.201†‡	.214†‡	.257*	.270*
−.178*	−.165*	−.038	−.034
−.017	−.024	−.056†	−.065*
−.035	−.040	−.046†	−.056†
. . .	. . .	. . .	. . .
.209*	.195*	−.012	−.032
.131*	.118*	−.028	−.028
§	§	.107¶	.076¶
.106*	.106*	−.033	−.032
.154*	.149*	.012	.002
.029	.022	.023	.023
	. . .		. . .
	.022		.050
	.067		.007
	.149†		.092†

TABLE 55 (continued)

	Ability 1 (N = 1806)		Ability 2 (N = 1396)	
Equation number	(1) M.A1	(2) M.A1	(1) M.A2	(2) M.A2
R^2	.040	.049	.079	.093
F	4.15	3.41	6.52	5.22
Accessibility within community (cont.):				
13 State college		−.124*		−.167†
14 Private college		.003		−.036
16 Junior college (public)		.115*		.010
17 Junior college (private)		.074†		.184*
26 Multiple		.031		−.086†
29 Charlotte		.025		−.022

* Significant $F_{.01}$, $t_{.05}$ (one-tailed).
† Significant $F_{.01}$ but not $t_{.05}$ (one-tailed).
‡ Includes 10 to 20 cases.
§ Includes no cases.
¶ Includes fewer than 10 cases.

TABLE 56 Regression analysis of college attendance rates of female 1966 North Carolina high school graduates by ability quarters

	Ability 1 (N = 2314)		Ability 2 (N = 1633)	
Equation number	(1) F.A1	(2) F.A1	(1) F.A2	(2) F.A2
R^2	.079	.084	.125	.134
F	10.98	7.76	12.79	9.20
Constant	.223	.224	.312	.314
Father's education				
1. Elementary	. . .	. . .	. . .	. . .
2,3. High school	.002	.006	.080*	.083*
4. College 1–3	.011	.014	.090*	.098*
5a. College graduate	−.021	−.013	.163*	.163*
5b. Postgraduate	.153†	.162*	.298*	.287*
NA.	−.059*	−.057*	.005	.005
Mother's education				
1. Elementary	. . .	. . .	. . .	. . .
2,3. High school	.059*	.058*	.094*	.089*
4. College 1–3	.354*	.350*	.239*	.232*
5a. College graduate	.362*	.362*	.402*	.395*
5b. Postgraduate	.287*‡	.281*	.548*‡	.530*‡
NA.	.041†	.038	−.032	−.045

Ability 3 (N = 1044)		*Ability 4 (N = 1127)*	
(1) M.A3	*(2) M.A3*	*(1) M.A4*	*(2) M.A4*
.076	*.083*	*.075*	*.087*
4.69	*3.38*	*5.02*	*3.90*
	.121¶		.231†¶
	.071		.034
	.003		.044
	.003		—.046
	—.014		.040
	—.016		—.037

Ability 3 (N = 1103)		*Ability 4 (N = 765)*	
(1) F.A3	*(2) F.A3*	*(1) F.A4*	*(2) F.A4*
.114	*.133*	*.086*	*.103*
7.78	*6.11*	*3.88*	*3.25*
.449	.493	.626	.686
. . .	. . .	. . .	. . .
.055†	.057†	.084*	.092*
.150*	.157*	.081†	.096*
.153*	.153*	.106*	.132*
.076	.083	.120†	.153*
—.220*	—.215*	.014	.032
. . .	. . .	. . .	. . .
.132*	.120*	.108*	.103*
.227*	.217*	.207*	.203*
.304*	.287*	.203*	.203*
.224*‡	.217*‡	.206*‡	.185†‡
.155†	.141†	.049	.065

TABLE 56
(continued)

	Ability 1 (N = 2314)		Ability 2 (N = 1633)	
Equation number	*(1) F.A1*	*(2) F.A1*	*(1) F.A2*	*(2) F.A2*
R^2	.079	.084	.125	.134
F	10.98	7.76	12.79	9.20
Father's occupation				
0. *Workman, service machine operator*	—.102*	—.106*	—.133*	—.147*
1. *Skilled craftsman, technician*	—.078*	—.083*	—.149*	—.161*
2. *Clerical, sales*	. . .	. . .	. . .	. . .
3. *Farm operator*	—.065†	—.066†	—.018	—.042
4. *Business proprietor*	—.092*	—.092*	.005	—.002
5. *Artist, entertainer*	¶	¶	.129§	.123§
6. *Manager, official, executive*	—.008	—.005	—.006	—.009
7. *Professional*	—.109*	—.116*	—.191*	—.200*
8. *NA*	—.129*	—.135*	—.073	—.088†
Accessibility within community				
00 *None: population 0–999*		. . .		. . .
01 *None: population 1,000–2,499*		.005		.006
02 *None: population 2,500–9,999*		.005		.068†
03 *None: population 10,000–20,000*		—.012		.091†
13 *State college*		—.082†		.261*‡
14 *Private college*		—.008		—.032
16 *Junior college (public)*		.047		—.054
17 *Junior college (private)*		.036		.030
26 *Multiple*		.091*		.095*
29 *Charlotte*		—.015		—.021

* Significant $F_{.01}$, $t_{.05}$ (one-tailed).
† Significant $F_{.01}$, but not $t_{.05}$ (one-tailed).
‡ Includes 10 to 20 cases.
§ Includes fewer than 10 cases.
¶ Includes no cases.

Ability 3 (N = 1103)		*Ability 4 (N = 765)*	
(1) F.A3	*(2) F.A3*	*(1) F.A4*	*(2) F.A4*
.114	*.133*	*.086*	*.103*
7.78	*6.11*	*3.88*	*3.25*
—.092*	—.114*	—.108*	—.128*
—.026	—.041	.016	—.001
. . .	. . .	. . .	. . .
.061	.034	.048	.006
.034	.015	—.030	—.052
—.032§	—.066§	¶	¶
.012	.003	.048	.041
.035	.012	—.007	—.024
—.099	—.111	—.002	—.011
	. . .		. . .
	—.047		—.046
	—.009		—.036
	.025		—.079†
	.287§		¶
	.000		—.038
	—.208*		—.108
	.116†		.000
	.105*		.038
	—.070†		—.109

TABLE 57 ***Regression analysis of college attendance rates of male 1966 North Carolina high school graduates by father's education***

	FED 1 (N = 1414)		FED 2 (N = 933)	
Equation number	*(1) M.E1*	*(2) M.E1*	*(1) M.E2*	*(2) M.E2*
R^2	.204	.207	.261	.280
F	21.03	14.45	17.92	13.52
Constant	.036	.035	.089	.044
Ability quarters				
1. *Low*	. . .	. . .	. . .	. . .
2.	.123*	.124*	.167*	.169*
3.	.401*	.403*	.388*	.390*
4. *High*	.509*	.511*	.574*	.583*
NA.	.121†	.121†	.027‡	.038‡
Mother's education				
1. *Elementary*	. . .	. . .	. . .	. . .
2. *High school 1–3*	.032	.031	.078*	.087*
3. *High school 4*	.088*	.089*	.122*	.130*
4. *College 1–3*	.131*	.133*	.299*	.321*
5. *College 4*	.176*	.174*	.225‡	.217‡
6. *College 5+*	.363§	.361§	.279§	.274§
NA.	—.166*	—.165*	—.007	.018
Father's occupation				
0. *Workman, service, machine operator*	.040	.039	—.065	—.051
1. *Skilled craftsman, technician*	.057	.057	—.033	—.026
2. *Clerical, sales*	. . .	. . .	. . .	. . .
3. *Farm operator*	.081	.079	.011	.016
4. *Business proprietor*	.074	.077	.097	.101
5. *Artist, entertainer*	¶	¶	—.059§	—.013§
6. *Manager, official, executive*	.182*	.181*	.045	.067
7. *Professional*	.171‡	.169‡	.099‡	.058‡
8. *NA*	.067	.066	—.010	.007
Accessibility within community				
00 *None: population 0–999*		. . .		. . .
01 *None: population 1,000–2,499*		—.004		.044
02 *None: population 2,500–9,999*		—.017		.051

FED 3 (N = 1128)		*FED 4 (N = 635)*		*FED 5 (N = 390)*	
(1) M.E3	*(2) M.E3*	*(1) M.E4*	*(2) M.E4*	*(1) M.E5*	*(2) M.E5*
.270	*.279*	*.205*	*.212*	*.261*	*.270*
22.84	*16.39*	*8.80*	*6.30*	*7.28*	*5.17*
.088	.091	.140	.176	.054	.077
. . .	. . .	. . .	. . .	. . .	. . .
.219*	.213*	.243*	.237*	.208*	.196*
.425*	.424*	.365*	.362*	.353*	.345*
.602*	.601*	.570*	.560*	.520*	.514*
.143†	.139	.069§	.071§	.480§	.483§
. . .	. . .	. . .	. . .	‡	‡
.152*	.162*	.075	.090	−.028	−.015
.190*	.202*	.149†	.154†	.342*	.353*
.186*	.203*	.172*	.185*	.303*	.316*
.329*	.337*	.219*	.223*	.321*	.332*
.421‡	.437‡	.142‡	.120‡	.410‡	.419‡
−.088	−.067	.083‡	.094‡	.296§	.312§
−.044	−.053	−.054	−.071	−.056‡	−.064‡
−.067	−.076	−.071	−.096*	−.054	−.052
. . .	. . .	. . .	. . .	. . .	. . .
.025	−.009	.079	.054	.333§	.308§
−.071	−.078	.069	.054	.067	.067
.010§	.054§	.118§	.079§	.084§	.089§
−.074	−.077	.041	.039	.030	.029
.104	.097	.025	.025	.070	.067
−.074	−.076	.121	.103	−.006	−.019
	. . .		. . .		. . .
	.037		−.035		−.033
	.015		.060		−.032

TABLE 57
(continued)

	FED 1 (N = 1414)		FED 2 (N = 933)	
Equation number	*(1) M.E1*	*(2) M.E1*	*(1) M.E2*	*(2) M.E2*
R^2	*.204*	*.207*	*.261*	*.280*
F	*21.03*	*14.45*	*17.92*	*13.52*
Accessibility within community (cont.):				
03 *None: population 10,000–20,000*		.094†		.079
13 *State college*		—.068		.008§
14 *Private college*		—.043		.027
16 *Junior college (public)*		—.030		.112
17 *Junior college (private)*		.012		.258*
26 *Multiple*		.003		—.094
39 *Charlotte*		.012		—.014

* Significant $F_{.01}$, $t_{.05}$ (one-tailed).
† Significant $F_{.01}$, but not $t_{.05}$ (one-tailed).
‡ Includes 10 to 20 cases.
§ Includes fewer than 10 cases.
¶ Includes no cases.

TABLE 58
Regression analysis of college attendance rates of female 1966 North Carolina high school graduates by father's education

	FED 1 (N = 1542)		FED 2 (N = 1079)	
Equation number	*(1) F.E1*	*(2) F.E1*	*(1) F.E2*	*(2) F.E2*
R^2	*.162*	*.172*	*.220*	*.228*
F	*17.32*	*12.56*	*17.56*	*12.47*
Constant	.177	.186	.241	.253
Ability quarters				
1. *Low*	. . .	. . .	. . .	. . .
2.	.073*	.071*	.116*	.114*
3.	.282*	.285*	.355*	.357*
4. *High*	.446*	.451*	.564*	.571*
NA.	.034	.041	—.053‡	—.052‡
Mother's education				
1. *Elementary*	. . .	. . .	. . .	. . .
2. *High school 1–3*	.062†	.054	—.033	—.032
3. *High school 4*	.164*	.152*	.024	.028
4. *College 1–3*	.311*	.309*	.212*	.219*
5. *College 4*	.275‡	.266‡	.346*	.372*
6. *College 5+*	.907§	.846§	.143§	.164§
NA.	.007‡	—.004‡	—.049	—.051

FED 3 (N = 1128)		FED 4 (N = 635)		FED 5 (N = 390)	
(1) M.E3	(2) M.E3	(1) M.E4	(2) M.E4	(1) M.E5	(2) M.E5
.270	.279	.205	.212	.261	.270
22.84	16.39	8.80	6.30	7.28	5.17
	.162*		.005		.105‡
	—.077‡		—.050§		—.066§
	.010		.027		.000
	.041		.078‡		.142‡
	—.010		—.094		—.075‡
	—.014		—.093		—.052
	—.059		—.050		—.038

FED 3 (N = 1130)		FED 4 (N = 744)		FED 5 (N = 348)	
(1) F.E3	(2) F.E3	(1) F.E4	(2) F.E4	(1) F.E5	(2) F.E5
.217	.231	.252	.269	.268	.277
17.11	12.75	13.60	10.16	6.71	4.73
.119	.092	.280	.331	.473	.476
...	...	...	...	...	...
.181*	.178*	.148*	.153*	.259*	.240*
.335*	.328*	.385*	.384*	.414*	.393*
.489*	.483*	.462*	.468*	.494*	.485*
.129‡	.125‡	.126‡	.128‡	.330§	.315§
...	...	...	...	§	§
.056	.067	—.039	—.022	—.249‡	—.277‡
.220*	.233*	.104	.130	—.132	—.134
.309*	.321*	.195§	.222*	.019	.022
.366*	.373*	.273*	.309*	.026	.023
.318§	.303§	.172§	.150§	.056‡	.070‡
—.003	.018	.014§	.073§	.228§	.243§

TABLE 58 ***(continued)***

	FED 1 (N = 1542)		FED 2 (N = 1079)	
Equation number	(1) F.E1	(2) F.E1	(1) F.E2	(2) F.E2
R^2	.162	.172	.220	.228
F	17.32	12.56	17.56	12.47
Father's occupation				
0. *Workman, service, machine operator*	—.084	—.084	—.077	—.089
1. *Skilled craftsman, technician*	—.022	—.018	—.059	—.073
2. *Clerical, sales*	. . .	. . .	. . .	. . .
3. *Farm operator*	—.010	—.005	—.099	—.028
4. *Business proprietor*	—.132*	—.125*	.017	—.002
5. *Artist, entertainer*	¶	¶	¶	¶
6. *Manager, official, executive*	.268§	.259§	—.072	—.074
7. *Professional*	.089§	.085§	—.128‡	—.133‡
8. *NA*	—.106*	—.110*	—.088	—.100†
Accessibility within community				
00 *None: population 0–999*		. . .		. . .
01 *None: population 1,000–2,499*		—.030		.020
02 *None: population 2,500–9,999*		.072†		—.046
03 *None: population 10,000–20,000*		—.064		.082
13 *State college*		—.017		.018
14 *Private college*		—.009		.040
16 *Junior college (public)*		—.127*		—.035
17 *Junior college (private)*		.028		.065
26 *Multiple*		.052		.106
39 *Charlotte*		—.001		—.054

* Significant $F_{.01}$, $t_{.05}$ (one-tailed).

† Significant $F_{.01}$, but not $t_{.05}$ (one-tailed).

‡ Includes 10 to 20 cases.

§ Includes fewer than 10 cases.

¶ Includes no cases.

FED 3 (N = 1130)		FED 4 (N = 744)		FED 5 (N = 348)	
(1) F.E3	(2) F.E3	(1) F.E4	(2) F.E4	(1) F.E5	(2) F.E5
.217	.231	.252	.269	.268	.277
17.11	12.75	13.60	10.16	6.71	4.73
−.027	−.040	−.087	−.113†	−.272*	−.288*
−.016	−.022	−.066	−.077	−.157†	−.158†
. . .	. . .	. . .	. . .	. . .	. . .
.154†	.143†	−.049	−.123	.230§	.200§
.025	.015	.056	.035	−.022	−.031
−.196§	−.216§	.231§	.148§	.300§	.295§
.055	.051	−.010	−.022	−.042	−.047
.007	−.000	−.122†	−.126†	−.024	−.040
−.123*	−.129†	−.217*	−.223*	−.257‡	−.262‡
	. . .		. . .		. . .
	.006		−.046		.022
	.064		−.024		.055‡
	.134†		.085‡		.081‡
	.184‡		.373§		.158§
	.002		.049		.227*
	.001		−.013‡		.283§
	.150*		−.031		.090
	.178*		.007		.075
	−.014		−.133*		−.008

paternal education (Tables 57 and 58), setting aside differentials among smaller and larger noncollege places. For the least able males, towns with public junior colleges do appear to induce the highest rates of college attendance, as they did when no controls on family background were used. And among males in the second category of ability, towns with private junior colleges take first place as before. But there is no obvious explanation for the latter results or for the lack of any clear associations among the most able boys. The one consistent result for girls, recurring in all four quarters of ability, is that college attendance is high in Charlotte but low in towns with public junior colleges.

The regressions within categories of paternal education clarify some interactive relationships between effects of paternal and maternal schooling. At each level of paternal education the chances that a boy would attend college were improved substantially if his mother had at least completed high school; among sons of men who had not attended college there were further substantial effects of having a mother with college training. Maternal education appears to have had a somewhat stronger and more consistent influence among daughters than among sons, especially among children of noncollege men. (The coefficients in Table 58, regressions for daughters of college graduates, take the expected monotonic form after adjustment for the misleadingly high value of the intercept.) For girls as for boys, ability was, of course, important throughout.

It has been remarked already that associations between college accessibility and rates of college going wane when we analyze relationships within categories of paternal schooling, especially if controls are used for ability and parental background. It would, then, be surprising were strong associations to emerge from Tables 57 and 58. Among sons of men who entered but did not complete high school, those residing in communities with private junior colleges were definitely the most likely to enter college. A less strong association is found between residence in a multiple-college place and going to college among daughters of men who had finished high school. But since we cannot give any more than weak post hoc explanations for such findings, they have to be clearly marked "tentative." What does persist, whatever the controls or the subsample, is the positive relationship between size of community of residence and rates of continuation into college among boys from noncollege communities; boys in the largest of these communities appear to be the most consistently oriented toward college, whatever their own ability or their fathers' schooling. That same conclusion, rather than any assertion about the effect of college location upon likelihood of attending college, is what emerges finally from examination of the North Carolina scene.

5. ACCESSIBILITY AND ATTENDANCE WITHIN ABILITY/STATUS CATEGORIES

There are two solid reasons for examining subsamples of the secondary graduates classified simultaneously by ability and by parental status when trying to identify the factors determining attendance at college—in the present instance, the factor of accessibility. First, ability and status are everywhere powerful determinants of the rate of college going, and their effects are interactive; unless their interaction is identified for various subpopulations, we will go astray in trying to explain the differential effects of college accessibility. A related question has been kept in the foreground: which subpopulations or which sorts of individuals are the responsible and marginal decision makers whose behavior is most sensitive to variations in college accessibility, and under which conditions? Our exposition stands now at a point that facilitates bringing together the evidence from Massachusetts, Illinois, and North Carolina in a three-way matrix similar to that used earlier for Wisconsin.

As is always the case with detailed cross-tabulations, we are enabled to observe unconstrained interactions, though we exacerbate problems arising from random variations in small subsamples. In line with the appropriate caution, we limit the logit analysis here to comparing noncollege with public junior college communities in Illinois. Aside from sporadic examples such as the urban sample for Charlotte, this Illinois category of communities with public junior colleges is the only subcategory large enough to obtain all 12 ability/status categories for each sex. The demand of the analysis with respect to cell numbers is aggravated by the fact that the classification of paternal occupation (FOC) puts a sizable majority of cases into a middle category, leaving smaller fractions at top and bottom. As a result, we face the risk of gaps in deviant cells, most especially in those representing low ability but high parental status. The choice was unavoidable, for it was not practicable to divide the cases into thirds, as with the scores on SES. On the other hand, the classification of occupational status (for Massachusetts, Illinois, and North Carolina) closely approximates the one used by Medsker and Trent (specified at the bottom of Table 64) so that we can more readily compare our findings with theirs.

Analysis of Variance for Illinois

The statistical advantages of an analysis using logit transforms were discussed in Chapter 4 and need not be repeated. The "main effect" results (using restricted male and female matrices that include only noncollege and public junior college communities on the access variables) are shown for Illinois in Table 59. Access effects for males turn out to be nonsignificant, as in the Wisconsin comparison for state colleges and Extension Centers. Among males, furthermore, even the status categories turned out not to have significant effects. Among girls, the main effect of paternal occupation was highly significant, though it was decidedly overshadowed by the explanatory power of ability, and ability proved to be even more important among girls than among boys. None of the interaction items included in the analysis was strong enough to be significant at the 5 percent level, but for both sexes the interaction between access and ability was high enough to suggest that isolated observations of distinctively high attendance rates in towns with public junior colleges may not be wholly fortuitous. This might also be true for some other comparisons and in other states, even where some particular access/ability paternal-occupation cells have too few cases for consideration.

A Search for Repeated Patterns

We now look across states, for each sex, to see whether by inspection we can identify any common relationships that would escape us when working with only one table or one state at a time. We still retain the distinction by sex used thus far in nearly every tabulation and regression. In seeking common patterns we remain alert also for contrasting patterns. Table 60 simply gives the numbers of cases from the SCOPE samples for each cell of Table 61; placing

TABLE 59 ***Analyses of between-cell variance in logits of proportions attending college; Illinois, 1966***

	(Matrix for access categories "none" and "junior college")						
				Males		*Females*	
	df	*F.95*	*F.99*	*Sum of squares*	*F*	*Sum of squares*	*F*
Access	1	5.99	13.75	0.0579	0.888	0.0029	0.154
FOC	2	5.14	10.92	0.2442	1.872	0.6488	17.255
Ability	3	4.76	9.78	6.8010	34.769	5.8169	103.138
Access/FOC	2	5.14	10.92	0.0604	0.463	0.0897	2.383
Access/Ability	3	4.76	9.78	0.6159	3.148	0.1969	3.489
Ability/FOC	6	4.28	8.47	0.1783	0.457	0.2596	2.303
Access/Ability/FOC	6			0.3912		0.1126	
TOTAL	23			8.3489		7.1277	

frequencies in the cells with the percentages would make it very difficult to identify any patterns in the table of attendance rates.[16]

The first row of percentages under each state in Table 61 is the benchmark for comparisons: namely, rates of attendance for youth from noncollege communities. For males, several facts that may not have been so evident before now stand out. First, the noncollege towns of Massachusetts seem to be remarkably "open" so far as concerns status selectivity into college; attendance rates rise sharply from one ability category to another, but only among boys of low-middle ability is attendance definitely higher for sons of high-status fathers than for those of low-status fathers. In this matter, North Carolina takes an intermediate position, somewhat closer to Massachusetts than to Illinois. Holding ability and status constant, young men from the noncollege towns of North Carolina attended college more often than did those in the samples for Illinois. In fact, low-ability boys generally and low-status boys in each category of ability were less likely to enter college if they came from noncollege towns in Illinois than if they came from such communities in either of the other two states. This means that Illinois towns with junior colleges would have to show a marked advantage over noncollege towns in that state just to bring them up to the level of noncollege communities in the other two states.[17]

Among girls, the college attendance rates for North Carolina residents of noncollege towns are even closer to those for Massachusetts than among boys, and again they equal or surpass the rates in corresponding cells for Illinois—with the exception of the top ability category. In contrast to boys, however, attendance among girls from noncollege towns does rise with family status in all three states.

In addition to data for communities with two-year colleges only (to which we return shortly), figures for the Boston sample and for three additional categories of college access for North Carolina have been entered in Table 61. Consistently, the more able Boston boys (and to a lesser extent girls) less often attend college than do comparable youth living in noncollege places—and often less frequently than youth residing in a town with a junior college. It may be that the specification of family status is too crude to reveal the most pertinent differences in backgrounds, or possibly the environ-

(Text continued on p. 230)

[16] In Table 61 we have excluded all cases in which the denominator would be less than 10 and we have footnoted all cases with denominators between 10 and 19.

[17] Or such is the case if we ignore possible differences in high school completion rates and set aside the important questions as to what determines interstate contrasts in distributions of ability and occupational status.

TABLE 60 ***Numbers of observations in selected cells of SCOPE samples for three states***

State and college-access category	*Ability 1*			*Ability 2*		
	Occupational status			*Occupational status*		
	Low	*Middle*	*High*	*Low*	*Middle*	*High*
						Males
Massachusetts						
Noncollege	64	146	21	94	245	46
Junior college (public)	11	37	1	22	43	8
Boston sample	23	32	5	36	54	14
Illinois						
Noncollege	53	105	12	66	175	28
Junior college (public)	50	80	15	53	145	17
Extension center	16	40	3	24	75	14
North Carolina						
Noncollege	388	514	27	199	530	50
Junior college (public)	12	22	1	11	31	3
Junior college (private)	24	35	2	9	32	8
Private four-year	48	87	5	24	59	8
Charlotte	151	215	21	56	173	41
Multiple, misc.	46	48	4	24	51	7
						Females
Massachusetts						
Noncollege	88	219	21	96	260	73
Junior college (public)	25	50	5	33	98	7
Boston sample	45	74	5	53	108	22
Illinois						
Noncollege	69	132	16	67	216	23
Junior college (public)	42	107	17	54	147	41
Extension center	21	48	3	15	81	11
North Carolina						
Noncollege	523	680	50	218	586	54
Junior college (public)	18	31	0	10	46	4
Junior college (private)	40	54	1	11	50	7
Private four-year	46	82	10	27	76	6
Charlotte	199	275	32	64	255	65
Multiple, misc.	39	49	7	17	64	12

Ability 3			*Ability 4 (High)*		
Occupational status			*Occupational status*		
Low	*Middle*	*High*	*Low*	*Middle*	*High*
68	271	80	100	393	154
29	61	13	45	119	37
48	91	13	60	130	30
44	153	27	43	171	59
51	147	45	47	154	66
13	70	8	13	67	32
90	349	53	51	336	88
7	29	4	5	23	8
11	25	9	5	24	11
10	37	11	11	44	11
30	171	72	28	229	118
10	52	12	10	37	10
72	252	65	44	201	138
17	66	17	13	67	47
54	99	36	54	120	63
38	151	29	18	107	25
36	131	34	19	109	37
10	63	11	7	47	14
84	407	67	38	212	59
9	23	2	3	17	1
6	33	11	3	23	9
8	49	7	11	20	5
28	194	69	25	151	82
17	45	10	5	34	15

TABLE 61 ***College attendance rates: summary in a selective three-way matrix, by sex, for three SCOPE states***

State and college-access category	*Ability 1*			*Ability 2*		
	Occupational status			*Occupational status*		
	Low	*Middle*	*High*	*Low*	*Middle*	*High*
						Males
Massachusetts						
Noncollege	16	23	14	31	34	50
Junior college (public)	27*	25	†	41	46	
Boston	4	16		28	28	56
Illinois						
Noncollege	8	11	0*	15	30	54
Junior college (public)	14	24	27	41	32	41
Extension center	0*	15		17	25	43*
North Carolina						
Noncollege	12	13	26	33	34	58
Junior college (public)	33*	23		18*	35	
Junior college (private)	17	23			56	
Private four-year	4	16		29	29	
Multiple colleges	15	13		25	25	
Charlotte	11	18	33	37	34	44
						Females
Massachusetts						
Noncollege	16	19	38	28	38	52
Junior college (public)	20	16		27	26	
Boston	7	8		23	21	50
Illinois						
Noncollege	6	17	25	30	33	48
Junior college	10	22	35	26	38	42
Extension center	5	10		13*	30	27*
North Carolina						
Noncollege	15	19	24	30	37	52
Junior college (public)	33*	16		40*	30	
Junior college (private)	5	33		37*	34	
Private four-year	20	16	30*	22	34	
Multiple colleges	26	33		41	45	75*
Charlotte	20	18	41	37	43	44

* 10 to 19 cases in the denominator.

† Cells with no entries had fewer than 10 cases in the denominator.

Ability 3			*Ability 4 (High)*		
Occupational status			*Occupational status*		
Low	*Middle*	*High*	*Low*	*Middle*	*High*
65	56	56	89	89	90
35	66	69*	88	84	84
48	45	54*	72	78	74
48	62	82	74	84	80
43	48	49	79	73	86
62*	49		85*	64	87
62	61	77	80	81	91
	49			91	
46*	64			79	82*
60*	65	81*	64*	84	100*
60*	59	75*	90*	78	100*
57	60	68	75	81	86
58	67	75	84	92	90
53*	64	82*	79*	88	97
54	54	69	78	84	86
45	49	83	83	87	88
61	57	62	63*	81	78
40*	46	64*		79	100*
54	60	76	71	85	85
	43			71	
	76	91*		87	
	67		73*	80	
71*	73	90*		91	100*
50	63	67	68	79	91

ments of the high school neighborhoods sampled are exercising a differential effect. But we would need more detailed data—especially longitudinal data—to pursue some of these more recondite puzzles.[18]

In order to facilitate an indentification of effects attributable to the presence of two-year colleges (especially junior colleges), the data of Table 61 have been converted into the differences shown in Table 62. To simplify the maze of data and reduce erratic variations in cells with sparse observations, some of the ability/status cells were combined by dividing the samples into lower and upper half in ability. We also added detail for some of the more populated ability/status cells.

The less able boys in all three states are more likely to attend college if they live close to a public junior college than if they live in a noncollege community; this does not occur if they come from a high-status home (regardless of ability) or if they are of high ability (regardless of status). Living in a North Carolina community with a private junior college seems also to exert some effect upon the young men of less than median ability—but only if their families are of middling (neither low nor high) status. It is for the extension centers of Illinois (which generally are found in communities with low college attendance rates for both sexes) that we find the strong impact sought by proponents of such kinds of college: a markedly higher rate of entry to college specifically among boys of more than average ability but from low-status homes (+ 24 percent).

Among girls, responsiveness to opportunities to attend college is not very similar to what has just been pointed out for boys. Thus, most of the positive effects found among boys living in communities with a public junior college fade away in the figures for girls. In Massachusetts, such positive differences for girls as one might think worth mentioning occur just where they are absent for boys: in access effects on college attendance among girls from higher status backgrounds among the more able. In Illinois, the figures for girls tend to parallel those for boys, but the junior college differentials are small. The North Carolina samples for communities with public junior colleges are small, but positive effects worthy of attention do seem to occur among girls of low measured ability who come from modest homes. Residence in North Carolina communities with private junior colleges seems consistently to favor all but the least able girls from the poorest homes.

[18] At each ability/status level, except the cell for ability 2 with high occupational status, the young men of Charlotte, North Carolina, were more prone to go on to college than were their counterparts in the Boston sample. This is not repeated for girls, however.

A Comparison with Medsker and Trent

From the immediately preceding discussion, as from evidence brought out at many points along the way, it must be evident that boys and girls do not always respond similarly to opportunities to attend college; in fact there are some notable contrasts in the patterns for the two sexes. On the other hand, where the sex differences appear erratically rather than systematically, combining the data for both sexes could smooth out irregularities due to small samples or to errors in the variables. Moreover, the main predecessor to this report (by Medsker and Trent) presents no data separated by sex simultaneously with a three-way classification by ability, status, and college-access profile; if we are to make comparisons, we must put our data for boys and for girls together. This could have been done by giving the same weight to each sex in the ability/status cells or by using the observed weights from the samples. However, there seem to have been some sex biases in the sampling of schools for the SCOPE inquiry that we used. We did eliminate some extreme discrepancies from Tables 60 through 62 simply by using only certain access types, but the sample weights by sex remain suspect. We chose the simpler alternative and counted the sexes as equal, despite the marked majority of boys in the highest ability rank that could be inferred from the numbers in Table 60. The outcome of this arbitrary operation is displayed in Table 63 (from which are excluded all cells with a male-female total of less than 20 cases or with *either* a male or a female count under eight). Table 63 is as nearly comparable to the Medsker and Trent data (given in Table 64) as we could make it.

With four exceptions the figures in each row fall quite tidily into line.[19] Making all reasonable allowance for nonsubstantive disparity among the many cells in the table, some generalizations

[19] The first exception is the low college attendance rates among Massachusetts young people of high-middle ability from high-status homes; and the second is the very high rate among similar youth in Illinois. Averaging across the sexes was not sufficient to correct for what appears to be definitely biased random errors in these two cases. Consequently, for the ability/status group involved there is a high positive differential for junior college communities in Massachusetts and an even higher negative differential for such communities in Illinois. The other two peculiarities occur in the North Carolina figures for attendance from communities with public junior colleges; there seems nothing beyond sampling error to explain the very high college attendance rate among the most disadvantaged youth—both in status and in measured ability—from these North Carolina towns. On the other hand, the college attendance rate from such towns among middle-status youth of ability class 3 is too low for the rest of the North Carolina pattern. These aberrations, if they are such, are again reflected in the associated differentials in college attendance rates.

TABLE 62 ***Analysis of percentage-point differences between college attendance rates from selected access types by ability/status categories, three states, 1966***

	Rates of attendance from noncollege places			*Percentage-point advantages over noncollege places*				
				Public junior college localities			*Private junior college; North Carolina*	*Extension centers; Illinois*
	Massachusetts	*Illinois*	*North Carolina*	*Massachusetts*	*Illinois*	*North Carolina*		
	Males							
Ability quarters 1,2								
FOC: Low	25	12	19	+11	+16	+7	−1	−2
Middle	30	23	24	+6	+6	+4	+15	−1
High	39	38	47		−4		−17*	+3
Ability quarters 3,4								
FOC: Low	79	49	69	−13	+11	+9*	−13	+24
Middle	75	65	71	+3	−9	−7	−1	−9
High	78	80	86	+1	−9	−1	−21	0
FOC Low								
Ability 1	16	8	12	+11*	+6	+21*	+5	−8
2	31	15	33	+10	+26	−15*		+2
FOC Middle								
Ability 1	23	11	13	+2	+13	+10	+10	+4
2	34	30	34	+12	+2	+1	+22	−5
3	56	62	61	+10	−14	−12	+3	−13
4	89	84	81	−5	−11	+10	−2	−20
FOC High								
Ability 3	56	82	77	+13*	−33			
4	90	80	91	−6	+6		−9*	+7
	Females							
Ability quarters 1,2								
FOC: Low	20	18	20	+4	+1	+16	−9	−10
Middle	29	26	27	0	+5	−8	+7	−4
High	47	38	38	−5*	+1			−17
Ability quarters 3,4								
FOC: Low	68	57	59	−8	+5	−7*		−4
Middle	78	65	69	−2	+2	−10	+11	0
High	81	85	80	+8	−15		+10*	−1

	Rates of attendance from noncollege places			Percentage-point advantages over noncollege places				
				Public junior college localities			Private junior college; North Carolina	Extension centers; Illinois
	Massa-chusetts	Illi-nois	North Carolina	Massa-chusetts	Illi-nois	North Carolina		
				Females (cont.)				
FOC: Low								
Ability 1	16	6	15	+ 4	+ 4	+18*	−15	− 1
2	28	30	30	− 1	− 4	+10*	+ 7*	−17
FOC: Middle								
Ability 1	19	17	19	− 3	+ 5	− 3	+14	− 7
2	38	33	37	−12	+ 5	− 7	− 3	− 3
3	67	49	60	− 3	+ 8	−17	+14	− 3
4	92	87	85	− 4	− 6	−14	+ 2	− 8
FOC: High								
Ability 3	75	83	76	+ 7*	−21		+15*	−19*
4	90	88	85	+ 7	−10			+16*

* 10 to 19 cases in one of the denominators.

do emerge. In brief, the public junior colleges do indeed draw into college some low-status and low-ability youth who otherwise, one infers, would not continue collegiate education after high school. This effect seems to disappear among youth above the median in ability and seems not to be exerted by the *private* junior colleges of North Carolina; the effect of the latter is focused among middle-status persons at all ability levels except the top, and comes through even when we combine boys with girls. Any effect of the Illinois extension centers among boys is neutralized by the absence of effect among comparable girls (and these schools are usually in areas marked by generally low propensities to attend college).

These figures differ considerably from those reported by Medsker and Trent (hereafter designated the M-T sample) for several reasons. First of all, the M-T subsample of noncollege communities was small, and the youth from those communities with low-status backgrounds display very much lower rates of college attendance (especially at higher levels of ability) than do the respondents in our data. Since the categories for ability differ in the two studies exact comparisons are not possible, but one would expect the

TABLE 63 ***Percentage rates of college attendance; sexes combined in selective three-way matrix for Massachusetts, Illinois, and North Carolina***

College-access categories and states	*Ability 1 (Low)*			*Ability 2*		
	Occupational status			*Occupational status*		
	Low	*Middle*	*High*	*Low*	*Medium*	*High*
	Percentage rates of college attendance; sexes combined (excludes all cells with fewer than 20 cases in denominator)					
Noncollege						
Massachusetts	16	21	26	29	36	51
Illinois	7	14	26	23	33	45
North Carolina	14	16	25	32	36	55
Public junior colleges						
Massachusetts	23	20		34	36	
Illinois	12	23	31	33	35	42
North Carolina	33	20		29	32	
Private junior colleges						
North Carolina	11	28		30	45	
Extension centers						
Illinois	3	12		15	28	
Multiple colleges						
Boston, Mass.	6	12		25	24	53
Charlotte, N.C.	16	18	37	37	39	44
Other, N.C.	20	23		33	35	
	Percentage-point excess over rate from noncollege places					
Public junior colleges						
Massachusetts	+ 7	− 1		+ 5	0	
Illinois	+ 5	+ 9	+ 5	+10	+ 2	− 3
North Carolina	+19	+ 4		− 3	− 4	
Private junior colleges						
North Carolina	− 3	+12		− 2	+ 9	
Extension centers						
Illinois	− 4	− 2		− 8	− 5	

Ability 3			Ability 4		
Occupational status			Occupational status		
Low	Medium	High	Low	Medium	High
61	61	60	87	90	90
47	56	83	78	85	87
58	60	76	76	83	83
44	65	76	84	86	85
52	52	55	71	77	82
	46			81	
	70	80		83	85
43	55		80	71	82
51	50	62	75	81	80
54	62	68	72	80	88
65	66	82		85	100
−17	+ 4	+16	− 3	− 4	− 5
+ 5	− 4	−28	− 7	− 8	− 5
	−14			− 2	
	+10	+ 4		0	+ 2
− 4	− 1		+ 2	−14	− 5

TABLE 64 ***College attendance rates; three-way matrix from Medsker and Trent study of 1959 high school graduates***

College-access category of high school community	Ability: Low 40%			Ability: Middle 20%			Ability: High 40%		
	Occupational status			Occupational status			Occupational status		
	Low	Middle	High	Low	Middle	High	Low	Middle	High
	Percentage rates of college entry								
Noncollege	5	20	69*	28	29	50*	22	45	80
Junior college	31	40	63	39	49	80	53	69	86
Extension center	13	14	48	18	31	57	35	51	80
State college	18	24	59	25	48	71	41	65	89
San Francisco	30	35	57	26	57	65	49	57	74
	Percentage-point excess over rate from noncollege places								
Junior college	+26	+20	− 6	+11	+20	+30	+31	+24	+ 6
Extension center	+ 8	− 6	−21	−10	+ 2	+ 7	+13	+ 6	0
State college	+13	+ 4	−10	− 3	+19	+21	+19	+20	+ 9
San Francisco	+25	+15	−12	− 2	+28	+15	+27	+12	− 6
	Number of observations								
Noncollege	44	105	14	21	66	16	52	161	36
Junior college	254	487	74	97	257	61	154	540	196
Extension center	320	659	74	136	377	74	218	870	236
State college	213	432	66	91	266	52	132	613	213
San Francisco	66	169	28	27	113	20	78	191	59

* 10 to 19 cases in the denominator.

NOTE: Occupational classifications were as follows:
High = Professional, managerial, and executive
Middle = Semiprofessional, small businessmen, sales and clerical, skilled manual, foreman, and farm operator
Low = Semiskilled and unskilled manual

"Ability" was measured by the School and College Ability Test (SCAT). Scores on this test are highly correlated with those on the Academic Ability Test (AAT) developed by the Educational Testing Service and used on the SCOPE survey.

SOURCE: Medsker and Trent, 1965.

lowest quarter of our sample to display lower attendance rates than the lower 40 percent of the M-T data; in fact those expectations are not upheld. The two studies appear to be working with quite dissimilar sets of communities. Moreover, between 1959 and 1966 there was a rise both in numbers and in proportions of American youth who completed high school and in the proportions of high school graduates who continued into college.[20]

[20] See Willingham (1970), Table E, pp. 202–203, and his comments on California, p. 53.

Second, while rates of attendance from noncollege communities are lower in the M-T than in the SCOPE data, the discrepancies for youth from towns having public junior colleges take on another pattern, and a complex one. M-T found higher rates of college going among the lowest 40 percent in ability than the SCOPE data show for the lowest quarter in ability—except for the low-status/low-ability set in North Carolina. For the second ability quarter in the SCOPE data, rates of attendance at junior college among lowest-status youth are about the same as in the lowest of the nine M-T categories. But the M-T rates for the low-ability/low-status combination run consistently above the SCOPE middle-status rates in the second ability quarter. For the two higher ability categories, the SCOPE rates are above those of the M-T sample, though by no means to the same extent as for noncollege towns.[21]

The net excess of college attendance rates in communities with a junior college over rates where there is no college is given in the second block of entries on Tables 63 and 64. Virtually throughout, Medsker and Trent found large positive differentials for the communities with junior colleges; even at the lowest ability-status levels, those differences exceeded the ones drawn from the SCOPE sample. Perhaps the most striking result from the M-T sample is the large differential for all three status groups among the upper 40 percent in ability. Remembering the heavy weighting of California in the junior college M-T sample and the reliance on two Midwestern towns for the noncollege sample, the contrasting outcomes from the two studies may be less puzzling.

What Medsker and Trent called "multiple colleges" was actually San Francisco; even allowing this unrepresentative instance, comparisons with the other three multiple-college rows is confounded by the noncommensurate categories for ability. It does appear, however, that a larger proportion of the low-ability youth in San Francisco continue into college than in the SCOPE cities selected out for comparison (in Table 63). All the way through these tedious comparisons of the two investigations of the effect of junior colleges we have to keep in mind that the college attendance rates for *noncollege* communities are astonishingly low for the M-T sample; valid or not, those rates go far to explain the

[21] Unfortunately, none of the state college samples within the SCOPE states of North Carolina, Illinois, and Massachusetts provided adequate data for such an analysis, although the state colleges were important in the evidence for Wisconsin analyzed in Chapter 4.

apparent support for the public junior college inferred from the M-T data. All in all, divergencies among communities and among state cultures and traditions can explain more about contrasting rates of college attendance than can proximity to one or another kind of college, even when we allow for the youth's ability and for the status of his family.[22]

6. COLLEGE SELECTION IN ILLINOIS AND NORTH CAROLINA

College experiences and their consequences may be very different according to whether a youth starts his higher education close to home in a locally oriented college or at a distance and in a more cosmopolitan environment—or for that matter, at a distance in a quieter and less urban setting than the asphalt maze in which he spent his childhood. Elusive as the clinching evidence may be, the proximity of one or another college may be more important for the ways in which it influences choice among colleges than in its tendency to raise the total proportion of youth in a community who decide to enter collegiate life. The importance of location substitution effects was stressed in the chapter on Wisconsin, as were selectivity effects in the types of school attended. These considerations are more important where greater cultural disparities or gaps in communication are associated with geographic remoteness, as tends to be the case in Appalachian areas especially.

Distance to College and Locational Substitutions

An initial perspective on locational substitution across categories of ability and parental status can be obtained by looking at the proportions of youth who attend a college that is more than 60 miles from home or out of state. (See the last row for each sex in Tables 65 through 68.)

Among Illinois youth who go to college from noncollege towns, those of lowest ability go the farthest; four-fifths of the low-ability boys and nine-tenths of such girls attending college from noncollege communities either leave the state or go at least 60 miles within the state (Table 65 and 66). For other categories of ability, the proportions going that far rise with ability, with youth in the top category of ability going the farthest, aside from youth in the lowest ability rank. Explanation of the irregularity in that trend is elusive; the answer cannot be that it is low-ability offspring of

[22] A striking difference between the M-T findings and evidence from the SCOPE survey is in the gradients of college attendance rates by status and by ability—quite generally, but most dramatically for the noncollege towns. In the M-T sample, father's occupational status was much more important than ability, whereas in the SCOPE samples, ability was by far the more important.

the rich who get into college, for there are not sufficient numbers of such individuals. Parental education had very little effect on proportions of college-bound Illinois boys from noncollege towns who went 60 miles or out of the state to school (Table 67), though sons of men with elementary schooling were less likely to go far than were sons of college graduates. There was no meaningful association between parental status and distance to college among Illinois girls from noncollege communities. By contrast there was a decided effect of parental education on proportions of both boys and girls from college towns who went out of Illinois to college. Parental education had more effect than ability on these migration patterns from college towns.

College-bound North Carolina youth were as likely as those in Illinois to travel at least 60 miles to school, and in the noncollege towns there was again a slight tendency for boys with least ability to go farther than those in the middle range of ability. The college 5+ category aside, education of parents made very little difference in proportions going to school at a distance. North Carolina youth rarely go outside the state to college, regardless of the type of community in which they reside, their ability, or their family background; this is in marked contrast to the sizable minorities of Illinois college-bound youth who attend college outside the state.

The home-rootedness of North Carolinians is pervasive. Differences in proportions attending college in another state are slight as between towns with and without a college (even among the ablest boys). Paradoxically, among the most able boys, attendance out of state is higher if the hometown has a college (15 percent) than if it does not (11 percent). Among girls, the contrasts between the two types of town are larger and persist further down the scale of ability. For both sexes, parental education outweighed the youth's ability. Withal, the highest proportion attending out of state in any North Carolina cell was no greater than the proportion for the entire Illinois male sample. But in Illinois as in North Carolina, the propensity to attend an out-of-state college was more frequent among those from towns having at least one college —again with the striking exception of the lowest ability quarter in each sex. Illinois sex differences in frequency of going to college in another state were large among relatively advantaged youth from noncollege towns but negligible among those whose community had a college. Among Illinois college goers in towns with a college, half the children of college-graduate parents of both sexes

(Text continued on p. 246)

TABLE 65 ***Distance distributions of college attendance of male and female 1966 Illinois high school graduates by ability quarters; college and noncollege communities***

College(s) in community	*Ability 1*		*Ability 2*	
	None	*One or more*	*None*	*One or more*
			Male graduates	
Total number of students	180	501	273	745
Number entering college	16	96	78	284
Percent entering college	8.9	19.2	28.6	38.1
Distribution of college entrants by distance:				
Within community		47.9		45.1
Within 20 miles	0.0	4.2	14.1	4.2
Between 20–60 miles	18.7	7.3	38.5	7.0
Greater than 60 miles	56.2	25.0	34.6	19.7
Out-of-state	25.0	15.6	12.8	23.9
Sum of percents beyond 60 miles and out-of-state	81.2	40.6	47.4	43.6
			Female graduates	
Total number of students	223	657	319	1010
Number entering college	26	109	105	326
Percent entering college	11.7	16.6	32.9	32.3
Distribution of college entrants by distance:				
Within community		52.3		37.4
Within 20 miles	7.7	11.9	12.4	11.3
Between 20–60 miles		2.7	19.0	5.8
Greater than 60 miles	65.3	20.2	53.2	26.4
Out-of-state	26.9	12.8	15.2	19.0
Sum of percents beyond 60 miles and out-of-state	92.1	33.0	68.4	45.4

* Totals include ability NA.

Ability 3		Ability 4		Total*	
None	One or more	None	One or more	None	One or more
229	824	282	1212	968	3305
142	495	231	1016	469	1892
62.0	60.1	81.9	83.8	48.4	57.2
	41.8		28.5		35.6
16.9	6.1	15.1	7.2	14.9	6.4
23.3	4.2	12.1	3.3	20.0	4.3
41.5	22.2	54.1	28.1	47.3	25.3
18.3	25.6	18.6	32.9	17.9	28.4
59.8	47.8	72.7	61.0	65.2	53.7
221	909	153	881	928	3485
115	529	132	728	381	1702
52.0	58.2	86.3	82.6	41.1	48.8
	32.4		20.8		29.6
13.1	19.3	7.6	11.9	10.5	12.0
15.6	4.7	14.4	3.7	15.2	4.3
52.1	24.6	61.3	30.6	56.7	27.2
19.1	26.1	16.7	33.1	17.6	26.9
71.2	50.7	78.0	63.7	74.3	54.1

TABLE 66 ***Distance distributions of college attendance of male and female 1966 North Carolina high school graduates by ability quarters; college and noncollege communities***

	Ability 1		*Ability 2*	
College(s) in community	*None*	*One or more*	*None*	*One or more*
			Male graduates	
Total number of students	1007	799	812	584
Number entering college	126	127	287	204
Percent entering college	12.5	15.8	35.3	34.9
Distribution of college entrants by distance:				
Within community		51.2		42.5
Within 20 miles	11.2	0.0	21.6	1.0
Between 20–60 miles	14.4	3.9	13.9	15.2
Greater than 60 miles	68.6	38.6	58.2	34.3
Out-of-state	5.7	6.3	6.3	6.9
Sum of percents beyond 60 miles and out-of-state	74.3	44.9	64.5	41.2
			Female graduates	
Total number of students	1310	1004	878	755
Number entering college	230	203	320	311
Percent entering college	17.6	20.3	36.4	41.2
Distribution of college entrants by distance:				
Within community		35.4		30.8
Within 20 miles	10.4	1.0	16.6	1.0
Between 20–60 miles	15.6	7.9	15.6	18.0
Greater than 60 miles	67.7	49.3	61.2	39.2
Out-of-state	6.2	6.4	6.6	11.0
Sum of percents beyond 60 miles and out-of-state	73.9	55.7	67.8	50.2

*Totals include ability NA.

Ability 3		*Ability 4*		*Total**	
None	*One or more*	*None*	*One or more*	*None*	*One or more*
519	525	498	629	2897	2584
327	324	412	520	1152	1175
63.0	61.7	82.7	82.7	40.4	46.0
	35.2		20.2		31.5
18.3	1.0	14.1	0.8	16.8	0.7
16.8	17.3	11.9	12.1	14.0	13.2
59.6	38.0	63.3	52.0	61.4	43.5
5.2	8.6	10.6	15.0	7.6	11.0
64.8	46.6	73.9	67.0	69.0	54.5
566	537	317	448	3106	2790
345	352	265	378	1171	1260
61.0	65.6	83.6	84.4	37.7	45.2
	24.1		16.1		24.9
16.5	1.4	12.8	1.3	14.3	1.2
13.9	16.2	17.0	14.3	16.3	14.5
62.0	43.9	64.2	51.8	62.7	46.6
7.6	14.2	6.0	16.4	6.6	12.6
69.6	58.1	70.2	68.2	69.3	58.2

TABLE 67 ***Distance distributions of college attendance of male and female 1966 Illinois high school graduates by father's education; college and noncollege communities***

	Father's education			
	FED 1 (Elementary)		FED 2 (H.S. 1–3)	
College(s) in community	None	One or more	None	One or more
			Male graduates	
Total number of students	261	521	188	573
Number entering college	90	214	76	279
Percent entering college	34.5	41.1	40.4	48.7
Distribution of college entrants by distance:				
Within community		45.3		49.1
Within 20 miles	14.4	7.9	17.1	6.1
Between 20–60 miles	25.6	6.1	15.8	4.3
Greater than 60 miles	50.0	22.9	55.3	25.4
Out-of-state	10.0	17.7	11.8	15.1
Sum of percents beyond 60 miles and out-of-state	60.0	40.6	67.1	40.5
			Female graduates	
Total number of students	268	556	143	668
Number entering college	67	175	42	255
Percent entering college	25.0	31.5	29.4	38.2
Distribution of college entrants by distance:				
Within community		42.8		40.0
Within 20 miles	7.5	14.3	4.8	16.1
Between 20–60 miles	17.9	4.0	11.9	6.7
Greater than 60 miles	49.2	22.8	71.4	25.8
Out-of-state	25.4	16.0	11.9	11.4
Sum of percents beyond 60 miles and out-of-state	74.6	38.8	73.3	37.2

FED 3 (H.S. 4)		FED 4 (College 1–3)		FED 5 (College 4)		FED 6 (College 5+)	
None	*One or more*	*None*	*One or more*	*None*	*One or more*	*None*	*One or more*
285	820	112	626	41	290	33	247
164	453	74	440	31	229	28	201
57.5	55.2	66.1	70.3	65.6	78.9	84.8	81.4
	43.7		30.0		20.5		12.9
15.9	7.1	16.2	6.6	6.4	3.1	7.6	6.5
18.4	5.1	17.5	4.3	19.2	2.2	28.4	2.5
49.2	22.5	47.4	32.5	32.5	25.4	21.3	22.9
16.5	21.6	18.8	26.6	41.8	48.8	42.7	55.2
66.3	44.1	66.2	59.1	74.3	74.8	64.0	78.1
267	833	123	707	39	299	26	180
138	400	78	436	23	230	23	153
51.7	48.0	63.4	61.7	59.0	76.9	88.5	85.0
	34.0		27.1		14.8		13.1
12.3	10.7	9.0	11.0	17.4	11.2	17.4	7.2
20.3	5.0	10.3	3.9	17.4	2.2	4.3	3.2
51.5	33.5	64.1	30.8	47.6	22.1	56.5	18.9
15.9	16.8	16.7	27.3	17.4	49.5	21.8	57.5
67.4	50.3	80.8	58.1	65.0	71.6	78.3	76.4

TABLE 68 ***Distance distributions of college attendance of male and female 1966 North Carolina high school graduates by father's education; college and noncollege communities***

	Father's education			
	FED 1 (Elementary)		*FED 2 (H.S. 1–3)*	
College(s) in community	*None*	*One or more*	*None*	*One or more*
			Male graduates	
Total number of students	920	494	481	452
Number entering college	259	141	178	173
Percent entering college	28.2	28.5	37.0	38.2
Distribution of college entrants by distance:				
Within community		36.1		42.8
Within 20 miles	20.1	2.1	18.5	0.0
Between 20–60 miles	19.3	10.0	13.5	9.2
Greater than 60 miles	53.9	45.4	59.0	42.2
Out-of-state	6.6	6.4	9.0	5.8
Sum of percents beyond 60 miles and out-of-state	60.5	51.8	68.0	48.0
			Female graduates	
Total number of students	1011	531	578	501
Number entering college	283	143	202	179
Percent entering college	28.0	26.9	35.0	35.7
Distribution of college entrants by distance:				
Within community		25.2		33.0
Within 20 miles	13.4	2.8	15.3	1.1
Between 20–60 miles	20.5	11.2	17.3	12.8
Greater than 60 miles	58.7	55.9	63.9	48.0
Out-of-state	7.4	4.9	3.5	5.0
Sum of percents beyond 60 miles and out-of-state	66.1	60.8	67.4	53.0

went out of the state to college. It is abundantly clear that any local effects that may come into play in these choices have a wider sweep than the local community and reflect larger environments, both educational and sociohistorical.

Turning these observations around, we can look at the proportions of college-going youth residing in college towns who attend at home. In North Carolina the gradients in this proportion by ability are systematic, dropping from 51 percent of the boys in

FED 3 (H.S. 4)		FED 4 (College 1–3)		FED 5 (College 4)		FED 6 (College 5+)	
None	One or more	None	One or more	None	One or more	None	One or more
553	575	267	368	129	261	66	98
309	298	181	240	95	200	43	73
55.9	51.8	67.8	65.3	73.6	76.6	65.2	74.5
	36.7		29.6		18.0		12.2
13.6	1.0	17.7	0.4	13.7	0.0	11.7	1.4
13.3	10.4	9.4	15.8	15.7	20.0	14.0	13.7
68.3	41.3	66.8	41.6	52.7	43.5	67.2	57.7
4.9	10.7	6.1	12.5	17.8	18.5	7.0	15.1
73.2	52.0	72.9	54.1	70.5	52.0	74.2	72.8
533	597	309	435	109	239	37	121
279	311	202	273	78	185	31	97
52.3	52.1	65.4	62.8	71.6	77.4	83.8	80.2
	29.3		21.3		18.9		16.5
12.9	1.9	17.4	0.4	12.8	0.0	6.4	2.1
13.6	14.4	12.8	19.0	16.6	13.5	3.2	14.4
67.7	45.3	63.3	43.5	55.1	44.4	74.2	38.1
5.7	9.0	6.4	15.7	15.4	23.2	16.2	28.9
73.4	54.3	69.7	59.2	70.5	67.6	90.4	67.0

the lowest quarter of ability to 20 percent of the most able, and among girls from 35 to 16 percent. Parental status was a less powerful factor, though offspring of college men less often went to college in the hometown.[23] The proportions by ability among

[23] This is in part, of course, a reflection of the particular communities in the sample, and the slack is taken by attendance at institutions in communities that were not included in the SCOPE survey—a complication we did not need to worry about with the Wisconsin sample.

Illinois girls closely approximate those for North Carolina boys, whereas ability was less important in distinguishing proportions attending school in the hometown among Illinois boys. College-going sons and daughters of college graduates were much less likely than other youth to attend a hometown institution in either Illinois or North Carolina, while children of men who had not completed high school were the most likely to attend locally. Among Illinois males, but not otherwise, parental education differentiated more in this respect than did ability.

Indexes of substitution effects were used to compare states in Chapter 3 and with more detail for Wisconsin in Chapter 4; they are computed for Illinois and North Carolina in Table 69. Columns (4) and (8), called "maximum net location effect," are just a repetition of the difference in percentage points between attendance rates among high school graduates in towns having colleges and rates for youth in noncollege places. We interpret these differences as maximum estimates of the net effects of proximity of a college upon college attendance. (Strictly speaking, they are not maximal if unspecified factors associated with college locations influence continuation rates perversely, as can sometimes occur.) Within ability categories most of the differences are negligible for both sexes in each state, in contrast to the modest but consistently positive 7 percentage points for Wisconsin—outside the near-zero differentials in the lowest quarter of ability. As we have seen earlier in Illinois it is among the *least* able (especially for boys) that residence in a town with a college stimulates college attendance, and by a considerable margin. When father's education is substituted for youth's ability, the two categories in Illinois that show up with positive differentials are, first of all, offspring of college men and then, more modestly, offspring of the least-educated parents.[24] Net location effects of college proximity do not emerge in North Carolina; effects of college location upon college attendance must operate, if at all, mainly through affecting where people go to college and what type of institution they attend.

The substitution index S_1, as before, is simply the difference in percentages of college goers who attend within 20 miles of home when they come from a college rather than a noncollege community.

[24] The differentials for the sons and daughters (especially daughters) of the college men were suspect, however, because the college-going proportions for children of college graduates living in noncollege towns were downward deviant relative to children of men with some college only.

TABLE 69 ***Indexes of locational substitution and maximum net location effects by ability and father's education; college and noncollege communities in Illinois and North Carolina***

		Illinois				North Carolina			
		Indexes of substitution effects			Maximum net location effects	Indexes of substitution effects			Maximum net location effects
		S_1	S_2	S_3		S_1	S_2	S_3	
					Males				
Entire sample		27.0	13.1	11.5	8.9	15.3	6.2	8.8	5.6
Ability quarter	*1*	52.1	4.6	−0.9	10.3	40.0	5.0	5.8	3.3
	2	35.2	10.1	7.7	9.6	21.9	7.7	15.2	−0.4
	3	31.0	19.2	27.0	−1.9	17.9	11.3	23.0	−1.3
	4	20.6	16.9	22.0	1.9	6.9	5.7	16.7	0.0
FED 1	*Elementary*	38.8	12.6	12.0	6.6	18.1	5.1	11.4	−1.1
2	*HS 1–3*	38.1	15.4	15.6	8.3	24.3	9.0	15.2	1.2
3	*HS 4*	34.9	20.1	26.4	−2.3	24.1	13.5	23.1	−4.1
4	*College 1–3*	20.4	13.5	16.8	4.2	12.3	8.4	21.9	−2.6
5	*College 4*	17.2	11.3	2.3	13.6	4.3	3.2	19.6	5.8
6	*College 5+*	11.8	10.0	13.9	−3.4	1.9	1.2	12.6	−3.6
					Females				
Entire sample		31.0	12.7	6.7	7.7	12.0	4.5	4.0	7.4
Ability quarter	*1*	56.5	6.6	3.8	4.9	26.0	4.6	9.9	2.7
	2	26.3	8.7	12.8	−.6	15.2	5.5	7.9	4.8
	3	29.3	15.2	12.3	6.2	9.0	5.5	11.2	4.6
	4	25.1	21.7	20.9	−3.7	4.6	3.8	12.8	0.4
FED 1	*Elementary*	49.6	12.4	6.9	6.5	14.6	4.1	6.5	0.3
2	*HS 1–3*	51.3	15.1	6.6	8.8	18.8	6.6	11.1	0.7
3	*HS 4*	32.4	16.8	20.0	−3.7	18.3	9.6	15.4	−0.2
4	*College 1–3*	29.1	18.5	18.4	−1.7	4.3	2.8	16.0	−2.5
5	*College 4*	8.6	5.1	−6.5	−17.9	6.1	4.4	11.7	3.0
6	*College 5+*	2.9	2.5	14.6	−3.5	12.2	10.2	3.9	9.3

NOTE: "Maximum net location effect" is defined as the percentage-point difference between rate of college attendance from college over noncollege communities.

S_1 = The percentage of all *college-going* youth from college towns who attended schools within 20 miles minus the proportion of all *college-going* youth from noncollege towns who attended schools within 20 miles.

$S_2 = C_o S_1$ where C_o is the proportion of youth from noncollege towns who entered college.

S_3 = The proportion of high school graduates of college towns who entered institutions of higher education in the home community minus the "maximum net location effect."

Since this index refers only to those youth who did enter higher education, it is independent of the proportions of high school graduates who do continue. If a local college practices an "open door" policy and if proximity to such a school enhances the decisions to enter college mainly among the least able youth, we should expect the value of S_1 to be larger among the lower-ability youth. This emphatically is what we find in Illinois, and in lesser degree, especially among girls, in North Carolina. In Wisconsin, by contrast, the value of S_1 was relatively stable across ability categories except for the least able men: 13 as against 25 percent in the higher categories of ability. The localization of attendance that is summed up by S_1 is associated also (negatively) with parental schooling among Illinois youth, especially among girls, whereas in North Carolina it is related less to parental schooling than to a youth's ability. With index S_2, which adjusts for proportions attending college, the associations with ability and status observed for S_1 are damped and in some cases reversed. We can interpret the values on S_2 to suggest that local attendance substitutes for attendance farther away among 15 to 20 percent of the more able Illinois youth who would in any case be attending college. Substitution effects so measured are much smaller for youth below the median in ability. In North Carolina the index ranged only from 5 to 10 percent for boys and 4 to 5 percent for girls.

The third index, S_3, simply asks how far attendance in the immediate local community among youth from college towns exceeds the overall differential in rates of attendance between the communities with and without a college. In view of the slight difference in the overall rates, most local college going will be substitutive in this sense. The main exception, of course, is for the lower-ability males in Illinois. Otherwise, net substitution effects by this index ran somewhat higher for boys than for girls in Illinois and in North Carolina, as in Wisconsin. Among Illinois youth of both sexes, this substitution rate exceeded a fifth of all high school graduates in the top ability quarter.

Accessibility Types and Destination Types

Relationships between the immediately available types of colleges and the actual choice of a college to attend are demonstrated clearly by data from the SCOPE samples. In reading the tables for Illinois, the most interesting questions center on university and public junior colleges as destinations classifying students by ability quarters and accessibility profiles (Tables 70 and 71). Young men from communities without a college or possessing only an extension center were the most inclined to attend the state university. Moreover, the proportions from noncollege communities who entered the state university rose consistently with ability. Though the sample from the vicinity of the university was poor, the pattern of attendance at the home university was unambiguous nevertheless, and again, especially among the most able. The public junior colleges absorbed at least two-thirds of those youth from towns with such colleges who went to college—except among the top quarter in ability, of whom a third entered the university and a fourth went out of state. The data for the city of Chicago display a similar adherence to the public junior college among the least able, and these colleges drew even more generally from youth in the subsample for the southern fringe of the metropolitan area. But as one moves up the ability scale, Chicago's youth manifest a tendency to spread out into diverse institutions. Once above the lowest level in ability, girls from Chicago display a more diverse set of destinations than boys, with public junior colleges claiming a smaller proportion of able girls from the city.[25]

Choice of a public junior college by North Carolina youth living in towns possessing such schools prevailed among the lowest quarter in ability only; with a rise in ability within each sex it faded out more markedly than in Illinois (Tables 72 and 73), but

(Text continued on p. 264)

[25] Tabulations on college-destination types classifying students by father's education instead of by ability (not shown) added a few further pieces of information not directly evident from other tables. Illinois sons of college men residing in noncollege towns were less likely to attend a public university than were other youth from those communities and much more likely to go out of the state to school. Among girls from noncollege towns, the pattern was very different; daughters of college men were no more likely to leave the state and were considerably more likely to attend a public university than were other girls from noncollege towns. In all other categories of residence in Illinois communities, whatever the college accessibility profile, there was a distinctively high propensity to leave the state for higher education if one's father was a college graduate—for girls as for boys. However, parental education had no systematic effects on proportions of boys or girls from Chicago who went to a public university or a public junior college—or on proportions from junior college communities who entered the University of Illinois. Being the son or daughter of a college graduate did sharply reduce the likelihood that a college-bound graduate from high school in a junior college town would enter a public junior college. In the sample for Chicago there was a clear falling off in proportions attending miscellaneous, more specialized postsecondary institutions—with progression from children (male or female) of high school graduates to those whose fathers had some college, and then again to those whose fathers were college graduates.

TABLE 70 Distributions of types of college attended by male 1966 Illinois high school graduates by within-community college-accessibility type and ability quarters

	Within-community college-accessibility type			
		University		*Junior college (public)*
	None	*State*	*Private*	
Ability quarter 1				
Percent entering college	8.9	0.0	25.0	18.1
Number entering college	(15)	(0)	(5)	(29)
Percentage distribution of college entrants by destination:				
11 University, public	26.7		0.0	10.3
12 University, private	0.0		0.0	0.0
16 Junior college, public	40.0		40.0	69.0
17 Junior college, private	0.0		20.0	3.4
18 Extension center	0.0		0.0	0.0
*19 Other**	6.6		20.0	3.4
Out-of-state	26.7		20.0	13.7
Ability quarter 2				
Percent entering college	28.6	39.3	64.3	34.7
Number entering college	(75)	(11)	(25)	(76)
Percentage distribution of college entrants by destination:				
11 University, public	32.0	27.3	24.0	7.8
12 University, private	1.3	0.0	20.0	0.0
16 Junior college, public	42.6	36.4	40.0	70.7
17 Junior college, private	1.3	18.2	4.0	0.0
18 Extension center	0.0	0.0	0.0	0.0
*19 Other**	9.3	9.1	8.0	3.0
Out-of-state	13.4	9.1	4.0	18.7
Ability quarter 3				
Percent entering college	62.0	54.5	86.0	47.5
Number entering college	(135)	(6)	(43)	(121)
Percentage distribution of college entrants by destination:				
11 University, public	43.6	66.6	41.8	15.7
12 University, private	9.6	0.0	16.3	2.5
16 Junior college, public	23.7	16.6	9.3	61.1
17 Junior college, private	0.7	0.0	0.0	0.8

Extension center (state)	Chicago City	Chicago Suburb (south)	Chicago Suburb (north)
11.1	34.0	12.5	21.6
(7)	(30)	(11)	(8)
42.9	6.7	0.0	25.0
0.0	6.7	0.0	0.0
0.0	63.3	81.9	25.0
0.0	6.7	0.0	12.5
0.0	0.0	0.0	0.0
0.0	13.2	0.0	0.0
57.1	3.3	18.1	37.5
25.2	45.5	35.8	32.1
(26)	(63)	(37)	(25)
38.4	14.3	8.1	12.0
0.0	7.9	2.7	0.0
0.0	49.2	78.5	24.0
0.0	4.8	0.0	4.0
7.7	0.0	0.0	0.0
7.7	4.8	0.0	4.0
46.1	19.1	10.8	56.0
52.1	73.3	59.7	65.6
(50)	(111)	(74)	(66)
56.0	19.8	5.4	28.8
0.0	20.7	1.3	7.5
2.0	17.1	66.2	10.6
2.0	19.8	6.8	6.1

TABLE 70
(continued)

	Within-community college-accessibility type			
		University		*Junior college (public)*
	None	*State*	*Private*	
Ability quarter 3 (cont.):				
Percentage distribution of college students by distination:				
18 Extension center	0.0	0.0	0.0	0.0
*19 Other**	3.0	0.0	4.6	1.7
Out-of-state	19.3	16.6	28.0	18.2
Ability quarter 4				
Percent entering college	81.9	89.7	92.2	77.6
Number entering college	(213)	(24)	(47)	(216)
Percentage distribution of college entrants by destination:				
11 University, public	57.9	91.9	31.9	33.8
12 University, private	9.9	4.1	31.9	4.2
16 Junior college, public	7.5	0.0	4.2	32.8
17 Junior college, private	0.9	0.0	0.0	3.2
18 Extension center	0.0	0.0	0.0	0.0
*19 Other**	3.7	0.0	0.0	0.5
Out-of-state	20.2	4.1	31.9	25.5

* Specialized technical, vocational, and religious institutions.

Extension center (state)	Chicago		
	City	Suburb (south)	Suburb (north)
16.0	0.0	0.0	0.0
0.0	0.9	4.1	0.0
24.0	21.6	16.2	47.0
73.3	88.7	81.1	88.3
(88)	(258)	(100)	(239)
44.3	19.0	23.0	34.3
4.5	19.0	6.0	8.8
4.5	3.5	37.0	1.3
0.0	25.7	13.0	0.0
8.0	0.0	0.0	0.0
0.0	1.9	2.0	2.5
38.6	31.0	19.0	53.0

TABLE 71 ***Distributions of types of college attended by female 1966 Illinois high school graduates by within-community college-accessibility type and ability quarters***

	Within-community college-accessibility by type			
		University	*Junior college*	*Extension center*
	None	*State*	*(public)*	*(state)*
Ability quarter 1				
Percent entering college	11.7	33.3	20.1	10.4
Number entering college	(26)	(5)	(35)	(8)
Percentage distribution of college entrants by destination:				
11 University, public	19.2	60.0	11.4	25.0
12 University, private	0.0	0.0	0.0	0.0
14 Private college	0.0	0.0	2.9	0.0
16 Junior college, public	11.5	0.0	71.5	0.0
17 Junior college, private	3.9	0.0	0.0	0.0
18 Extension center	0.0	0.0	0.0	12.5
19 Other†	38.4	20.0	11.4	12.5
Out-of-state	26.9	20.0	2.9	50.0
Ability quarter 2				
Percent entering college	32.9	48.3	36.7	28.2
Number entering college	(105)	(14)	(92)	(31)
Percentage distribution of college entrants by destinations:				
11 University, public	35.2	50.0	16.3	32.2
12 University, private	4.8	0.0	1.1	0.0
14 Private college	1.9	0.0	2.2	3.2
16 Junior college, public	20.0	7.2	51.1	3.2
17 Junior college, private	0.0	0.0	2.2	0.0
18 Extension center	0.0	0.0	0.0	22.6
19 Other†	22.8	35.6	14.1	3.2
Out-of-state	15.2	7.2	13.0	35.6
Ability quarter 3				
Percent entering college	52.0	53.1	63.1	57.1
Number entering college	(115)	(17)	(135)	(52)
Percentage distribution of college entrants by destination:				
11 University, public	45.2	76.6	21.5	28.8
12 University, private	4.3	5.9	4.4	7.7

	Chicago			
Multiple two-year	City	Suburb (west)	Suburb (south)	Suburb (north)
13.5	16.0*	14.0*	17.2	17.8*
(5)	(19)	(6)	(23)	(8)
20.0	0.0	16.7	0.0	25.0
0.0	0.0	0.0	0.0	0.0
0.0	0.0	16.7	0.0	0.0
40.0	47.3	66.6	82.6	0.0
0.0	0.0	0.0	0.0	0.0
20.0	0.0	0.0	0.0	0.0
0.0	47.3	0.0	8.7	12.5
20.0	5.3	0.0	8.7	50.0
26.7	29.6‡	33.3‡	25.3‡	36.7
(12)	(60)	(26)	(38)	(51)
66.8	11.7	3.8	7.9	29.4
0.0	11.7	11.5	0.0	5.9
8.3	5.0	15.4	0.0	0.0
8.3	20.0	38.4	63.2	0.0
0.0	3.3	0.0	0.0	7.9
8.3	0.0	0.0	0.0	2.0
8.3	35.0	27.0	15.8	7.9
0.0	13.3	3.8	13.2	47.0
45.9	53.8§	57.9§	48.4	64.8
(17)	(86)	(55)	(46)	(116)
53.0	20.9	23.7	15.2	26.8
5.9	19.8	10.9	2.2	6.9

TABLE 71 (continued)

	Within-community college-accessibility by type			
	None	University State	Junior college (public)	Extension Center (state)
Ability quarter 3 (cont.):				
Percentage distribution of college entrants by destination:				
14 Private college	3.5	0.0	3.7	1.9
16 Junior college, public	12.2	0.0	40.7	0.0
17 Junior college, private	0.0	0.0	0.0	9.7
18 Extension center	0.0	0.0	0.0	17.3
19 Other†	15.6	11.8	11.1	1.9
Out-of-state	19.2	5.9	18.6	32.8
Ability quarter 4				
Percent entering college	86.3	85.7	79.2	85.9
Number entering college	(132)	(18)	(141)	(67)
Percentage distribution of college entrants by destination:				
11 University, public	61.3	55.6	26.2	38.8
12 University, private	6.8	5.5	11.3	10.5
14 Private college	5.3	11.1	4.3	4.5
16 Junior college, public	5.3	0.0	32.6	0.0
17 Junior college, private	0.0	0.0	1.4	2.9
18 Extension center	0.0	0.0	0.0	7.4
19 Other†	4.5	0.0	2.2	2.9
Out-of-state	16.8	27.8	22.0	32.9

* Contains 10.5, 16.6, and 12.5 percent attendance at teachers college respectively.
† Specialized technical, vocational, and religious institutions.
‡ Contains 11.7, 19.2, and 2.6 percent attendance at teachers college respectively.
§ Contains 10.5 and 23.6 percent attendance at teachers college respectively.
¶ Contains 12.5 and 13.1 percent attendance at teachers college respectively.

	Chicago			
Multiple two-year	*City*	*Suburb (west)*	*Suburb (south)*	*Suburb (north)*
0.0	5.8	16.4	2.2	5.2
5.9	19.8	12.7	58.7	0.9
0.0	0.0	0.0	4.4	3.4
5.9	0.0	0.0	0.0	0.0
0.0	17.4	31.0	2.2	3.4
29.4	16.3	5.4	15.2	53.3
81.3	75.6¶	86.0¶	85.9	84.7
(26)	(96)	(92)	(67)	(216)
50.0	26.0	25.0	32.8	23.1
3.8	13.6	17.4	5.9	8.8
0.0	7.3	19.6	0.0	9.7
0.0	3.1	9.7	29.9	0.4
0.0	0.0	0.0	9.0	0.4
3.8	0.0	0.0	0.0	0.0
0.0	14.6	17.4	4.5	4.2
42.4	35.4	10.9	17.9	53.4

TABLE 72 ***Distributions of types of colleges attended by male 1966 North Carolina high school graduates by within-community college-accessibility type and ability quarters***

	Within-community college-accessibility type					
		Four-year colleges	Junior college		Multiple private colleges	
	None	Private	Public	Private		Charlotte
Ability quarter 1						
Percent entering college	12.5	13.5	22.9	20.3	15.7	16.4
Number entering college	(126)	(20)	(8)	(13)	(17)	(68)
Percentage distribution of college entrants by destination:						
11 University, public	15.1	5.0	12.5	7.7	0.0	5.9
12 University, private	0.8	5.0	0.0	0.0	0.0	0.0
13 State college	8.7	10.0	0.0	7.7	0.0	2.9
14 Private college	4.7	20.0	0.0	15.4	29.4	1.5
16 Junior college, public	17.5	5.0	75.0	0.0	0.0	70.5
17 Junior college, private	8.7	10.0	0.0	7.7	5.8	2.9
*19 Other**	39.0	35.0	0.0	61.5	58.8	8.9
Out-of-state	5.5	10.0	12.5	0.0	5.8	7.4
Ability quarter 2						
Percent entering college	35.3	30.9	33.3	54.0	26.4	37.1
Number entering college	(291)	(29)	(16)	(27)	(23)	(105)
Percentage distribution of college entrants by destination:						
11 University, public	16.4	17.3	31.2	18.5	4.3	14.3
12 University, private	0.0	0.0	0.0	0.0	0.0	0.0
13 State college	11.1	0.0	0.0	0.0	0.0	1.0
14 Private college	7.3	20.6	6.2	3.7	39.3	2.9
16 Junior college, public	19.2	3.4	31.2	7.4	13.0	51.3
17 Junior college, private	15.7	13.8	12.5	29.6	13.0	16.2
*19 Other**	24.0	41.5	18.7	33.3	26.1	4.7
Out-of-state	6.3	3.4	0.0	7.4	4.3	9.5
Ability quarter 3						
Percent entering college	63.0	67.8	56.1	63.0	59.8	61.6
Number entering college	(327)	(40)	(23)	(29)	(49)	(178)
Percentage distribution of college entrants by destination:						
11 University, public	40.4	22.5	30.4	31.0	24.5	33.1
12 University, private	0.6	0.0	0.0	0.0	2.0	0.6

	Within-community college-accessibility type					
		Four-year colleges	Junior college		Multiple private colleges	
	None	Private	Public	Private		Charlotte
Ability quarter 3 (cont.): Percentage distribution of college entrants by destination:						
13 State college	5.7	0.0	4.3	0.0	0.0	0.6
14 Private college	13.2	37.5	8.7	3.4	30.6	9.5
16 Junior college, public	9.5	0.0	26.1	6.9	4.1	27.5
17 Junior college, private	15.6	12.5	8.7	27.6	8.2	20.2
*19 Other**	9.8	25.0	8.7	10.3	16.4	2.2
Out-of-state	5.2	2.5	13.0	20.7	14.3	6.1
Ability quarter 4						
Percent entering college	82.7	84.9	82.1	79.1	84.4	82.2
Number entering college	(412)	(62)	(32)	(34)	(54)	(333)
Percentage distribution of college entrants by destination:						
11 University, public	61.4	69.4	56.2	53.0	53.6	56.6
12 University, private	4.3	3.2	9.4	5.9	7.4	7.5
13 State college	2.9	3.2	0.0	0.0	0.0	0.3
14 Private college	11.6	17.8	9.4	8.8	24.2	5.7
16 Junior college, public	1.0	0.0	15.6	2.9	1.8	4.5
17 Junior college, private	6.3	1.6	3.1	20.6	3.7	3.9
*19 Other**	1.7	3.2	3.1	2.9	5.5	0.0
Out-of-state	10.7	1.6	3.1	5.9	3.7	21.3

* Specialized technical, vocational, and religious institutions.

TABLE 73 ***Distributions of types of colleges attended by female 1966 North Carolina high school graduates by within-community college-accessibility type and ability quarters***

	Within-community college-accessibility type					
		Four-year colleges	*Junior colleges*			
	None	*Private*	*Public*	*Private*	*Multiple private colleges*	*Charlotte*
Ability quarter 1						
Percent entering college	17.6	17.9	21.6	21.4	28.7	19.1
Number entering college	(230)	(26)	(11)	(22)	(33)	(105)
Percentage distribution of college entrants by destination:						
11 University, public	13.1	23.1	9.1	18.2	3.0	11.4
12 University, private	0.0	0.0	0.0	4.5	0.0	0.0
13 State college	12.6	15.4	0.0	0.0	0.0	1.9
14 Private college	6.6	11.5	0.0	4.5	45.5	11.4
16 Junior college, public	14.8	0.0	81.9	18.2	3.0	33.3
17 Junior college, private	6.6	11.5	0.0	9.1	3.0	12.3
*19 Other**	39.6	23.1	9.1	41.0	45.5	21.9
Out-of-state	6.6	15.4	0.0	4.5	0.0	7.6
Ability quarter 2						
Percent entering college	36.4	32.7	26.7	38.9	49.0	43.1
Number entering college	(320)	(36)	(16)	(28)	(48)	(171)
Percentage distribution of college entrants by destination:						
11 University, public	21.2	27.8	12.5	3.6	4.2	21.0
12 University, private	0.0	0.0	0.0	0.0	0.0	0.0
13 State college	6.6	5.5	0.0	17.8	10.4	0.6
14 Private college	11.8	30.6	18.7	14.3	25.0	7.0
16 Junior college, public	9.4	0.0	25.0	0.0	4.2	17.5
17 Junior college, private	14.4	8.3	25.0	50.0	20.8	28.0
*19 Other**	30.0	22.2	18.7	7.1	33.3	8.8
Out-of-state	6.6	5.5	0.0	7.1	2.1	16.9
Ability quarter 3						
Percent entering college	61.0	64.6	35.3	81.5	74.7	63.6
Number entering college	(345)	(42)	(12)	(44)	(56)	(194)
Percentage distribution of college entrants by destination:						
11 University, public	37.9	40.5	58.3	18.2	37.5	41.6
12 University, private	0.3	0.0	0.0	0.0	0.0	0.0

	Within-community college-accessibility type					
		Four-year colleges	Junior colleges		Multiple private colleges	
	None	Private	Public	Private		Charlotte
Ability quarter 3 (cont.):						
Percentage distribution of college entrants by destination						
13 State college	3.7	0.0	0.0	2.5	0.0	1.0
14 Private college	13.6	31.0	8.3	13.5	25.0	9.3
16 Junior college, public	6.1	2.4	25.0	6.8	7.1	8.2
17 Junior college, private	14.2	7.1	0.0	38.6	8.9	13.4
*19 Other**	16.5	9.5	8.3	9.1	16.2	6.7
Out-of-state	7.5	9.5	0.0	11.4	5.3	19.6
Ability quarter 4						
Percent entering college	83.6	82.9	68.2	92.1	94.9	82.6
Number entering college	(265)	(34)	(15)	(35)	(56)	(238)
Percentage distribution of college entrants by destination:						
11 University, public	58.3	56.0	40.0	37.1	48.2	48.3
12 University, private	5.3	2.9	13.3	2.9	3.6	5.1
13 State college	1.9	0.0	0.0	2.9	0.0	0.4
14 Private college	15.2	35.3	6.6	22.8	28.5	16.0
16 Junior college, public	2.2	0.0	13.3	0.0	0.0	1.2
17 Junior college, private	3.8	0.0	0.0	22.8	5.3	3.8
*19 Other**	7.1	2.9	26.6	5.7	5.3	2.5
Out-of-state	6.0	2.9	0.0	5.7	9.0	22.7

* Specialized technical, vocational, and religious institutions.

was less strongly associated than in Illinois with father's education (not shown). In Charlotte, as in Chicago, the public junior college was important, though few of the more able (or of the higher status youth) preferred it. Among low-ability youth, the other major destination (almost irrespective of the pattern of local institutions) was that miscellaneous set of technical and vocational collegiate institutes that have grown up in the state.[26] The private junior colleges are widely scattered and draw from many other communities; they recruit 20–30 percent of the college-going youth in their home communities who were above the lowest quarter in ability. Although attendance at colleges of the same type the home community possessed (and presumably at that same institution) usually was above random expectancy within each ability quarter, there is little evidence for North Carolina of selective effects by local colleges on the kind of college chosen. This being the case, there are relatively low substitution effects in North Carolina compared with either Wisconsin or Illinois.[27]

Commonalities across these states are numerous, but so are the signs of distinctive heritages that influence college going, from the setting from which educational options emerge or are inhibited, and out of which educational policies and problems take on a distinctive local color.

[26] Few sons or daughters of college men went to these institutions, which were favored primarily by children of men who had not graduated from high school. There was little association between parental education and proportion of college-bound North Carolina youth attending either private junior colleges or public four-year colleges and universities. However, among North Carolina males, the likelihood of attending four-year institutions was substantially higher if one's father was a college graduate, regardless of community of residence.

[27] An examination of tables similar to those we have just discussed, but organized by father's education instead of by ability, added nothing of further interest, except the negative fact that parental education had remarkably little selective impact on type of institution attended in either the Illinois or the North Carolina samples. These tables have therefore been omitted.

6. *Conclusions*

The problem set for this study, stated in simple terms, was to examine the effects of college accessibility upon attendance at college. "Accessibility" is defined in the layman's geographic sense, and the analysis uses comparisons across towns or communities (whether a village of a few hundred people or a metropolis). Accessibility *within* large metropolitan conurbations could not be considered, given the nature of the data available to us; indeed, in such communities accessibility has special meanings and its analysis requires special sorts of data. We have dealt with college proximity and with rates of college attendance among high school graduates, contrasting communities without colleges and those with various college-access profiles. Even without considering the special difficulties of this sort of investigation in the special conditions of the giant city, we can reach an understanding of responses to proximity of colleges only as the notion of accessibility becomes refined, and as it is related back to the pertinent parameters of individual decision making with respect to entry upon postsecondary education. Among the first concerns in this sphere, societally speaking, must be what kinds of opportunities are made available, what benefits those opportunities bring, and which subsets of high school graduates display the most sensitive response at the decision margins as new collegiate options open up.

Implicit in this study are presumptively societal judgments, of which we infer two to be critical: (1) geographic proximity of a college is an important dimension of opportunity for a college education (whether or not that opportunity be taken), and (2) schooling at least to the fourteenth grade would be desirable for large numbers of youth who heretofore have not attended college. Other basic but latent values and policy issues could be brought out for mention and scrutiny, and some of them cannot be avoided. We will come back to that fundamental level of deliberation (what one might call the tacit or shadow issues) at the end of this conclusion.[1]

The topic upon which our empirical research is centered is not new. Neither, in its more pristine forms, is it particularly expressive of the configuration of contemporary academic controversies. Over the last two centuries the placement of colleges on the landscape has been a topic of conscious policy among those who were given, or who had assumed, responsibility for implementing the society's commitment to expanding the supply of collegiate places. In another of its aspects, the problem is also old and is shared by all modern or would-be modernized societies in varying degrees: the aspiration for a more democratized educational system. That the more able youth, especially those who have grown up in disadvantaged families or communities, should be given every encouragement to attend college is an idea that has won progressive support, and much deliberation has been given to the most suitable means for implementing this goal. Neither in abstract reflection nor in empirical fieldwork is it easy to identify where the roadblocks to wider opportunities lie, which strategies for removing them would be most effective, what the priorities in this sphere might be, and what the explicit and the hidden trade-offs may be for given policies. There are persisting tensions also between the pursuit of excellence and the democratization of academic opportunity, almost irrespective of measured ability or academic performance. These tensions, both latent and overt, have risen to a new level of stridency in the past few years. There are pressures toward ever more diffused spatial accessibility of colleges because college attendance has come to be associated with open-door policies. This range of disputes has centered on the junior college in particular and is thereby tied in with issues concerning the place of junior versus four-year colleges in the network of higher institutions—sometimes called a "system." It is not at all clear, however, that things are what they seem to be. In fact, the correlation between enrollment trends in the colleges of the various states and the seeming or reputed openness of state systems of higher education is impressively low.

[1] Throughout, however, we will refrain from exposition or debate over the many conceptions of "equality of educational opportunity." Also, we have not undertaken any exegetical inquiry into the different meanings this phrase has been given during the last century, when our system of higher education expanded manifold.

1. THE HIGH COST OF KNOWLEDGE

It would be easy to make a list of what pass for axioms in educational policy, widely accepted either as "obvious" or as "proven" by empirical observations. But the history of every body of learning is that empirical generalizations, when reexamined, often do not stand up to the sharper questions or the more copious body of evidence. As more states and nations begin to reconstruct their systems of higher education according to deliberative procedures based on empirical evidence, the list of questioned truisms lengthens. The basic question for this study could have been: How much substance is there in the mountain of numbers, how much support for the widely held belief that college proximity significantly affects rates of college attendance? The search for answers to this question has proved to be costly in time, even without collecting a whole archive of fresh data. As we were beneficiaries of an unusual pair of academic courtesies, we were able to analyze large bodies of data assembled by others: for Wisconsin high school graduates of 1957 and for the four-state SCOPE survey of high school graduates for 1966.

Our answers on some points challenge established opinion, mainly in a negative direction. Our simplest conclusion, in brief, is that spatial accessibility to one or more colleges has little effect, for most youth, on whether they will attend college—be the accessible school a junior college, an open-door four-year college, or a more selective institution. This conclusion has large practical implications; at a minimum, if our reasoning has been sound, the case for implanting junior colleges thickly over the landscape probably will have to stand on other grounds—or that sphere of policy be thoroughly reformulated. But there are important exceptions to that conclusion for particular categories of youth who live in particular settings.

Any careful statements affirming positive effects of the nearness of one kind of college or another (or mixture of colleges) upon rates of college going must be complex because one must allow for widely varying circumstances that affect unequally the responses of particular categories of youth. Response to accessibility can and does differ with the ability and family background of youth and with the structure of higher education in a given state. The straightforward but crude relations between accessibility and attendance reported in most of the earlier studies were appealingly simple, but most of them were misleading on at least two counts. (1) The analysis confounded associations between the socioeconomic features of the residents of a community and its possession of one or more colleges. (2) During recent years there seems to have been a marked narrowing of the gap in raw college attendance rates between youth from communities without colleges (or beyond commuting distance) and youth residing in towns possessing one or more colleges. A necessary, though not sufficient, condition for circumvention of the first difficulty is to use individuals as the units of observation and distinguish them by traits such as ability and family status, which have repeatedly proved to be strong predictors of the likelihood of continuation into higher institutions, whatever the accessibility of colleges to the home community.

In the present study we have benefited from the availability of extensive data that enabled us to analyze patterns within states, each viewed as an entity, and also to compare states with each other. Techniques included cross-tabulations, multiple regressions (taking ability and father's education in turn as design variables), and variance analysis of logit transforms of the percentages of college goers in specified ability/status/accessibility categories. We have also related college accessibility to the college destinations of youth who did enter some sort of higher school. The resulting outputs from computers and other generators of printouts demonstrate that it is important to specify generalizations for an interlocked set of cells characterized by types of schools, by types of communities from which students go to college, by types of colleges to which they go as enrollees, and by characteristics of youth who enter college and those who do not. That statement actually is the most general finding of the study. Along with the more narrowly or particularly specified findings, it has important implications for the choice of educational policies in a diverse, variously affluent, and education-prone society.[2]

We believe our findings are rich, though our topic was narrow and quite undramatic. While the data were superior to any ever used for this question, not all our aims could be served by the source materials at our disposal. Only the Wisconsin sample had an unbiased statewide coverage; the SCOPE survey was not designed to provide any complete geographic sampling. Data

[2] We have dealt with proportions of secondary graduates who attend college, not with percentages of an age cohort. Some of the consequences of so narrowing our focus come out in the "tacit questions" of which we have spoken briefly above and to which we will return at the end of this chapter.

like those for Wisconsin are needed for assorted other states and of a more recent date. But we explicitly do not urge the compilation of a national sample; we are convinced that it is more important to analyze the response patterns of youth in particular states, each of which has a distinctive educational history, ethnic mixture, and economic situation. Analysis of other aspects of demands for higher education, such as the difficult instance of large metropolitan centers, might well deserve priority before any elaboration of the paths we have opened up are retraced. New data are emerging from rapidly multiplying investigations of college going, but the need is less to establish broad outlines than better to identify the impact of specific parameters relevant to decisions about college going and the sequels to those decisions.[3]

2. THE CONTEXT OF DECISIONS

That educational expansion has been continuous and that it has moved with a breathless pace in the upper ranges of our system of higher education needs no documentation. Some states have moved faster or further than others. In some states, the system has been almost exclusively composed of public institutions; in others, private colleges and universities have been important or even dominant. And collegiate education is only one of a variety of postsecondary learning and training options that range from the most formally academic to the most informal modes of learning at work. Individual decisions about educational careers are made in a particular context—a context colored by a historical heritage of customs and institutions brought up against the swirling contemporary forces of educational and societal change. Some brief remarks concerning those settings are in order before we go on to the more particularized evidence relating to youths' responsiveness to college proximity in the particular configurations of today's circumstances.

The Varieties of Postsecondary Education

A complete enumeration of all varieties of instruction (quite apart from the even more varied learning) exists for no society. Because it is academic men who carry out most investigations, education

[3] One major topic that we touched upon only peripherally is the effect of type of high school attended and of college proneness among peers and neighbors, given the individual's parental background. Also, we did not attempt any direct analysis of evidence relating to information and attitudes as these may relate to and be affected by college proximity. Some clues on these points could have been extricated from the SCOPE materials had we had the time and funds.

tends to be defined as formal schooling. Although there is widespread awareness that many sorts of education and training are available to individuals after they have completed secondary school, for most people the mental picture of those options has come to have a predominantly academic or collegiate cast. The present investigation has been carried out in a society possessing an especially rich system of postsecondary schools. It is a society also that can seriously contemplate providing "universal" schooling for a majority of youth until they have reached at least the third decade of life.

A by no means negligible proportion of our youth, to be sure, fail to complete secondary school, and many who do have barely gone through the motions of learning during most of their academic careers—an ironic label to use, indeed. Of these secondary graduates, a large though diminishing proportion choose immediately to take a job or to enter upon some other noneducational activity. For those who elect to take more schooling, there are many and diverse training programs, and this training can be deferred for some years. Enrollment in academic or collegiate schools (colleges for short) expands steadily.[4]

Using the better-than-average instance of Wisconsin, the sample of high school graduates for that state enables us to make some estimates of how individuals distribute themselves among these various courses of life. Thus about one-eighth of the boys and one-sixth of the girls obtained some sort of noncollegiate instruction within seven years after finishing high school. They made up respectively one-fourth and two-fifths of all who received any formal postsecondary instruction. These individuals are by no means uniformly "culls"; though typically less able than the collegiate set, many had good test scores and parents with better-than-average schooling and status. As has been known for half a century, the correlation between a youth's ability and the type of postsecondary activity he chooses (including the type of college

[4] We are not discussing what may be the most important postsecondary training of all—both the formal training and the more informal but critically important learning on the job that takes place in many employment situations and occupations. Postsecondary training in vocational schools and institutes almost certainly is more important than is usually realized, though we are not able to trace this through our data with any degree of precision. Moreover, the boundary between what is and what is not regarded as "collegiate," and counted accordingly, is a somewhat arbitrary one, differing from one time and state to another.

attended) is only moderate, and the ability distributions vary less by type of college (though not between individual pairs of colleges) than most persons would assume.[5]

Historical Convergence in College Attendance

Though the quality of the statistical sources leaves something to be desired, we do have recurrent enumerations of college students that go back for a century and from which we can estimate the approximate attendance rates for each state at different dates. The states of the nation have become progressively more alike in college attendance rates, even as there have also been a few decided shifts in rank. Northern New England, for example, has lost relatively, as has most of the Southeast, while the Plains and Mountain states have forged ahead. Southern New England and the mid-Atlantic states, along with the Pacific Coast, have continued in strong relative positions, regardless of the striking contrasts in their systems of education.

Meanwhile, there has been geographic convergence on a smaller scale as well. A clear example is Wisconsin, where rates of attendance from noncollege communities have become virtually equal to those from college towns, a marked convergence during one decade. College going, we may be confident, is a practice and a set of attitudes that diffuse among the population much in the manner of electric refrigerators or TV sets, or if you prefer, the

[5] Some incidental evidence on this for Wisconsin is included in Table 37 (1957). In this connection, Windham (1970, pp. 38–39), in his survey of students in Florida colleges, showed that the percentage distribution of family incomes for junior college enrollees was quite similar to that for parents of students in other colleges, except for a discernible but not dramatic excess of the latter from families with incomes over $15,000. In a classification by income categories, the index of dissimilarity in percentage distributions of parents of youth in the two-year and the four-year institutions was only 5 percent. Windham (p. 45) commented on these findings in the following words. "The net effect of the junior college system is somewhat surprising. There is very little difference between this system and the university system in the way it affects low-income groups. Although the system of junior colleges has received substantial popular support because of its supposed ability to provide greater opportunities to a wider range of students, the distribution of the students' family incomes was not very different from that of the universities; but, once again, this situation may result from the higher percentage of urban students attending junior colleges. Moreover, because the state provides a larger share of the total cost—financed from more regressive taxes than those forming the basis of federal support—the effect of the financing may be *more* regressive than that for the universities. The net result for junior colleges alone is still that those earning less than $10,000 pay a larger share of the costs than they receive in benefits."

accelerating liking for Danish-style furniture. The propensity to stay in school for more and more years has been permeating more deeply into the general population and into particular various subpopulations once they have begun to use collegiate services.[6]

To what extent colleges have induced or to what extent they have reflected, the spread of the custom of college going cannot be definitively settled by our data. On the whole, however, there can be little doubt about the push up from the secondary schools and the cumulative rise in proportions completing that level of school. And it is as yet by no means clear just what continuation beyond high school will come to mean. However that may turn out, there is in any case the question of how far new college places follow the demand, or induce and reshape it, even among states with the highest rates of continuation into college. Has California attained its position because of its enormous system of junior colleges or has it acquired the latter because of the pressures for entry into its bulging four-year colleges? Comparing California with Massachusetts forces one to accept the foregoing query as a serious one. In California, 75 percent and in Massachusetts, 66 percent, of the 1968 high school graduates continued directly into postsecondary institutions. In California, 60 percent went to public free-access schools and 15 percent to other types of schools. Four-fifths of all college youth in California were in public institutions. In Massachusetts, on the other hand, only 11 percent attended the free-access schools, whereas 55 percent, or five-sixths of all enrollees, entered more selective and usually more expensive private colleges. Moreover, in Massachusetts, remarkably high proportions of low-status youth and children of comparatively uneducated fathers entered college; the status gradients with college entry in that state are exceptionally low, despite its educationally elitist reputation.

3. ABILITY, STATUS, AND ACCESSIBILITY

It would be difficult to support the assertion that spreading attendance at college among the nation's various subpopulations should be attributed in major degree to the greater local availability of

[6] Compulsory education laws did not precede the rise in the age at which children left school; they followed it—except for a small group of laggard children. Also, there has been an astonishingly high propensity among Negroes to continue in school, despite low returns on that investment in discriminatory job markets. But that is not the topic here; indeed, we have been severely handicapped by a lack of data needed to analyze location and college attendance among black youth.

colleges. Neither the sweep of historical change nor the cross-community data of more recent times would bolster that assertion. Indeed, family status and personal ability outweigh accessibility in explaining variations in college attendance rates, despite large overlapping in the ability distributions for college and noncollege youth. If we begin with indexes of accessibility, adding family or ability factors into a multiple regression brings clear gains on predictability of college attendance; if we begin instead with sets of variables for ability and family status, addition of indexes for accessibility brings virtually no addition in the proportion of variance explained. This result was unequivocal for each sex for each of the states and samples observed.[7] There was generally also a higher gradient on ability among boys and on parental status among girls, expressing gradients simply in terms of arithmetic increments in rates of college attendance. Being the daughter of a college man was in most instances especially important, regardless of family status and the college-accessibility profile of the hometown.

That college accessibility plays a minor part in stimulating attendance was supported further by analyses of variance using logit transforms of percentages attending college in the cells of a three-way matrix that categorized high school graduates simultaneously by ability, status, and selected college-access types.[8] The poor showing on accessibility for Illinois boys is the more

[7] In noncollege communities, the range in college attendance rates between the lowest and the highest quarter on ability were, for males and females respectively: Wisconsin, 12 to 60 percent and 9 to 42 percent; Massachusetts, 21 to 89 percent and 19 to 90 percent; Illinois, 9 to 82 percent and 12 to 86 percent; North Carolina, 12 to 83 percent and 18 to 84 percent. With the exception of Massachusetts, the rates for the lowest-ability quarter were somewhat higher in the college than in the noncollege communities; this was most emphatically the case for Illinois males, who had the highest college-town rate for the lowest-ability quarter (19 percent). Ranges in college attendance rates were narrower between children of men who had not gone beyond elementary school and children of college graduates. Grouping by father's education, the lowest of the 1966 rates was for girls from noncollege Illinois towns whose fathers had not gone beyond elementary school (25 percent); yet among daughters of college men living in these same towns, the rate of continuation into college or university was 89 percent, making this decidedly the widest range across levels of father's schooling.

[8] The variance analysis was carried out for three pairings of college-access types, two in Wisconsin (state college against noncollege, and Extension Center against noncollege) and one in Illinois (public junior college against noncollege). For discussion of the method and findings, see Chapter 4, pp. 112–115, and Chapter 5, pp. 224–225.

notable in view of the fact that the access categories used were noncollege communities and communities with public junior colleges. These observations say nothing, however, about the selective impact of college accessibility upon particular subgroups of youth. It is in our use of analytical refinements to identify more particularized relationships that we most need an analytical framework that will order our thoughts and interpret the data in more than an ad hoc fashion.

4. DECISION PARAMETERS AND COLLEGE PROXIMITY

Schools render their services mainly in a particular place; education is not normally disseminated through space in the manner of radio or television. And the families of potential students are also distributed in particular settlement clusters. The composition of these settlements varies in distributions of measured ability of youth, the quality of previous schooling, the education or social status of their parents, and so on. In this situation, educational space can be looked at in two ways. It is possible, as many college administrators and planners of state higher education systems must do, to put oneself at the site of a college (or future college) and attempt to map its recruiting field. From what places do or might students come? Could this pattern be altered by changing tuition, or by trying innovative courses of study, or in some other way bringing about "product differentiation"? Educational space can be looked at also by standing successively at secondary schools (for convenience within a given state) and looking out upon the field over which their graduates customarily have scattered themselves by their choice of one or another type and place of higher education. One could go on to consider alternative secondary curricula, guidance procedures, interaction between high schools and colleges about admission policies, and so on. As should by now be evident, the second stance has been chosen for the present report. Using samples of high school graduates, we tried to ascertain whether the presence of a collegiate institution of one kind or another in a community will increase the proportion of that community's youth who go on to college—or to what extent the response may be also (or instead) a substituting of local attendance for what would have been attendance farther from home.

We have asked, more particularly, whether youth of a certain academic ability or family background are more likely (or even less likely) to go on to college, given one or another college-accessibility profile in the home community or nearby. But thereby we also are asking the complementary question of whether the ability of a youth or the status of his family will alter the pulling power of a given set and combination of opportunities to enter college. Ultimately these two perspectives (from the college outward to its catchment basin and from the hometown outward to colleges) must converge. For even when we take a market-area point of view—be students "raw material" or "clients"—it may be necessary to work back into the communities of origin and to the individuals and families residing in those communities. Recruitment areas, effects of proximity of a college on attendance, and substitution effects with respect to the distances that students travel to college are intertwined—whether our aim be to explain behavior or to guide educational policies. And as soon as we think of the students or their families as decision makers, we must look behind the statistical associations both to test what we may predict a priori and to interpret what we have observed.

Predictions from Model 1

Having accepted the terms of reference for this investigation, we set down a conceptual decision-framework to help in organizing our thoughts. In its core version (as Model 1), that framework is the simplified economic model of the student decision maker as an investor in education, though we do use an enlarged notion of returns to include nonmonetary rewards and the access to preferred occupations that college graduation may confer. All the determinants usually considered when examining the decision to enter college are imbedded in that model, along with some elements that often are neglected. It includes costs of attending each of a number of colleges (local or nonlocal), the ability of the individual to pay for his education, any nonmonetary constraints that limit his access to some colleges (especially ability cutoffs), and his expected future benefits from choosing one college over another. The relationships are all interactive. The effects of the presence of a particular college in a community will depend upon the individual's access to other colleges at varying distances and on the characteristics of those colleges, along with the characteristics of the home community in the general sense. Furthermore, costs will be more important to youth from low-income families. But this model pays no attention to tastes or to adequacy of information about college options. Though Model 1 is a simplification, it has brought us some distance. Let us see just how far by asking what it would imply in selectivity of response to the proximity of one or another institution of higher education.

1 Unless the local institution provides a unique education (in which case its location effect is spurious), the main impact on attendance will be through effects upon costs of continuing into higher education. There is no necessary connection between free access and local accessibility, and the comparatively small cost advantage in location will be of negligible importance to high-status, well-off families. Furthermore, exceptionally able youth will have a better chance of securing scholarships elsewhere than will mediocre youth, so the cost advantages to the former of going to a local college will be less. We should then expect (a) relatively little effect of a nearby college on rates of college going among the economically advantaged youth of either sex, and (b) limited effects among the highly able youth of modest backgrounds.

2 When the local college is also an open-door or free-access institution for both ability and tuition, it will minimize the costs of continuing into college, especially for youth in the lower half of the ability distribution. Even assuming that nearness of a college has no effects with respect to diffusion of information or the formation of tastes (which are not specified in Model 1), this should lead us to expect that the response will be greatest in the lower ability, lower-to-middle brackets of economic status. It is among these youth that we would look for the largest net differentials in the overall rate of college attendance from (free-access) college over noncollege communities—not merely the substitution of attendance in one locale or type of institution for another.

3 Sex-selective effects of local proximity may appear even within the confines of Model 1 if returns to higher education are seen as higher for boys than for girls. Such a difference normally would show up in maximal marginal responses to college proximity at levels of ability and family status that are lower among boys than among girls.

4 The net effect from proximity of a high-quality college upon college attendance rates among the youth of a community would be mainly a locational-substitution effect, which would be operative among the more able local youth regardless of sex. This stems from the proposition that the relatively small cost effects of attendance at school in one's home community will be insufficient to alter college-going decisions among able youth who can afford to go away to school; the comparatively few among such young people who are marginal decision makers with respect to college attendance will normally be marginal on grounds other than costs.

Responses at the Margins

Some of our findings concerning responses at the margins are as follows:

1 The first of our a priori hypotheses—that college accessibility in the spatial sense would have little impact on college attendance rates among able

youth from advantaged backgrounds—is fully sustained for the highest ability-status category in all cases. Positive differentials began to show up immediately below those levels in the state college towns of Wisconsin (1957), but in the SCOPE data for Massachusetts, Illinois, and North Carolina, effects of accessibility do not show up until we push considerably further down the ability and status scales (if then).[9]

One of the most interesting findings was that the Wisconsin Extension Centers had a strongly positive effect upon rates of college going among the most able boys from modest homes. This finding is better understood when we remember that these centers are branches of the University of Wisconsin, uphold the same standards for entry, and are regarded as a normal route to the university. They are a comparatively low-cost route, and draw in just those boys for whom the centers were created. By contrast, the Illinois extension centers are not selective, and male differentials for places with these schools were strongly negative in the upper half of the ability distribution. They were positive in Wisconsin. Among girls in both states the differentials were erratic but negligible at each ability quarter.

2 The second a priori proposition was that less able youth of humble or modest backgrounds would more often continue into colleges when such institutions were located on their doorsteps. We could add (from item 4) that we expect such effects to be stronger among the males than the females within the low-status, modest-ability category, even without bringing in cultural or taste factors. The result would then be a strong male and a weak female responsiveness to the presence of public junior colleges among the less able half of youth finishing high school, especially when they are offspring of relatively uneducated parents in humble occupations or of modest SES. Indeed, it is among just such youth that we find positive differentials in the data for males in the three SCOPE states that we studied, whereas effects among females were in all cases negligible.[10]

There is a clear contrast between our findings and those of Medsker and Trent so far as response to the presence of a junior college among the more able youth is concerned. They come out with strong positive differentials in this as in the lower ability and status ranges, whereas we did not get such results. In fact, our differentials in the high-ability range were as often negative as positive, for Illinois, North Carolina, and Massachusetts alike. Considering both the logic of the situation and the nature of the various samples, the Medsker and Trent findings for the high-ability

[9] North Carolina girls of better-than-average ability and in the middle range in social status were an exception, displaying strong positive differentials for private (not public) junior college towns.

[10] The small subsamples of low-status/low-ability girls in public junior college towns of North Carolina are the exception, showing remarkably high college attendance rates as compared with similar girls from noncollege communities.

categories seem to be dubious both for junior colleges and for other categories of college accessibility.[11]

Following the kind of logic we have just applied to the instance of the public junior colleges we might have predicted that the Wisconsin county teachers colleges would mainly attract girls of low or modest ability residing close to the college. In fact, it was only in the towns with teachers colleges that college entry rates among girls of low ability exceeded rates in noncollege communities.

3 The third inference that we drew from Model 1, and the most tentative, was that the maximum responsiveness among girls would appear at higher levels of ability and status than among boys. This was unambiguously the case for Wisconsin as of 1957. The clearest overall differentials in college attendance rates between college and noncollege towns were among top-ability girls and middle-ability boys. Also, while sons as well as daughters of college graduates were overall more likely to attend college if they lived in a community having a college, there were equally big differentials for boys, but not for girls, from the most humble homes. In the 1966 figures for the SCOPE states, the college attendance rates among the most able girls were uniformly very high and overall differentials between college and noncollege towns were small. If something like the Wisconsin process operated in those states in the past, it has by now worked itself out, even as the gaps between college attendance rates for noncollege and college towns have been narrowing. What does show up in both Massachusetts and Illinois is higher attendance among sons than among daughters of the least educated men, regardless of the proximity of a college. This, of course, is another facet of the same phenomenon that lay behind our inference (4)—that college is viewed as an investment to a greater extent by boys than by girls, especially when the youth come from comparatively humble homes.

4 Finally, we suggested that the net effect of the proximity of a high-quality college would be reflected mainly in a locational substitution effect, so long as influences beyond those stipulated in Model 1 were excluded. This hypothesis is upheld by the overall measures of net substitution effects on the two indexes that are relevant as a test, taking all the college places together in a comparison with noncollege communities. For both men and women in all the states on which these figures were worked out (Illinois, North Carolina, and Wisconsin), these two indexes are substantially higher

[11] Their results were strongly biased against the noncollege towns, only two of which were in their sample; both of those towns had exceptionally low college attendance rates among high school graduates compared with rates for such towns in other surveys. Also, the sample for public junior college communities was heavily weighted with high schools in California. (See Tables 7 and 64 and our discussions about them.)

for the two upper quarters of ability than in the lower quarters, and despite wide variations among the states in the differential rates of college attendance from college and noncollege towns among the less able youth. However, there were some special instances of significant positive differentials in rates of college attendance for some college-access situations, instances that could be explained only by elaborating the conceptual framework to include Models 2 and 3.

Preferences, Information, and Decision

In the second and third conceptualizations of our decision models we introduced tastes or preferences and the diffusion of information, both of which were treated as endogenous variables in Model 3. It is specified thereby that the presence of a college (or set of colleges) in the immediate vicinity of a youth's home will affect the formation of tastes and the awareness of and level of information about college options and their implications. Furthermore, these effects may be lagged, in which case the impact of establishing a new college in a community may be greater after some years than initially. This last model almost certainly is the most realistic one, but it also requires the most data to test relationships. Unfortunately, we lacked longitudinal data for particular towns. Many public junior colleges are quite young, and the samples were not large enough to cross-compare communities that have new and old junior colleges. To test these relationships properly, it would be necessary to consider circular effects—not only how far the proximity of a college may affect rates of college going but also to what extent local interest in higher education may account for the presence of the college—a theme that was developed a few pages back.[12]

Consideration of tastes and of lagged diffusion effects of college proximity can modify the a priori hypotheses suggested by the simpler Model 1 only if we suppose these effects to be very strong indeed. There is the very real danger that the effects of historical and cultural inheritances will be confounded with indirect effects of college proximity in the attribution of causal influences. We could inject into the more complex models some assumptions about

[12] More recently there have been interactive processes in the establishment of new institutions that could work both ways so far as effects on statistical observation are concerned. The new effort to extend opportunity to populations heretofore not served by local institutions has encouraged consideration of their establishment in places where we might expect a weaker educational tradition. Running counter to this is the fact that the interest of local people in having such an institution plays a significant part in location decisions.

tastes and how they affect college attendance rates, but such arguments would tend to be ad hoc. It would be easy to get trapped in a game of self-fulfilling prophecies that infers attitudes from revealed behavior and then explains the behavior by the imputed attitudes. For example, to attribute to the presence of private junior colleges the differentially high college attendance rates among some categories of North Carolina girls living in the communities with such colleges might run directly contrary to the actual effects. When we come to these complexities in the interpretation of geographically specified data, it is essential that any specification of operational hypotheses concerning cultural factors be brought into the analysis from exogenous sources, quite independently of the data on individuals or high school classes.

Elaboration of the models to incorporate tastes and various sorts of changes is valuable nevertheless; indeed, we must do it if we are to remain alert to important influences upon our empirical observations that we must consider as we interpret our findings. It is important, also, in leading us back to a longer and broader perspective. For the dynamics of the diffusion process is a critical matter for educational policy, and once fully appreciated may give special meaning to our notions of what is local or accessible. Over time it may come to encompass considerably wider areas than those circumscribed by the distances over which people commute daily. Indeed, we have long known that information and tastes relevant to college-going decisions may emanate out of a highly visible college some distance away and diffuse among a population with greater impact than that exercised by a local institution with local orientations. The extent to which this does occur, and in which sectors of the population such effects will be greatest, must depend upon the sorts of tastes, information, and opportunities involved.

5. DISTANCE PATTERNS AND COLLEGE ATTENDANCE

It is prudent to begin consideration of this relationship by a reminder that the proportion of students who cross state borders to attend college has remained comparatively constant since at least the 1920s. The much-discussed revolution in transportation systems and habits seems mainly to affect mobility within a state, if at all— apart from trips to demonstrations, ski holidays, or trips home on weekends.

At the same time, the proportion of people living within conurbations has expanded, automatically increasing the proportion of youth residing near a college, even as it may also increase the amount of time many students spend commuting. These shifts in settlement patterns give an appearance of the importance of accessibility that is quite spurious. That is, a large proportion of individuals from Seattle who attend the University of Washington would almost certainly have attended that same university if economic history had been different and their parents continued to reside in outlying parts of the state.

Thus, the basic questions about the effects of college location are as follows: When a new (or branch) institution of a particular kind is established in a community, what effect does its presence have on where young people of the vicinity go to college? To what extent will local attendance be a net addition to or a substitution for attendance elsewhere? And, lastly, what are some of the implications, for individuals or society, of one pattern of migration or the other?

Locational Substitution

Despite many irregularities, the data do indicate that individuals tend to choose the nearer option in attending college, but that this preference is usually weak and for some sets of youth may even be reversed. What happens depends on both the characteristics of colleges in the immediate vicinity and the traits of the potential students and their families. Such would be the situation even within the limitations of Model 1, and not only because of constraints from costs or from entry requirements. When viewed as channels to future jobs and earnings, colleges differ in what they may seem to promise for youth of varying characteristics. Typically, we should expect, and we find, that the more able youth from the economically most advantaged homes will be the most likely to go to college, not only at a distance but in another state. This presumption is strengthened when we add consideration of tastes and preferences to the decision model. The more able youth from such homes seek the nationally prestigious colleges, private or public, and the least able among the privileged youth select colleges that provide social advantages, whatever the intellectual and academic limitations. At the same time, it appears that some groups in some parts of the country desire to keep girls near home, whereas elsewhere the emphasis may be on sending daughters to "live in," even as boys from similar homes commute. Among many youth who have grown up in remote rural areas, there is unquestionably a strong preference, regardless of sex, for the security of the familiar and personalized environment. Of critical importance is a complicating factor that, for lack of data, cannot come within our purview: selectivity of college going within large metropolitan areas and the relationships of ethnic preferences and associated college features to patterns of intra-urban migration. These distinctions may seem superficial or minor on the surface even when they are in fact subtly and profoundly important.

Setting intrametropolitan questions aside, we found that the presence of a college in a town made very little difference with respect to the geographic range over which youth will go to college. But there are also marked differences over the states by type of college close at hand, and, in some instances, by sex.

In summarizing results, it will be convenient to look at two groups: those who attend college in the home community and those who attend out of state. The first of these entails local attendance in the narrow sense, but this is the sense in which most of the literature on accessibility has conceived it. The inverse of the second can also be used as an index of localism, but in the sense of in-state rather than in-community attachment. We consider first the more narrowly local measure—applicable only to communities with colleges—and report the proportions attending a home institution among those who go to college.

In Wisconsin, the college attendance rate among girls was consistently lower than among boys. But once we take sex difference into account by considering only the college-bound youth within each ability or parental-education category, sex differences in proportions attending college within the hometown are generally negligible. Overall, the associations with ability and with parental status are erratic, though they come out incidentally as a facet of the traits of colleges in one compared to another community. Among residents of Madison, for example, proportions of college-bound youth who attend the university are quite small among those in the lowest quarter of ability, but rise from three-fifths in the second ability quarter to five-sixths at the top. Among residents of towns with regional state colleges, attendance was highly localized in those institutions, more nearly corresponding to the low-ability Illinois males of towns with public junior colleges than to any other of the situations we could observe.[13] Proportions ran between 80 to 90 percent, except for the top quarter, where they

[13] However, the Wisconsin four-year colleges had a smaller representation from the lowest quarter of high school graduates.

dropped back to two-thirds. Sex differences in localism appear only where there also are strong sex contrasts in types of institutions attended: boys of above average ability to the Extension Centers and girls of low ability to the county teachers colleges. The latter accounts for the fact that among all low-ability girls who entered college from towns with colleges, the proportions attending locally tend to be higher than in other ability groups.

The patterns for 1966 in Illinois and North Carolina were much more clear-cut so far as attendance in the local community is concerned. The most able fourth of the young people were consistently least likely to attend college at home, as were offspring of the more highly educated men. Local proportions for the highest ability quarter ranged from 16 percent of North Carolina girls to 29 percent of Illinois boys. Among Illinois males, ability difference above the lowest quarter made little difference, but among the Illinois girls, and for both sexes in North Carolina, there was a decidedly higher rate of local attendance among the least able youth; this was especially marked in Illinois among girls and in North Carolina among boys, majorities of both going to schools at home. For Illinois, the concentrations of localism in attendance were among both sexes going to public junior colleges, whether from towns in which those were the only institutions or from Chicago and its vicinity. The higher local proportions in North Carolina among the least able boys again were attributable mainly to the impact of public junior colleges, whereas localism among girls was damped by their lack of response to these institutions and their adherence to the private junior colleges (which were both somewhat more selective and less local in recruitment).

These findings were summed up in the indexes of "locational substitution effect" among the more able young people. That effect in Illinois was especially strong among youth from modest homes. In North Carolina, the substitution effects were smaller, but the differentials between college and noncollege communities were consistently nonsignificant to start with. Putting all this another way, and more harshly: The much-desired expansion of attendance by able youth from low-status families cannot dependably be increased through the implanting of colleges closer at hand.

The presence of a college in a town seems to have little effect on the proportions of college-bound youth who attend colleges in other states. To be sure, in Wisconsin a slightly larger proportion of youth from noncollege communities left the state; this pattern occurred for most categories of ability and parental education, and in both sexes, but the effects were slight. Moreover, associations with ability were modest, although youth from more favored families tended more often to attend out of state. The highest proportions (among offspring of college graduates and postgraduates) ranged from a fourth to somewhat more than a third from college and noncollege towns alike. These wide-ranging youth were spread over the full range of ability and they evidently were seeking a wide diversity of college opportunities.

Illinois youth were much more likely to go outside of the state than were the Wisconsin youth, whereas North Carolina youth were more home-abiding. These generalizations from the SCOPE survey are in accord with information covering the whole population of 1963 and 1968 high school graduates in these states.[14] Moreover, in both Illinois and North Carolina, for most categories of college-bound youth (classified by either ability or by parental background), the proportions from towns with collegiate institutions who nevertheless attended schools in other states were higher than proportions from towns without colleges. The exceptions for Illinois were among the least able youth of both sexes and, more significantly, among the daughters of men who had no college experience. The only North Carolina exceptions were sons and daughters of men who had not gone beyond elementary school. But what is more important about North Carolina is the very small proportions of youth who went out of state for college, whatever their personal or community characteristics. Over half the college-bound children of Illinois college-graduate fathers and a third of the most able went out of state to college (whether from college or noncollege towns); even at the lowest ability level a sixth of the males and a seventh of the females did so. The ability gradients are systematic for both sexes in Illinois; those against parental status are steeper and monotonic for boys, but less striking among girls (especially from the noncollege towns). In North Carolina, by contrast, proportions of girls who went out of the state run at about 6 percent of all ability levels irrespective of type of community; for boys, they are about the same, except among the most able, where they reach a maximum of 15 percent—the same as the lowest figures for Illinois. When our locational perspec-

[14] On this, see especially Gossman et al. (1968).

tive is the state rather than the town, the pervasive home-rootedness of the college-bound youth of North Carolina stands out.

Community Ethic and College Attendance

Because states differ so widely in the customary level of college going and because settlement patterns and community traits have quite diverse historical backgrounds, we have been able to examine a considerable diversity of situations. One dimension of these diversities is in associations of community size with college profiles, socioeconomic composition of the population, and orientations toward higher education.

Simple regressions on community size (in five categories) predicted rates of college going in Wisconsin as well (and as poorly) as similar regressions using nine variables to represent different college-accessibility profiles. Moreover, this performance as a substitute for the college-accessibility set was repeated with the introduction of variables to control for ability and for father's education and occupational status.[15] Without other variables in the equation, the relationships were monotonic: college going for boys rose from 30 percent for communities with fewer than 2,500 residents to 43 percent for places with 25,000 to 99,999, and just under 60 percent for Madison, yielding a differential of 28 percent between Madison and the smallest places. Controlling for the ability of a youth and the education and occupation of his parents, there was little difference by size among communities under 25,000, the differentials dropping from a maximum range of 28 to just over 8 percent. Given the correlations between community size and college-access profiles, we are, of course, picking up both elements, whichever equations we use. It is clear, however, that there was an essential homogeneity with respect to college-going behavior across rural Wisconsin and the smaller towns. Madison is less distinctive when we introduce controls for ability and parental background.

For North Carolina and Illinois, community size was introduced into the regressions in a different way; we subclassified the noncollege towns according to their populations, treating these as subcategories within the college-accessibility set. In the data

[15] To avoid confounding observed relationships for the rest of the state by the heavy weighting of the Milwaukee metropolitan area, it was excluded from the regression analyses for Wisconsin (though analyzed with separate equations to delineate relationships within Milwaukee alone).

for Illinois, size made very little difference, except that the smallest farming communities did better for the most part than did somewhat larger noncollege places. There is nothing to suggest a communication ranking by size, but it would appear that farm youth in Illinois may be more education-prone than other residents of rural places.

The picture is quite different for North Carolina, and it is of special interest in two respects. First, there is a consistent positive relationship between size of noncollege place and rates of college going that seems concordant with settlement patterns in the state, which range from the lowlands to the Piedmont and the less-developed mountain counties. But, second, the larger noncollege towns of 10,000 to 19,000 inhabitants manifest a distinctively high propensity to send their youth to college. Back of this lies a history of distinctive relationships between socioeconomic status clusters and college implantations. The public institutions were not initially welcomed in the leading towns of North Carolina, and even today the state university community is marked by a large proportion of families of low economic status and limited schooling. At the same time, private colleges, in particular junior colleges, were scattered in spots accessible to the more advantaged sectors of the population, away from the main urban centers. The dotting of two-year public colleges and technical institutes over the state has come only recently.

In sum, many of the factors we have identified statistically apply rather uniformly nationwide, and many of them could be generalized to the higher educational systems in other advanced societies. This, indeed, should be expected if the propositions derived from Model 1 are valid. We have, we believe, also identified situations that make college going something distinctive in different regions or states that are part of our enormous educational system. Despite common roots in the colonial settlements on the Eastern seaboard, many common frontier experiences, a common constitutional structure of central-local relationships, and the shared experiences accompanying the development of urban life and the markets for high-level manpower, we come out near the end of the twentieth century with a set of surprisingly diverse state systems of colleges as well as a diversity of customs about who should use them and how the different colleges should complement each other. Identifying response to local college accessibility in its common as in its disparate manifestations requires specification of the conditions that affect the decision parameters among the youth involved.

Propensities to attend college are spread by many influences, but college proximity is among the least influential factors bringing about the diffusion of college going among members of a community. Both low-cost tuition and the elimination of ability constraints on entry are more relevant than school location to those youth who are at the decision margins. In particular, evidence that a new local college will increase college attendance among youth from disadvantaged families is weak. There is some evidence that local open-door colleges will increase the attendance of youth of below-average ability and socioeconomic status—sometimes. But that response may raise as many problems as it seems to resolve, if indeed it resolves any problems at all. And there may be much less isomorphism than most writers have casually assumed between the map of schools and the map of travel for the use of those schools among people who have reached an age that allows them to vote and subjects them to the draft.[16]

Localism and Cosmopolitanism

The inauguration of a new college in a particular location may have very different implications for those who attend it instead of going to college elsewhere—depending upon the nature of the college, the nature of the surrounding community, and the thinness or density of the communications that link the community (or that segment of it represented by potential students and their families) with other places. The substitution effect is important, in other words, not only for what it tells us about the net as compared with the direct effect on the college-going behavior of local residents, but also for what choice of the nearby college may mean.

For the young man or woman who grows up in Madison, to attend the home university is nevertheless to participate in a broadening and cosmopolitan experience that goes well beyond the immediate environment—though this experience certainly varies among individuals in its quality and its intensity. But if the nearest college to a youth is determinedly "local," the college

[16] One suspects that the "mobility" of students who travel to political demonstrations, wander from campus to campus as academic vagabonds, or fly to the ends of the earth during holidays represents a distinctive cluster of conventions almost wholly unrelated to the readiness of youth to enlarge the radius within which they choose a college. This may be so partly because these youth are not by any means the same individuals (save by a small overlap) as those most newly drawn into the college-going streams.

experience can be less emancipating. The latter college will have a quite different recruitment area and a more provincially limited student body. Introducing a new college into an Appalachian mountain town may lead a number of youth to enroll in it who otherwise would have traveled to a state college or university; and that choice may rest not only upon financial grounds. For many youth, the local school is comfortable and they do not have to depart from familiar surroundings into a strange outer world. But by the same token it is also limiting in what it contributes, both directly and indirectly, toward the enlistment of young people in the wider society. Lack of strong communication links and a limited capacity to move from a back eddy into the mainstream reduces future mobility and is likely to diminish the contribution that the young man or woman will make to the society's future production, creativity, or welfare. Or so, in the perspective of cosmopolitanism, it would seem.[17] There are, then, serious reservations to be expressed about both the effectiveness and the desirability of inserting new colleges into Appalachian valleys or Chicago slums—or even into the climax agrarian country of the corn belt.

6. EDUCATIONAL OPTIONS AND THE SOCIAL INTEREST

This is a moment in the sweep of educational expansion when Americans may take an opportunity to reexamine national options in higher education. Indeed, that is the overriding aim of the Carnegie Commission. The tides have been running strongly almost since before World War I, and some choices may seem already to have been foreclosed. Yet at the same time there is a new and pressing awareness of limitations in the financial resources that would be needed to meet the stupendous demands that seem to lie ahead; even if the solidity of those demands should turn out to be largely imaginary, the challenge is there. When apparently strong demands come up against constraints, as in the present

[17] There is a countervailing argument—in fact, a two-edged one. It may be argued that a halfway house, as it were, is what is needed for a happy adjustment by many rural young people—that they would be better off in that kind of institution, and further, that only as they stand close enough to the traditional end of the cultural bridge can they function as effective cultural intermediaries. At any rate, the argument continues, we need some people in that situation, as a part of a communication continuum. In a still more traditional (and youthful?) vein, it might also be argued that only by providing distinctively local institutions can we possibly preserve values of nonmetropolitan life that are fast disappearing from the scene—though the possibility of saving and revitalizing the values of a face-to-face society seems remote in any case.

moment in our national history, perhaps the time is ripe to examine where we have been, where we seem to be going, and the alternatives that could await our readiness to consider societal implications in an untrammeled spirit.

A hoard of latent issues are inextricably associated with pressures to expand college facilities and to locate new institutions or branches in accordance with a not-very-carefully-examined criterion of accessibility. The most that we can do here is to raise a few questions that need extensive scrutiny before new public policies are formulated or major undertakings are implemented. We group them under three main heads: (1) localization, locational substitution, and community service; (2) inequities, equalization, and excellence; and (3) looking behind the twelfth year.

Localization, Locational Substitution, and Community Service

On our extended reading of the evidence, we have concluded that the popular argument that immediate proximity of a college will increase college attendance among local youth rests on weak grounds, certain special cases aside. Moreover, those who respond to such new opportunities have usually not been the bright sons and daughters of poor men. (Hence, our repeated refrain that tempting people into local colleges may be to shortchange them educationally.) We have raised some questions, also, as to how far locational substitution was in fact the main result, and what the implications in that eventuality might be. That discussion was only to edge up to the matter, however. For there can be many reasons for both dispersal of colleges widely over space and the deliberate localization of orientation in at least some of the educational services of such colleges—as there can be arguments against localization of other services or activities. We suggest that the arguments are actually very different according to the kind of college considered and whether its role is as an intervening link in a regular academic sequence—a transitional stage in conventional education—or as a community institution serving many people, old and young, through diverse educational activities attuned to many interests.

Two very general sorts of questions are entailed here. First is the question: Does deliberate localization of postsecondary academic education at the junior college level satisfactorily serve the interests of either the students or the society? Is this a better way to make such education available to less advantaged youth than arrangements that would encourage them to participate in higher education more remotely placed from their homes? The answer can hardly be obvious, but we have commented sufficiently on this question already.

The second question is more crucial. What educational (and related) services should be developed to serve a local community and raise its quality of life, whether in economic or noneconomic terms? It seems clear that there could be justification for a set of widely available schools to serve as auxiliaries to the many specialized social welfare functions and agencies needed in a complex society: training for local planning agencies, training for paramedical, paraeducational, or paralegal and police work, and so on. More ambitiously, there unquestionably is a place for community colleges that would serve mainly as institutions for interested adults (including young school dropouts) and would offer nondegree and nontransfer programs. The localization of these services is tied up with the situation of the people they would serve, on the one hand, and with their possible community roles (whether in rural places or in urban slums), on the other hand. But if we push on to technical and polytechnical institutions and junior colleges offering regular associate degrees—with or without privilege of transfer—the case for localization as a deliberate goal fades away. Schools may still be located, as they will be, where demands are strong, but not for the purpose of *creating* the demand so much as for responding to it. And geographic dispersal of schools may then be seen as a way of relieving the anomie of huge and immensely impersonal educational complexes, as much to draw people away from congested centers as to serve residents in the vicinity of the new school. These are not just exercises in semantics, for wherever institutions are located, it is clear that their characteristics, the clientele they come to serve, and the functions they perform in the society will depend largely upon how those functions are conceived—including how location and localization or wider recruitment are related to those functions.

Inequities, Equalization, and Excellence

These problems and issues have aroused many a forum and lucratively supported many a platform lecturer from ocean to ocean. While we can hardly take space for a theoretical and logical exposition, neither can such basic issues be ignored if the implications of our main report are to be seen in what we regard as the proper context.

One has to ask, for example, whether open postsecondary

collegiate establishments will function mainly to siphon off the less-than-brilliant individuals so that the intellectually elitist colleges and universities may continue in their usual way. If the students of new local colleges turn out to be halfhearted or inept in their academic work, those colleges will become known as second-rate places. Not only will they safeguard the self-chosen mission of the selective schools from being swamped by "unsuitable" students; we may confidently anticipate a rise of whole cadres of counselors whose main function will be to smoothly divert presumably unsuitable students away from the reputedly superior colleges or universities. Equity, in practice, does not turn out to be a very clear idea. Neither is it at all clear what "equalization of opportunity" means in a situation in which a large majority of high school graduates may continue through an extra one or two years in school only to find at the next step, by which they might extricate themselves from the indifferent mass, a closed door. It is not accidental that in California, with its immense establishment of free-access junior college, the bottleneck to opportunity is a stage further along.[18]

Meanwhile the certification game seems to have become increasingly contentious, and with it the pejorative distinction between degree-credit or collegiate schools and higher technical-vocational schools or institutes. The better part of gamesmanship seems to be to get your institution transferred to the college, and then to the university, category. Yet some of the genuine technical institutes may in fact be superior, despite limited transfer potential to four-year colleges. Perhaps we should take yet another look at such options, not as local institutions but as institutions of wider appeal standing in their own right.[19] In all the current debates about policy for higher education (and not only in this country), almost

[18] A related issue that has broken open recently is the matter of who really pays the cost of college and who benefits—including how far those who can afford to do so *should* pay for college (as for a bigger or better house, for example). Among recent contributions on this theme, see especially Windham (1970) and Hansen and Weisbrod (1969).

[19] The curious lack of attention to technical institutes—almost regardless of their quality—in the work of recent "task forces" or in the reports of committees and commissions concerned with higher education is all the more curious in view of the emphasis that has been given in some writing to "vocational" education at the high school level. Whether this is academic ignorance, the academician's biased notion of what is "higher," or the elusiveness of data is not clear; but plenty of data have been gathered for more conventional purposes.

no attention has been given to returning to the practices of the day before yesterday as possible superior options, at least in some respects. The day before yesterday, in this instance, includes the vast array of remedial courses in public colleges or universities and also the many examples of technical education at various levels in some European systems.

Inevitably we must ask also whether the junior college will come to be conceived of mainly as an extension of secondary education. A closely related question is whether the junior college, using this term generically, is viewed mainly as a form of remedial education for students who were sluggards in earlier years of school, even though of high potential. It clearly cannot become a sort of American "sixth form" that prepares an academic elite for elite universities. But junior colleges could conceivably come to be much more diversified, and some of them might eventually play the "sixth form" role in a world in which college begins with the fifteenth year in school.

Looking Behind the Twelfth Year

Once one shifts his viewpoint to consider what happens before college, opening his mind to elementary and secondary school alternatives balanced against all the fine plans for higher education, the whole problem revolves into a new configuration. It could then be easy to justify enormous increases in investments to improve the learning increments in our secondary schools. Improving secondary achievement might well yield more benefit, to both the individual and to the society, than adding years of mediocre pseudocollege onto our present mediocre watered-down twelve-year common schools.[20]

With even more justification, one might contend that higher education now receives a sufficient proportion of the education dollar. Even the most academic among us have learned that the major holdup in educational progress for most youth occurs during the earliest grades or even before entry to school. Equal chances for all ethnic groups to share in positions of leadership is one sort of equalization and a crucial one; but it is not served merely by lower qualifications or by providing open entry. Our educational system needs more resources earlier if such ends are to be realized. More resources earlier are needed from the point of view of dis-

[20] Even if the latter are better than they were 50 years ago, that is not relevant to the issues being raised here.

advantaged individuals as well. However many the defects in our system of higher education, and however wise the proposals for remedying those defects, investment of resources for the purpose of thickening the network of colleges, on our reading of the evidence, is indefensible. For the bottleneck that is the most serious of all lies back of the twelfth grade, with the "students" who never were.

We have an opportunity, which we badly need, to reexamine our national options on education. But in doing so we must consider not only options for implementation. We must also consider options in aims, resisting intellectual fashions and the momentum of received opinion that foreclose crucial discussion about those aims. In particular, we must make sure that large decisions now do not unduly preclude better decisions in the near future.

References

The Advisory Committee on Junior Colleges: *Community Junior Colleges: Summary Report,* a report prepared for the Committee on Education, Kansas Legislative Council, State Printer, Topeka, Kansas, 1964.

Anderson, C. Arnold: "Social Class as a Factor in the Assimilation of Women into Higher Education," *Acta Sociologica,* vol. 4, no. 3, 1959, pp. 27–32.

Anderson, G. L., and T. J. Berning: "What Happens to Minnesota High School Graduates?" *Studies in Higher Education,* University of Minnesota, Minneapolis, 1941, pp. 15–40.

Beezer, R., and H. Hjelm: *Factors Related to College Attendance,* Cooperative Research Monograph No. 8, Department of Health, Education and Welfare, Washington, 1961.

Bock, Darrell, and Lyle Jones: *Measurement and Prediction of Judgment and Choice,* Holden-Day Inc., San Francisco, 1968.

Bowman, Mary Jean: "The Land-Grant Colleges and Universities in Human-Resource Development," *Journal of Economic History,* vol. 24, no. 4, 1962, pp. 523–546.

Brumbaugh, A. J.: *Higher Education and Florida's Future,* a report prepared for the Board of Control, Florida Institutions of Higher Learning, Tallahassee, vol. 3, 1956.

Cartter, Allan M.: *New Approaches to Student Financial Aid,* Cartter Panel's final report to the College Scholarship Service, College Entrance Examination Board, New York, March 1971.

Cobun, Frank E.: "The Educational Level of the Jacksonians," *History of Education Quarterly,* vol. 7, 1967, pp. 515–520.

College-Going Rate of New York State High School Graduates: 1968–1969, The State Education Department, Albany, 1969.

Coster, H. L., and L. W. Wager: "The Multivariate Analysis of Dichotomized Variables," *American Journal of Sociology,* vol. 70, no. 4, 1965, pp. 455–466.

Cowen, Philip: *A Study of Factors Related to College Attendance in New York State,* University of the State of New York Bulletin No. 1329, University of New York Press, Albany, 1946.

Daughtry, Alex A., and Richard Hawk: *A Report on the Post-Graduation Activities of the 1956 Kansas High School Graduates,* Kansas State Teachers College, Emporia, 1957.

Geographic Distribution of Freshmen Enrolled in Wisconsin's Public and Private Colleges and Universities, Fall 1959–Fall 1967, Wisconsin Coordinating Council for Higher Education, Madison, 1968, table 1.

Gossman, Charles S., et al.: *Migration of College and University Students in the United States,* University of Washington Press, Seattle, 1968, chap. 12.

Griffith, Coleman, and Hortense Blackstone: *The Junior College in Illinois,* a joint publication of the Superintendent of Public Instruction and the University of Illinois Press, Urbana, 1945.

Groat, Theodore: "Internal Migration Patterns of a Population Subgroup: College Students, 1887–1958," *American Journal of Sociology,* vol. 69, no. 4, 1964, pp. 383–394.

Hägerstrand, Torsten: *Innovation Diffusion as a Spatial Process* (translated by Allan Pred), University of Chicago Press, Chicago, 1967.

Hägerstrand, Torsten: "Quantitative Techniques for Analysis of the Spread of Information and Technology," in C. Arnold Anderson and Mary Jean Bowman (eds.), *Education and Economic Development,* Aldine Publishing Co., Chicago, 1965.

Hamilton, C. Horace: *Community Colleges for North Carolina: A Study of Need, Location, and Service Areas,* North Carolina Board of Higher Education, Raleigh, 1962.

Hansen, W. Lee, and Burton Weisbrod: *Benefits, Costs, and Finance of Public Higher Education,* Markham Publishing Co., Chicago, 1969.

Hawthorne, Phyllis, and L. J. Lins: *Geographic Distribution of New Freshmen Enrolled in Wisconsin's Public and Private Colleges and Universities, Fall 1959–Fall 1967,* Wisconsin Coordinating Council for Higher Education, Madison, 1968 (processed).

Henmon, V. A. C., and M. J. Nelson: *The Henmon-Nelson Test of Mental Ability,* Houghton Mifflin, Boston, 1942.

Hoenack, Stephen A.: "The Efficient Allocation of Subsidies to College Students," *American Economic Review,* vol. 61, 1971, pp. 302–311.

Hoenack, Stephen A.: *Private Demand for Higher Education in California,* unpublished doctoral dissertation, University of California, Berkeley, 1967.

Judd, Charles, et al.: *Report of a Survey of the State Institutions of Higher Education in Indiana,* W. B. Burford, Indianapolis, 1926.

Kariel, H. G.: "Student Enrollment and Spatial Interaction," *Annals of Regional Science,* vol. 2, no. 2, 1968, pp. 114–127.

Keller, R. J., R. A. Kehl, and T. J. Berning: "The Minnesota Public High School Graduates of 1945—One Year Later," *Higher Education in Minnesota,* University of Minnesota Press, Minneapolis, 1950, pp. 88–89.

Kentucky Council on Public Higher Education: *Kentucky High School Graduates Who Went to College, 1957,* New Capitol Annex, Frankfort, 1958.

Koos, Leonard: *A Community College Plan for Oregon,* a report to the Interim Committee on Post-High School Educational Facilities, State Printing Office, Portland, 1950.

Koos, Leonard: *The Junior College,* University of Minnesota Press, Minneapolis, 1924, pp. 134–135.

Landis, Paul H.: *Washington High School Graduates in Depression and in War Years,* Washington Agricultural Experiment Station, Bulletin 463, Pullman, Washington, May 1945.

Little, J. Kenneth: *Explorations into the College Plans and Experiences of High School Graduates: A Statewide Inquiry,* School of Education, University of Wisconsin, Madison, 1959.

Maton, Jef: "Regional Differences in Educational Participation: A Regression Analysis of Cross-sectional Data on Participation Coefficients," *Sociology of Education,* vol. 39, no. 3, 1966, pp. 276–287.

McConnell, Harold: "Spatial Variability of College Enrollment as a Function of Migration Potential," *The Professional Geographer,* vol. 17, no. 6, 1965, pp. 29–37.

Medsker, Leland L., and Dale Tillery: *Breaking the Access Barriers: A Profile of Two-Year Colleges,* McGraw-Hill, New York, 1971.

Medsker, Leland L., and James Trent: *The Influence of Different Types of Public Higher Institutions on College Attendance from Varying Socioeconomic and Ability Levels,* Center for the Study of Higher Education, University of California, Berkeley, 1965.

Meeting the Enrollment Demand for Public Higher Education in California through 1977, California Coordinating Council for Higher Education, Sacramento, 1969.

Miller, Leonard S.: "Demand for Higher Education in the United States," a paper for the Conference on Education as an Industry, sponsored by the Universities-National Bureau Committee for Economic Research, Chicago, June 1971.

Nelson Associates: *A Study of Factors Related to Change in Freshmen Enrollment at Private Colleges in New York State, 1961–1966,* a report submitted to the New York State Education Department, 1967 (processed).

Paige, John, and John D. Russell: *Migration of College Students to and from New York State,* University of the State of New York Bulletin No. 1304, The University of New York Press, Albany, 1945.

Patterson Education 1957–58, Educational Directories, Inc., Chicago, Illinois, 1957.

Plunkett, H. Dudley, and Mary Jean Bowman: *Elites and Change in the Kentucky Mountains,* University of Kentucky Press, Lexington, 1972.

Ravenstein, E. G.: "The Laws of Migration," *Journal of the Royal Statistical Society,* vol. 42, no. 2, 1885, pp. 167–235.

Reeves, Floyd, et al.: *The Liberal Arts College,* University of Chicago Press, Chicago, 1932, pp. 28–35.

Russell, J. D.: "Geographic Origins of Michigan College Students," Staff Study No. 2 in *The Survey of Higher Education in Michigan,* Michigan Legislative Study Committee on Higher Education, Lansing, 1955.

Russell, J. D.: "Geographical Origins of Students Attending College in Virginia," Staff Report No. 3, Virginia Higher Education Study Committee, Richmond. 1965.

School to College: Opportunities for Postsecondary Education (SCOPE), Center for Research and Development in Higher Education, University of California, Berkeley, 1966.

Sewell, William H., and Vimal P. Shah: "Social Class, Parental Encouragement, and Educational Aspirations," *American Journal of Sociology,* vol. 73, no. 5, 1968, p. 562.

Sewell, William H., and Vimal P. Shah: "Socioeconomic Status, Intelligence, and Attainment of Higher Education," *Sociology of Education,* vol. 40, no. 1, 1967, pp. 1–23.

Stewart, John Q.: "Empirical Mathematical Rules Governing the Distribution and Equilibrium of Population," *Geographical Review,* vol. 37, 1947, pp. 461–485.

Stouffer, Samuel: "Intervening Opportunities: A Theory Relating Mobility and Distance," *American Sociological Review,* vol. 5, no. 6, 1940, pp. 845–867.

Stouffer, Samuel: "Intervening Opportunities and Competing Migrants," *Journal of Regional Science,* vol. 2, no. 1, 1960, pp. 1–26.

Strayer, George D.: "Public Education in Washington," report to the legislature, Seattle, 1946.

Theil, Henri: "On the Estimation of Relationships Involving Qualitative Variables," *American Journal of Sociology,* vol. 76, no. 1, 1970, pp. 103–154.

Tillery, Dale: *School to College: Distribution and Differentiation of Youth,* Center for Research and Development in Higher Education, University of California, Berkeley, 1969, pp. 59–61 (processed).

Tillery, Dale, Denis Donovan, and Barbara Sherman: *SCOPE: Four-State Profile, Grade Twelve, 1966,* College Entrance Examination Board, New York, 1966.

Tobin, James: "Estimation of Relationships for Limited Dependent Variables," *Econometrica,* vol. 26, no. 1, 1958, pp. 24–36.

Tuckman, Howard: "College Location and Student Choice," an unpublished paper written for the Institute for Social Research, Florida State University, Tallahassee, 1969.

Willingham, Warren W.: *Free-Access Higher Education,* College Entrance Examination Board, New York, 1970.

Windham, Douglas M.: *Education, Equality, and Income Redistribution,* D. C. Heath and Company, Lexington, Massachusetts, 1970, pp. 38–39, 45.

Zipf, George: "The P_1P_2/D Hypothesis on the Intercity Movement of Persons," *American Sociological Review,* vol. 11, no. 6, 1946, pp. 677–686.

Index

This book was set in Vladimir by University Graphics, Inc. It was printed on acid-free, long-life paper and bound by The Maple Press Company. The designers were Elliot Epstein and Edward Butler. The editors were Nancy Tressel and Cheryl Allen for McGraw-Hill Book Company and Verne A. Stadtman and Sidney J. P. Hollister for the Carnegie Commission on Higher Education. Alice Cohen supervised the production.